JOHN KEATS

MASTERS OF WORLD LITERATURE SERIES

GENERAL EDITOR: LOUIS KRONENBERGER

Published:

GEORGE ELIOT by Walter Allen
JOHN MILTON by Douglas Bush
JONATHAN SWIFT by Nigel Dennis
HONORÉ DE BALZAC by E. J. Oliver
DANTE by Francis Fergusson

In Preparation:

PROUST by William Barrett
FLAUBERT by Jacques Barzun
COLERIDGE by W. J. Bate
SAMUEL JOHNSON by James L. Clifford
YEATS by F. W. Dupee
JOYCE by Leon Edel
D. H. LAWRENCE by Monroe Engel
CONRAD by Elizabeth Hardwick
THOREAU by Granville Hicks
HARDY by Irving Howe
SHAKESPEARE by Frank Kermode
JANE AUSTEN by Louis Kronenberger
EMERSON by Alfred Kazin
POE by Dwight Macdonald
FIELDING by Midge Podhoretz
HENRY JAMES by Richard Poirier
TOLSTOY by Philip Rahv
GOLDSMITH by Ricardo Quintana
MELVILLE by Harold Rosenberg
BEN JONSON by Raymond Rosenthal
WORDSWORTH by Lionel Trilling

John Keats

HIS LIFE AND WRITINGS

Douglas Bush

WEIDENFELD AND NICOLSON
5 Winsley Street London W 1

00025780

Printed in Great Britain by
Lowe & Brydone (Printers) Ltd., London

TO
Walter Jackson Bate,
OLD FRIEND, OLD PUPIL, AND NEW MASTER

CONTENTS

PREFACE

WHILE ONE has small hope of saying anything about Keats that is both new and true, there may still be room for a small book which, after a fashion, covers both his life and his poetry. This one is, to be sure, a skiff sailing in the wake of W. J. Bate's richly laden ship, *John Keats* (1963); to that work I have been constantly and happily indebted. In a book of the present kind it is impossible to refer to countless writings, large and small, which have been of help; some are cited in notes and more are listed at the end.

If there are readers who like to float on a stream of broad impressions, they may skip occasional pages that take some account of two kinds of details, Keats's revisions and his echoes of other poets. But many readers are interested in concrete evidence of the ways in which a great poet's mind works, and, if such data are welcome in studies of Yeats, Pound, Eliot, and Auden, they may be likewise even in a summary survey of Keats.

For the abundant quotations from Hyder E. Rollins' masterly edition of Keats's *Letters* (2 vols., 1958), I am indebted to the generosity of the Harvard University Press.[1] For those readers who may want to see the context, references are normally given (by volume and page only, without title). It has seemed best to reproduce the text exactly, with Keats's

---

1 *The Letters of John Keats 1814–1821*, ed. Hyder E. Rollins, Cambridge, Mass.: Harvard University Press; copyright, 1958, by the President and Fellows of Harvard College.

often hasty and erratic spelling and punctuation, which im-
pose no real difficulty upon the reader and help to preserve
the writer's vital identity. For quotations from Rollins' *The
Keats Circle* (2 vols., 1948), I am also obliged to the Harvard
University Press;[2] these items are indicated by "*K.C.*" I am
indebted to Southern Illinois University Press for permission
to quote from *The Major English Romantic Poets: A Sym-
posium in Reappraisal,* edited by Clarence D. Thorpe, Carlos
Baker, and Bennett Weaver; and to the Houghton Mifflin
Company for quotations from *John Keats: Selected Poems
and Letters.*

One obligation, partly stated at the beginning, must be
enlarged. To two interpreters of Keats, W. J. Bate and David
Perkins, my colleagues and friends, I am in debt not only for
their writings but for their careful reading of my manuscript,
from which it has profited—although, of course, they are not
responsible for any erroneous opinions that may remain.

Finally, I am grateful to Louis Kronenberger, the ideal
general editor, whose generous warmth is always inspiring.

D.B.

[2] *The Keats Circle: Letters and Papers 1816–1878,* ed. Hyder E. Rollins,
Cambridge, Mass.: Harvard University Press; copyright, 1948, by the Presi-
dent and Fellows of Harvard College.

INTRODUCTION

JOHN KEATS died four months after his twenty-fifth birthday, and, because of the active onset of illness, his last year counted only in terms of mental and physical suffering. No other major English poet would be a major poet if he had been cut off so soon. And the miracle is all the greater since Keats was not at all a precocious poet. Indeed his early artistic development was rather slow than rapid, partly on account of his relative lack of literary education, the time he spent in medical studies, and the prevailing poetical modes that were his first inheritance and medium. In spite of such disadvantages, he became in a few years not only one of the principal voices of English and European romanticism but—what is more important—a poet whose stature has grown through all the vicissitudes of taste and outlook that have marked the past century and a half.

That is not to say that modern poets write like Keats or would or should try to do so; and the several "axioms" for poetry that Keats listed in a letter to his publisher are not those of our age.[1] But his poems and letters have been more or less absorbed by modern poets and critics, who recognize him as one of themselves, a poet and critic driven by that kind of insight and integrity that remains a vital force. The anti-romantic reaction of the second and later decades of our

1 They are quoted below, on the last page of Chapter 3.

century (which in retrospect may look more like another wave of romanticism) left Keats undamaged, in fact much stronger; our image of Keats, of a man and poet of realistic and philosophic awareness, has been established mainly during the last forty or fifty years. What "romantic" weaknesses he had—such as an open and unembarrassed passion for beauty, if that is one—have appeared as minor in comparison with the combination of qualities that made him unique and that bind him and his ideas and problems to cur time. In many letters and some major poems he seems to speak to us directly, whereas we instinctively take a more or less historical approach to Coleridge and Wordsworth, Byron and Shelley. Keats's letters have become more and more a testament of critical and human wisdom (witness T. S. Eliot's tribute of a generation ago, or W. H. Auden's later one), and dozens of ideas and phrases are current coin in our critical language. Nowadays Keats is, as W. J. Bate has said, "a part of our literary conscience." In reading the letters, however, we must remember that Keats's moods and attitudes shifted, that many of his most quoted utterances on poetry and life were not fixed and final; in the letters, more obviously than in the poems, he was, as Ian Jack puts it, discovering his own identity. One of the things about him that are congenial to us is that his poetic and intellectual beliefs and intuitions were constantly beset by his own skeptical questionings.

One immediate and lasting reason for Keats's hold upon his friends and upon us is his extraordinarily winning personality. On the dark day when he sailed for Rome, Fanny Brawne said, in her first letter to Fanny Keats: "I am certain he has some spell that attaches them to him, or else he has fortunately met with a set of friends that I did not believe could be found in the world."[2] Along with his poetic gifts and fine intelligence, we feel his affectionate warmth and loyalty, his honest understanding of himself and others, his

2 *Letters of Fanny Brawne to Fanny Keats 1820–1824*, ed. Fred Edgcumbe (London: Oxford University Press, 1937), p. 4.

courage, magnanimity, geniality, and realistic common sense,
his freedom from the egotism, dogmatism, and other faults
that we have to allow for in his old and young contempo-
raries.

On the literary plane, there is the fascinating phenomenon
of Keats's artistic growth. When at the age of eighteen he
began to write, he fell naturally into a meretricious style, the
style of a swarm of now obscure or forgotten versifiers of his
time and earlier decades. Leigh Hunt was only one of the
better influences of that kind, although his personal relations
with the novice have given him a bad eminence. It took
Keats several years to work free of that conventional idiom, a
flaccid, sentimental, erratic mixture of "poetical" language
both rhetorical and familiar. At first even the Elizabethan
and Jacobean poets he was reading were rather assimilated
into that vein than used to purify and strengthen it. And
Keats could have momentary lapses after he had attained his
mature, individual, and often perfect language and tone. To
emphasize his long apprenticeship is not to disparage him; it
is only to suggest the extent and the rapidity of his later
growth. The nature of his ripe endowment and achievement
was finely distilled by Robert Bridges, in words that might be
said to amplify Matthew Arnold's more general comments.
Keats's highest gift, the highest gift of all in poetry, Bridges
said, was

the power of concentrating all the far-reaching resources of lan-
guage on one point, so that a single and apparently effortless ex-
pression rejoices the aesthetic imagination at the moment when
it is most expectant and exacting, and at the same time astonishes
the intellect with a new aspect of truth. This is only found in the
greatest poets, and is rare in them; and it is no doubt for the
possession of this power that Keats has often been likened to
Shakespeare, and very justly, for Shakespeare is of all poets the
greatest master of it; the difference between them here is that
Keats's intellect does not supply the second factor in the propor-
tion or degree that Shakespeare does; indeed, it is chiefly when he
is dealing with material and sensuous objects that his poems
afford illustrations; but these are, as far as they go, not only like

Shakespeare, but often as good as Shakespeare when he happens
to be confining himself to the same limited field.[3]

Finally, there is the growth of Keats's insight and wisdom
in regard to the nature and aims of poetry and ethical and
philosophic questions, practical or speculative. We may re-
member that the two generations of romantic poets found
themselves in a position markedly different from that of the
long line of their predecessors; they were the first great poets
who were, and knew they were, more or less alienated from
the religious and political convictions of the country at large.
The older poets, from Chaucer up to Pope, had stood on
firm ground, conscious of having an accepted place in both
society and poetic tradition, of holding beliefs and opinions
held by most or many of their cultivated readers and fellow
citizens. But poets no longer had such firm supports. Various
currents of thought and action—rationalistic skepticism, the
French Revolution, science and the Industrial Revolution—
had been creating new and divided worlds with opposed sets
of values; and the romantic poets (whatever the eventual
conservatism of Coleridge and Wordsworth) were relatively
isolated individuals who stood outside traditional orthodoxies
and had to grope for working philosophies of their own.

When we look at the young Keats in this large perspective,
we see that some central romantic attitudes and ideas, which
in other poets may be—for us if not for them—partial liabili-
ties, took in his mind a moderate and tentative form that we
more readily comprehend and accept. Like Blake, Keats be-
lieved in the holiness of the heart's affections and the truth
of imagination, but he was not a militant and eccentric
prophet of revolt. Like Coleridge and Wordsworth, he found
sensuous and imaginative inspiration in nature, but he did
not find there a moral guide or metaphysical doctrine. Like
Shelley, Keats was—up to a point—a believer in progress, but
he was no crusader, no "Godwin-methodist" (as he called his
friend Dilke); he knew that the nature of man and the world

[3] *Poems of John Keats* (London: Muses' Library, Routledge; New York:
Dutton, 1896), I, xci–xcii.

will not admit of perfectibility. The mature Keats recoiled from the mature Byron as a cynical poseur and showman rather than a real poet of imagination. These brief and unqualified contrasts are not of course foolish disparagements of the other great poets; they are only reminders that Keats, for all his gifts and intensities, was a sensible middle-of-the-road man. As I once remarked (adapting a gimmick from Lord David Cecil), "if we can imagine ourselves contemporaries, and in urgent need of wise advice, we would never think of consulting Shelley or Byron or Blake or Coleridge or even Wordsworth, but we would turn with confidence to Keats, the youngest of the lot."

Keats's developing and changing ideas will be touched in the pages that follow, and only one will be registered here: that is, man's movement out of the world of illusion into the world of reality. This is, to be sure, a universal idea and theme, but every artist has his own conception and experience of it; and Keats, characteristically, sees such growth as essential for the artist and for everyone alike. In this he goes along with such very different contemporaries as Jane Austen and the Scott of the Scottish novels, to name two representatives of realistic sanity. Keats's early craving to "burst our mortal bars," to attain through the senses and imagination some kind of supramundane or transcendental beauty and truth, was eventually subdued and chastened by a sober acceptance of the human condition. The denial of human limits was a main impulse of romanticism, and Byron and Shelley battered their wings in struggles both to deny and to accept such limits. Keats's development was quieter and wiser. In Sleep and Poetry, written when he had just become twenty-one, he recognized his present stage, the delighted, half-escapist response of his senses to nature and art, but a vast idea rolled before him, and he looked forward ten years to a nobler kind of poetry (he was to have only three years). The journeyings of Endymion took him theoretically from ideal abstraction to earthly reality. When in Hyperion Keats reworked the same theme, the nature of the poet, immature and mature ideas appeared together: Oceanus' faith in the law of beauty and the providential march of history was superseded by Apollo's attaining a tragic vision of beauty, the beauty born of the knowledge of suffering. That vision furnishes the ground or background, indeed it is the measure, of the greater odes. And the dreaming that in *Endymion* led to reality proved in *Lamia* to be a fatal illusion.

Keats's letters on the mansion of life and the vale of soul-making are expositions of humanitarian and ethical insight and growth which, however unoriginal and unimportant in the history of thought, are of prime importance for Keats and for his readers. Those two parts of his creed were joined and sharpened in his last attempt to define his ideal of poetry, *The Fall of Hyperion.* Thus Keats's earlier and purely aesthetic ideal of "negative capability" gave way to the need of a stable ethical identity disciplined by experience. But if acceptance of the human condition meant seeing both nature and man as involved in everlasting process, Keats did not acquiesce in any kind of determinism; unlike Coleridge, Wordsworth, and Shelley, he seems to have been untouched by current doctrines of Necessity. Feeling and thinking man must and can partly disentangle himself from natural process and thereby nourish and mold his humanity. Thus, while most of Keats's major poems and letters are about poetry and might seem limited to an audience of connoisseurs, in fact, as we all know, they make a wide and strong appeal to all who are concerned with the meaning of experience.

I

Childhood, Apprenticeship, and
First Poems (1795–1815)

M EN OF GENIUS have usually sprung from families
and circumstances of which no such offshoots could
have been predicted. (Some five weeks after the birth of John
Keats appeared another infant not outwardly favored by an-
cestry or the stars, the long-lived Thomas Carlyle.) Our very
limited knowledge of Keats's forebears would suggest no
more than that he might—like his brother George—have in-
herited the capacity for prospering in the middle-class busi-
ness world which was possessed by his father and by his
maternal grandfather; the latter, with other connections, was
rooted in the East End of London, on the edge of the City.
The origins of his father, Thomas Keats, are unknown; he
came to London perhaps from Cornwall or Dorset, at any
rate from the West Country. He was employed at the Swan
and Hoop, a public house and livery stable in Finsbury, and
he seems to have had, without the priggishness, the abilities
and the success of the virtuous apprentice; good judges de-
scribed him as attractive, sensible, and well-bred. On October
9, 1794, when he was twenty, Thomas Keats married Frances,
the nineteen-year-old daughter of his employer, John Jen-
nings; the ceremony had no less fashionable a setting than St.
George's, Hanover Square. On his father-in-law's retirement,
Thomas Keats managed the business. The young couple re-
sided for some years at the livery, 24 Moorfields Pavement

Row, just north of the City. There John Keats was born on October 31, 1795. His brother George was born on February 28, 1797; Thomas on November 18, 1799; in 1801 a boy who died in infancy; and Frances (Fanny) on June 3, 1803. In 1798 the family had moved a short distance northward, to a house near the City Road; by the end of 1802 they were back at the Swan and Hoop.

We have only a glimpse or two of Thomas Keats, who died on April 16, 1804, as the result of a fall when his horse slipped on the cobblestones. John and George were old enough to feel the loss, and there followed quickly the loss of precious familial solidarity. On June 27, 1804, ten weeks after her husband's death, the young widow married—again at St. George's—a bank clerk named William Rawlings, of whom little is known and nothing good. The chief picture of her comes from the prejudiced Richard Abbey (later the children's guardian) and must be heavily discounted; George remembered her as a generous and doting mother. We get the impression of a pretty, lively, intelligent, and rather impetuous and passionate young woman. The best evidence on her behalf is John's deep attachment. Whatever the motives and circumstances of her remarriage, her disapproving mother, Mrs. Jennings, took the children to live with her and her husband at Ponder's End, near Enfield, ten miles north of London. In March, 1805, John Jennings died, and in the summer Mrs. Jennings moved her family to Edmonton, two miles south of Enfield. John Jennings had left £1,000 to be divided, with interest, among the four Keats children as they came of age. The provisions made for his wife and his own children quickly led to trouble. In April, 1805, Mrs. Rawlings and her husband lodged a complaint in Chancery that her mother and her brother Midgley Jennings were withholding money due to her under the will. In 1806 the suit was decided against the plaintiffs. It was perhaps in this year that Mrs. Rawlings left her husband; some time later— Robert Gittings suggests that it was after Midgley's death in November, 1808—she became reconciled with her mother and spent with her and the children the short remainder of her life.

In 1803 John and George, aged seven and six respectively, had been sent to a school of about seventy-five boys kept by the excellent John Clarke at Enfield, which the two Jennings sons had attended. They were joined in time by the youngest brother, Tom. John's earlier years at school were notable mainly for an addiction to fighting that did not lessen his popularity; he was given to openhearted explosions of both rage and laughter. With "terrier courage" he fought anyone on general principles or in defense of his brothers (whom he also fought with); once he assailed a teacher who had boxed Tom's ears. The younger but bigger George often, laughingly, held down the small fire-eater. Boyish pugnaciousness, normal enough except in its intensity, was heightened by emulation: the fatherless John and his brothers made a family hero of their uncle, Midgley Jennings, a naval officer and a glamorous figure in the great outer world of the Napoleonic War. In later years in London Keats, though still small of course, could—in a fight of nearly an hour—trounce a big butcher's boy who was maltreating a kitten.

During 1809, when he was thirteen, early adolescence brought a shift from fighting to equally ardent reading. In the newly discovered realms of gold the boy may have found some alleviation for the grief that came upon him with the death of his mother in March, 1810. Her health had long been declining and she died probably of tuberculosis. John, during his holidays, was a devoted nurse and a jealous guardian of her sickroom; and no one can forget the picture of him at school taking refuge under the master's desk to be alone with his misery. He was now, at fourteen, the male head of the family; his only elder was his grandmother.

Keats was fortunate in having as a literary mentor and friend Charles Cowden Clarke, the son of the headmaster and an assistant teacher. Clarke—who lived until 1877 and became a minor man of letters—was eight years older than Keats and a cultivated reader. His recollections, set down

much later, tell us most of what we know about the school-
boy's early interests.[1] We hear of his sitting at the communal
supper table with Gilbert Burnet's folio *History of His Own
Times* propped up in front of him. Another large and sober
item, William Robertson's *History of America,* is of special
note because it welled up in his mind when he wrote the
sonnet on Chapman's *Homer.* Instinct somehow led Keats to
eager assimilation of such not very inviting handbooks of
classical myth—boyhood favorites also of the older Leigh
Hunt—as Andrew Tooke's old *Pantheon,* John Lempriere's
Classical Dictionary, and the school abridgment of Joseph
Spence's *Polymetis.* While we know little about his formal
studies, he evidently acquired competent French and a good
grounding in Latin; he began, as a voluntary enterprise, a
prose translation of the *Aeneid,* which he finished after he
had left school. Keats's scholastic career, or the latter part of
it, does not support the conventional idea of the genius who
is above conventional study. He worked hard, even on holi-
days, and won several first prizes. One of these, John Bonny-
castle's *Introduction to Astronomy,* contributed, along with
Robertson, to the sonnet on Chapman. Keats's mind and im-
agination expanded rapidly with advancing age and in a
congenial atmosphere. He was indebted to the Clarkes also
for the sprouting of his political liberalism; they subscribed
to Leigh Hunt's paper, *The Examiner,* and Hunt was no
friend of the Establishment. Then, although music was not
to be a major element in Keats's experience, he delighted—
as he recalled in his verse epistle to Clarke of September,
1816—in hearing his friend play Mozart, Arne, Handel, and
Moore's *Irish Melodies.* Later he said that the lines in *The
Eve of St. Agnes* (stanza 29) about the door shutting off fes-
tive music embodied a memory of listening, in bed, to the
sounds floating upstairs from Clarke's piano.

[1] In 1846 Clarke wrote some memoranda for Monckton Milnes to use in
his *Life, Letters and Literary Remains of John Keats*—these are printed in
The Keats Circle, II, 146–153—and enlarged them for his and his sister's
Recollections of Writers (1878). Both versions are quoted by Keats's biog-
raphers and critics.

In July, 1810, after Mrs. Rawlings' death, Mrs. Jennings set up a trust fund which allotted about £1,625 to each of the four Keats children and named as their guardians a J. N. Sandell and Richard Abbey, a London tea merchant (the latter she had known in Lancashire before her marriage).[2] The solicitous grandmother's choice of guardians proved unfortunate. Sandell did not take an active part and died in 1816, and authority remained with Abbey, who was at best a philistine businessman. There was money enough to send Keats to Oxford or Cambridge (the ambitious parents had thought of Harrow), but such a possibility would never have occurred to Mrs. Jennings or her adviser, since the universities were as remote from their world—and the world of most of Keats's later friends—as Olympus; and perhaps, in view of Keats's temperament and short life, even Cambridge, the nursery of poets (and mathematicians), would not have been good for him. The decision to article Keats to an apothecary-surgeon, Thomas Hammond of Edmonton, must have seemed judicious, perhaps generous, to his elders (George was being given a desk in Abbey's office), and possibly to Keats himself this lesser branch of the medical profession seemed as accept-

2 A footnote cannot properly summarize the complications of John Jennings' and his widow's bequests, which have been carefully worked out by W. J. Bate (*John Keats*, Cambridge, Mass.: Harvard University Press, 1963, pp. 14–15, 24, 705–712). Various advances from capital to John came to about £1,000, but he was entitled to about £1,735 that he never received. Abbey's authoritarian meanness was evident during John's lifetime; his incontestable duplicity (Bate's phrase) came out later, when Fanny Keats, her husband, and Charles Dilke and James Rice pressed him for an accounting. Fanny's phrase for Abbey was "consummate villain."

The tangled business of the Jennings wills and their aftermath has been examined afresh by Robert Gittings (*The Keats Inheritance*, London, 1964; summarized by Mr. Gittings in *The Listener*, LXXII, 1964, pp. 631–632). He exonerates Abbey from niggardly or fraudulent handling of Mrs. Jennings' bequest to the Keats brothers (though not from the attempt to swindle Fanny), on the ground that market values of the stock fluctuated; his estimates of money available and received differ from Bate's. The other money left by John Jennings was held in trust by Chancery and would have been available to Keats and to George when they came of age, if they had applied for it. But they knew nothing about it; nor, says Mr. Gittings, did Abbey, who was concerned only with Mrs. Jennings' bequest. Not all readers may be convinced of Abbey's ignorance and innocence.

able a means of livelihood as anything within reach. An apothecary-surgeon did not need a university degree and combined the more ordinary functions of a modern general practitioner and dentist; we may remember the "intelligent, gentlemanlike" Mr. Perry, the oracle of Emma Woodhouse's valetudinarian father. As an inmate of his chief's household, the apprentice studied books under direction while he gained practical and technical knowledge as an assistant. Keats began his new mode of life in the late summer of 1811, when he was a little short of sixteen. We know almost nothing of his reactions to Hammond and medical studies during the next four years. The chief item has uncertain implications: in a letter to George and his wife of September 21, 1819—apropos of the old idea that the human body renewed itself every seven years—Keats exclaimed ". . . seven years ago it was not this hand that clench'd itself against Hammond." That incident would have occurred at about the end of his first year; presumably it was unusual, since he would hardly have nursed active rebellion through three more years, and there is no good evidence of Hammond's having been other than a capable and worthy man.

Whatever his resentments and loneliness and possible boredom, Keats had a solace and stimulus in visiting about once a week with Clarke at Enfield. He could borrow books and talk them over with a sympathetic and knowledgeable guide whose seniority was not great enough to check the free outpouring of personal opinions. In the epistle of 1816 Keats gave abundant thanks to the friend who "first taught me all the sweets of song"—Spenser and Milton, the sonnet and the ode, the epigram and the epic. After a walk through country lanes, "at night-fall among your books we got"; at the end of a full evening Clarke would accompany him to a point "Mid-way between our homes," and Keats would go on alone, his friend's voice still in his ears. It was in this period, 1811–1815, that Clarke saw Keats's love of poetry developing, and the prime agent—as Charles Brown also reported later, on the authority of both Keats and his brothers—was Spenser (who had awakened other young poets in the past). When Keats had just read the *Epithalamion* and asked for the loan of *The Faerie Queene,* Clarke thought the boy had got a bit above himself, but he was soon undeceived: Keats went through the poem "as a young horse would through a spring meadow—ramping!" Since one signal gift of the mature Keats is his command of the suggestive and reverberating epithet, critics have noted Clarke's emphasis on his special response to the "felicity and power" of Spenser's epithets: "He *hoisted* himself up, and looked burly and dominant, as he said, 'what an image that is—*sea-shouldering whales!*' "

We can readily imagine the excitement with which Keats essayed what seems to have been his first poem, the *Imitation of Spenser,* written probably at the beginning of 1814, when he was somewhat past eighteen. This piece, in four Spenserian stanzas, sets out to be a Bower of Bliss, a scene of luxuriant—though ideal and innocent—beauty, and it has some authentic bits, but both nature and Spenser are seen through a tissue of eighteenth-century "Spenserian" clichés and conceits. Along with clear or possible Miltonic echoes there are strained allusions to Dido and King Lear. It was almost inevitable that a novice, however active his own senses, should fall into the language of faded plush that was the standard medium for fifth-rate versifiers of his generation; indeed, to the eager aspirant this fustian may well have appeared fresh and moving. Most of what he was to write in the next two years was more or less bad in more or less the same way; and we cannot measure the achievements of 1818–1819 unless we take fair account of his relatively long journey through weakness to strength.

The feeble sonnet *On Peace,* probably of the spring of 1814, testifies to an awareness—derived no doubt from the *Examiner*—of the hopes that attended Napoleon's confinement on Elba. The sonnet *To Lord Byron* (December, 1814) was a wholly sympathetic tribute, in the conventional "plaintive" style, to the great image and voice of romantic melancholy. In the same month came a sonnet, "As from the darkening gloom," on the death of Mrs. Jennings, who since 1804 had been a second mother to Keats and his brothers and sister. His genuine affection and gratitude hardly emerge from the picture of heaven and the language of orthodox piety; at the time he may have at least nominally shared such piety, or he may have known no other mode for the occasion.

Of poems written in 1815, two, dated February, and *To Chatterton*, of about that time, must be given a word. The *Ode to Apollo* was Keats's first enthronement of the god whose name, the most banal of mythological counters, was to remain throughout his career a symbol of vital reality. The first line, "In thy western halls of gold," looked forward to his one great early poem. The ode was a miniature "progress of poesy," in the declamatory tradition of Dryden and Gray (and some of Collins—witness "The Passions—a terrific band"). *To Chatterton* is about as bad as *To Lord Byron,* but it was Keats's first recognition of the young poet-suicide (d. 1770) who had been for Coleridge and Wordsworth and was to be for Shelley the type of unfulfilled genius—and whose pure English Keats was later to overestimate. The sonnet *Written on the Day that Mr. Leigh Hunt Left Prison* (February 2, 1815) is, as poetry, perhaps a little better. It was a sincere tribute to the courageous liberal who had had two years in prison (a martyrdom not without literary and do-mestic comforts) for giving in the *Examiner* a truthful por-trait of the Prince Regent at the age of fifty. Keats handed the sonnet to Clarke with a "conscious look and hesitation" when the latter was on his way to congratulate Hunt on his release. It was the first intimation Clarke "had received of his having committed himself in verse."

Keats's term of apprenticeship was to have run the normal five years, but the fifth year was canceled and in the summer of 1815 it was arranged that he should go on to the next stage of medical work, a sort of student internship at Guy's Hos-pital in London. Work with Hammond may have grown monotonous. Also, Tom was now established with George in Richard Abbey's office and Fanny lived with the Abbeys, so that John may have wanted to be near them. Especially after their grandmother's death the four orphans were bound closely together by mutual affection and need.

2

London, Medicine, and Poetry
(October, 1815–March, 1817)

O N O C T O B E R 2, 1815, four weeks before his twentieth
birthday, Keats was registered as a student at Guy's
Hospital. (His name was followed by that of a young Ameri-
can, John White Webster, who in 1849, at the Harvard
Medical School, was to murder a colleague, an oppressive
creditor.) Keats, after four years of semi-solitude in quiet
little Edmonton, was now thrown into a round of lectures,
study, and hospital work, along with a swarm of other stu-
dents, in a busy and dingy part of London. Southwark, "the
Borough," just south of the river and London Bridge, still
had something of the squalor of the Elizabethan Bankside,
"a beastly place in dirt, turnings and windings," Keats wrote
to Clarke (October 9, 1816). Near neighbors of Guy's Hospital
were three prisons. While Keats and his associates were more
serious students than Mr. Pickwick's young friends Bob Saw-
yer and Benjamin Allen, their lodgings and surroundings
were much as Dickens described them twenty years later—a
scene where there was no possible "inducement to look out
of the window" (though Keats was said to have always sat by
one) or to look inside either. So Keats became, in the words
of the Dickensian landlady, one of "a parcel of young cutters
and carvers of live people's bodies," who got along with what
sweetness and light they could muster.

At the start the most famous of lecturers and surgeons,

Astley Cooper (later a baronet), somehow discerned Keats's lonely bewilderment—though he was one among several hundred—and asked a senior student to look after him. Keats's surviving notes on Cooper's lectures suggest some initial difficulties in grappling with unfamiliar demands. At the end of the first month he was made a "dresser"; this meant the daily cleaning and bandaging of surgical wounds and other routine practice. The surgeon Keats assisted, William Lucas, was described by a fellow student as good-natured but bungling. Although Guy's Hospital and the associated St. Thomas' Hospital seem to have been well abreast of contemporary medical science, it is not now easy to imagine— even if we pass by the torments and the mortality of patients —the experience of attending and assisting at, and after, operations in the grim era before the use of either anesthetics or antiseptics. Whatever Keats's early troubles, he must, to judge from the outcome, have put in a good deal of efficient work.

But, unlike his fellow students, he was increasingly distracted by the seductive and imperative claims of poetry. One indication is the exuberance with which, on receiving his certificate, he fled from the Borough to Margate and writing. Another is the memory of his last operation, the opening of a man's temporal artery, which he had done "with the utmost nicety," but while his mind had wandered far away. There is, too, the account written by an able fellow student and roommate, Henry Stephens, of Keats's continual talk of poetry, "the zenith of all his Aspirations—The only thing worthy the attention of superior minds." Stephens, as more literary than others, had a larger share of Keats's confidence (though sometimes resentful of his assumption of authority): Keats greatly admired Spenser, liked Byron, thought Pope only a versifier; and while Stephens relished bold rhetoric, Keats was attracted by imagery.

The fullest and best evidence of Keats's state of mind is of course the verse that he wrote during this period. In the sonnet "O Solitude," of November, 1815, he turned away

from "the jumbled heap/Of murky buildings" (an unwont-
edly realistic phrase) to "Nature's observatory," the flowery
dell, the river, the wild bee in the foxglove bell; if this last
image was prompted by "Nuns fret not at their convent's
narrow room," it would apparently be Keats's earliest echo
of Wordsworth. The "two kindred spirits" who flee to soli-
tude in the sonnet's last line were Keats and his literary
friend George Felton Mathew. Chiefly through his sociable
brother George, the diffident John had begun to extend his
acquaintance before he entered the medical school. Three
young friends were Caroline and Anne Mathew, who occa-
sioned some Mooreish verses, and Mary Frogley, who—antici-
pating the scholarly zeal of her cousin, Richard Woodhouse
—collected copies of Keats's poems; she was addressed in
"Hadst thou liv'd in days of old," in its first version a valen-
tine written for George Keats's use. The Mathew girls'
cousin, George Mathew, was a prim, conventional, senti-
mental, and conceited versifier who, in the absence of better
minds, seemed for a while a kindred spirit. In the month of
"O Solitude," November, Keats wrote *To George Felton
Mathew*, his first epistle in verse and his first piece in heroic
couplets. He may at this time have known Drayton's epistles
and the similarly colloquial couplets of William Browne's
Britannia's Pastorals; and he had a doubtful contemporary
model of informality in Leigh Hunt. In this, as in most other
poems of 1815–1816, Keats's intoxication with the idea of
poetry is all the more touching because of his often quite
inept powers of expression; as we have observed already, he
naturally fell into the idiom of a bad age which had not yet
been purified by the great romantic poets. But what matters
is the long process of Keats's self-education—long, that is, in
proportion to his brief career. With "genius-loving heart" he
sees Mathew and himself as another Beaumont and Fletcher.
They will write and think of Chatterton, Shakespeare, Mil-
ton, Burns; there are phrases quoted from Milton and Spen-
ser. The young liberal also works in some of his stock heroes,

King Alfred, William Tell, and William Wallace. Poetry is one refuge, nature is another. In contrast with "this dark city" is set

> Some flowery spot, sequester'd, wild, romantic,
> That often must have seen a poet frantic.

(The first line of this execrable couplet may echo a popular poem that was to stay in Keats's memory, William Sotheby's translation of Wieland's *Oberon*.)[1] And Keats here makes his first identification of classical myth with living nature: medical studies have held him so long in thrall

> That I am oft in doubt whether at all
> I shall again see Phoebus in the morning:
> Or flush'd Aurora in the roseate dawning!
> Or a white Naiad in a rippling stream. . . .

These items, however weak and thin, are not merely bookish; they belong to the new romantic way of seeing and feeling both myth and nature.

In March, 1816, came another relatively good sonnet, "How many bards gild the lapses of time!" The octave rehearses the pleasures of reading and writing poetry, the sestet those of nature in her quiet evening moods (suggested perhaps by a descriptive catalog on an early page of Mrs. Radcliffe's *Mysteries of Udolpho*). But now Keats's ambitions were given a new turn by Leigh Hunt's long romance, *The Story of Rimini,* which appeared in February. Keats had read the "Spenserian" tales of James Beattie and Mrs. Tighe, *The Minstrel* (1771–1774) and *Psyche* (1805)—he was to look back on his early admiration for these as bad taste—but Hunt opened a new and modern vein with a tragic story of real persons, told with spirit and in colloquial language and loosely colloquial couplets. It was one of Hunt's defects that he did not feel the inappropriateness of his jaunty manner for a narrative of Dante's Paolo and Francesca—though the poem is better than its most notorious lines:

[1] See Werner W. Beyer, *Keats and the Daemon King* (New York: Oxford University Press, 1947).

The two divinest things this world has got,
A lovely woman in a rural spot!

Hunt's style and versification—along with the parallel influ-
ence of such Jacobeans as William Browne—were to affect
Keats for a long time to come, in part, as he later recognized,
because his earlier and weaker self had much in common
with Hunt; and both reflected their period. Meanwhile, in
this spring of 1816, Keats wrote two pieces, of 68 and 162
lines respectively, *Specimen of an Induction to a Poem* and
Calidore: A Fragment, in which he tried, not very happily,
to blend pseudo-Spenser with Hunt. In *Calidore* there are
clear-cut touches of natural observation—until the tinsel
characters appear.

May 5, 1816, brought the kind of event that stands out in
every young author's memory, his first appearance in print,
in this case the publication in the *Examiner* of Keats's sonnet
"O Solitude," written in November. In June came another
sonnet of escape, "To one who has been long in city pent."
Here, as in "How many bards," the pleasures of nature were
joined with those of art, art being apparently represented by
the *Story of Rimini.* Keats also made a beginning on what
was to be "I stood tip-toe upon a little hill." But the ex-
amination was looming up and he must have bent to his
medical books. On July 25 he passed with a success that
surprised his fellow students; he was now licensed to practice
—when he became twenty-one—as an apothecary.

Whether or not Keats intended to seek a professional open-
ing at the legal time, he had a stretch of enforced freedom
before October 31, and he hastened from London to Margate,
a resort on the southeastern coast, where Tom soon joined
him. Margate was not a resort of the Muses, but to Keats,
having his first sight of the sea, all things seemed possible and
exciting. The sonnet *To My Brother George,* written in
August, begins "Many the wonders I this day have seen," and
goes on with a happy picture of the sky and the mysterious
ocean; and Keats's beloved moon assumes the guise she is to
have in "I stood tip-toe" and *Endymion.* There followed an

epistle to George of 142 lines. It opens with an admission of dismay and bewilderment: freedom and novel sights have not yielded the expected inspiration, the effort "to think divinely" has not brought Apollo's song. But, invoking Spenser and Hunt, Keats rouses himself to describe the "wonders" the poet sees and the richer joys of "posterity's award." Though his only equipment is his senses and ambitious naïveté, he has grown since the epistle to Mathew.

In the epistle *To Charles Cowden Clarke* (September), Keats does not feel such a disturbing want of inspiration— "I slowly sail, scarce knowing my intent" (and, as often, rhyme can be his rudder). For this poem, as we have seen, was a tribute both to Clarke and to the poets Clarke had put in his way. Allusions and echoes, sparing in the epistle to George, naturally multiply here and bring in at least Cowper, Tasso, Spenser, Wieland, Hunt, Milton, Campbell, Moore (to follow the order of their appearance). And recollected pleasure rises to critical awareness:

> Spenserian vowels that elope with ease,
> And float along like birds o'er summer seas;

and

> Who read for me the sonnet swelling loudly
> Up to its climax and then dying proudly?

—a description to be greatly fulfilled in Keats's next poem.

At the end of September he returned to London and the Borough, where, for some weeks, he lived on Dean Street near the Hospital. Clarke, who had moved from Enfield to Clerkenwell in north London, was lent a folio copy of Chapman's *Homer,* and one evening the pair—who had known Homer only in Pope's elegant version—settled down to read the "famousest" passages, among them the account of Odysseus' shipwreck (which included the free and virile metaphor that delighted Keats, "The sea had soakt his heart through"). The story of that October night everyone knows, but it can never grow stale. At dawn Keats walked the two miles back to Dean Street and by ten o'clock that morning

Clarke received the sonnet. It was Keats's first masterpiece; he had so far done nothing that approached it and he was not to approach it for a long time afterward. Viewed in another way, as modern critics have viewed it, the sonnet was the first culmination of the exciting voyage of discovery that Keats had begun when as a boy he turned eagerly to books, and the process, the assimilation of "wonders," had been going on ever since. Now a climactic inspiration brought with it an original and masterful rightness and strength of form, style, images, and rhythm. The sonnet is, by the way, a rebuke to those who say that a writer must always go to "life"—as if great books were not a great part of life, and notably of Keats's. The theme of Odysseus' voyaging, transposed into Keats's own experience of discovery, drew together memories from his earlier years: Apollo, a symbol he had made his own; from Robertson, the Spaniards' quest of American gold and Balboa's first sight of the Pacific from Darien (Panama)—by a slip the more prominent Cortez displacing Balboa; from Bonnycastle, Sir William Herschel's discovery of the planet Uranus. These vivid, concrete, "heroic" examples reinforced and widened the particular theme stated in the octave. The power and tone of the conclusion were finely suggested by Leigh Hunt when he spoke of "that noble sonnet . . . which terminates with so energetic a calmness, and which completely announced the new poet taking possession. . . . The last line . . . makes the mountain a part of the spectacle, and supports the emotion of the rest upon a basis of gigantic tranquillity."[2] Keats's capacity for inspired revision, immediate or subsequent, was revealed chiefly in some later poems, but it began here. The original "Yet could I never judge what men could mean" he pronounced "bald, and too simply wondering"; his metaphorical revision caught up "pure serene" from Coleridge's *Hymn Before Sun-rise*. And the pallid "wond'ring eyes" of line 11 became—fired perhaps by a thought of Titian's portrait of Cortez—the metaphorical and pictorial "eagle eyes."

[2] *Lord Byron and Some of His Contemporaries* (1828), I, 410, 412.

Since the word "eagle" was used of Keats's own expression by Joseph Severn the painter, and since he came of age, poetically and legally, in this October of 1816, we might pause to look at the figure he presented to his friends and the world. He was five feet and three-quarters of an inch in height and broad-shouldered. He commonly had more important things to think about than his shortness (and average height then was less than it is now), but the chief references in his letters—which were made during his northern tour (June 4 and 27 and July 22, 1818)—suggest that it was often in his mind: he "never forgot" his stature "so completely" as in the presence of the northern mountains, and it was one cause of his feeling awkward in the presence of women. Keats's hair was reddish brown. He had his mother's wide mouth. What especially evoked comment was his expressive face and eyes. Mrs. Procter (wife of the poet "Barry Cornwall") said his face "had an expression as if he had been looking upon some glorious sight." Severn was impressed by the serene intensity of his delight in watching the wind blow over a field of grain. Keats's eyes, which Clarke and Severn said were hazel, were described by Hunt as "glowing; large, dark, and sensitive"; Benjamin Bailey spoke of their varying tender softness and "fiery brightness," and Severn of their "wine-like lustre." Bailey told Milnes that Keats's head was like that of a fine Greek statue, that it realized for him, more than any head he had ever seen, that of "the youthful Apollo." In December, 1816, Haydon made the life mask that is familiar in pictures and reproductions; it of course shows Keats's face in repose, not in its usual warm mobility.

In this month of October Keats met three men who were to be important through much of his active life: Leigh Hunt, already long admired from a distance; Benjamin Robert Haydon, the fervidly ambitious painter; and John Hamilton Reynolds, poet and miscellaneous writer, who was only a little more than a year older than Keats and was to be closer to him in spirit than any other friend. Clarke, having shown Hunt some of Keats's poems, was asked to bring him to

Hunt's cottage in the Vale of Health on Hampstead Heath. Keats's earliest extant letter (October 9, 1816) was a joyful reply to Clarke's message: " 't will be an Era in my existence." Hunt, eleven years older than Keats, was a well-known figure in the world, at least as a liberal editor; he was also a minor poet, an easy, charming talker—and listener—on books and art, and a generous encourager of young talent. The two made an immediate conquest of each other and henceforth, as poems of this autumn remind us, Keats was a frequent visitor at Hunt's fireside, where, with his host and others, he had abundant and exhilarating talk about poets and poetry. One such reminder is the sonnet describing his homeward walk from Hampstead, "Keen, fitful gusts are whisp'ring here and there." On December 1 Hunt printed in the *Examiner* an article on *Young Poets* (Shelley, Reynolds, and Keats), in which he quoted the sonnet on Chapman.

At Hunt's house Keats met Hunt's complete opposite, the painter Haydon, Keats's elder by nine years and, like Hunt, already a personage. He had fought a strenuous battle against mistaken orthodoxy in defense of the Elgin Marbles, the figures and friezes from the Athenian Parthenon which Lord Elgin had bought and thereby saved from probable destruction. Haydon was sublimely confident of winning immortality through his huge historical canvases—though what survives is his volcanic autobiography and diary. Just now he was working on *Christ's Entry into Jerusalem* and was conferring immortality on Wordsworth, Lamb, and Hazlitt— with whom Keats was to be joined—by using their heads for some of his figures. His debts (which were later to bring harassment on Keats) were likewise huge, though not for him overwhelming, and prolonged defeat and suicide were far in the future. Haydon's enormous ardor at once embraced Keats and his grandiose vehemence inspired heroic visions beyond Hunt's compass. On November 20, wrought up after spending the previous evening at Haydon's studio, Keats sent his host the sonnet "Great spirits now on earth are sojourning."

With something of Haydon's grandiosity he celebrated Wordsworth, Hunt, and Haydon and, tyro though he was, distilled the significance of the romantic movement and his own aspirations:

> And other spirits there are standing apart
> Upon the forehead of the age to come;
> These, these will give the world another heart,
> And other pulses. . . .

Some days earlier Keats had moved from the Borough to live with George and Tom at 76 Cheapside, in the City, and November 18, Tom's birthday, he had marked with the quiet sonnet *To My Brothers*—"Small, busy flames play through the fresh laid coals." Two sonnets of December came from the political and the religious liberal. Praise of the Polish patriot Kosciusko brought in the inevitable King Alfred. The last line, "To where the great God lives for evermore," goes along with the unwontedly anti-Christian *Written in Disgust of Vulgar Superstition* (December 22) and other evidence to suggest that Keats, now and later, might be given the loose label of "Deist." Through Hunt, he had lately been seeing Shelley, and the sonnet—which was done in fifteen minutes and is below Keats's usual level of human sympathy —may reflect their skepticism (they were given to baiting the staunchly Christian Haydon); the positive interest of the sonnet is in Keats's assumption that the only religion is poetry. Less ambitious and much better than either of these was a sonnet he wrote on December 30 in one of those informal competitions occasionally held in Hunt's circle. Keats quickly produced that fresh and charming report of simple sensation, *On the Grasshopper and Cricket*, which begins "The poetry of earth is never dead." The octave describes the summer pleasures of the grasshopper and switches gracefully to the cricket's song

> On a lone winter evening, when the frost
> Has wrought a silence . . .

At this last phrase the enthusiastic Hunt, who had hailed the "prosperous opening," broke out with "Ah! That's perfect! Bravo Keats!"

This autumn and early winter saw the completion of "I stood tip-toe" and the composition of *Sleep and Poetry*. These, the longest poems Keats had yet written, are poetical and personal documents that together explain his early view of the nature of poetry and the poet. In matter and manner as well as in chronology they are bridges between the juvenilia and *Endymion;* in fact "I stood tip-toe" was a first effort toward the long narrative and Keats referred to it as "Endymion." The epigraph from *The Story of Rimini*—"Places of nestling green for Poets made"—and the opening lines prepare us for

> a posey
> Of luxuries bright, milky, soft and rosy,

for loving, lavish, and wayward description of all "Nature's gentle doings" that Hampstead Heath can yield to eager senses. Simply as description, the writing is stronger than in the early epistles, and there are felicities to set against lapses. But the catalog of luxuries turns into something more, through that Keatsian agent, the moon,

> lifting her silver rim
> Above a cloud, and with a gradual swim
> Coming into the blue with all her light.
> O Maker of sweet poets, dear delight
> Of this fair world . . .
> . . . .
> For what has made the sage or poet write
> But the fair paradise of Nature's light?

The world of the senses is not abandoned but is carried into the ideal world, and the last hundred lines are given to the triple association or identity of nature, poetry, and myth, to the nature that inspired poets to conceive of Psyche, Pan, Narcissus, and Endymion and Cynthia. In reviewing the *Poems* of 1817, Hunt remarked on the affinity between

Keats's and Wordsworth's conception of myth; and Keats's more sensuous feeling was also akin to Hunt's own. Whether through affinity or through influence or both, Wordsworth's "Authentic tidings of invisible things" (*Excursion*, iv.1149)[3] become "Shapes from the invisible world" that visit "The wanderer by moonlight." The poet who created Endymion was a poet and a lover who surely "had burst our mortal bars." This phrase may be remembered as a vital clue to *Endymion* and other poems; it is Keats's version of that striving toward the infinite which was a central motive of European romanticism. And the general and personal prophecy of the sonnet to Haydon is heard again in the final question about the union of Endymion and Cynthia: "Was there a Poet born?"

The much longer *Sleep and Poetry*, diffuse and uncertain as it is in structure and style, is an explicit assessment of Keats's present and future and of the state of modern poetry. Whatever ideas he owes to Wordsworth, Hunt, and Hazlitt he has made intensely his own. Beginning with another catalog of nature's beauties, he sees them as elevated and consecrated by the poetic imagination. As a humble aspirant, he hovers between what his instincts now make him and what he longs to be, and even his ambition wavers between those two poles. Within the same paragraph (47–84) he would "die a death/Of luxury" and also would seize "the events of this wide world . . . /Like a strong giant." At the moment he is dwelling in the purely sensuous realm of Flora and old Pan, "And can I ever bid these joys farewell?" "Yes," he goes on,

> I must pass them for a nobler life,
> Where I may find the agonies, the strife
> Of human hearts.

These two stages have long been seen as Keatsian parallels to the second and third stages of development in *Tintern Abbey*, the adolescent and purely aesthetic passion for nature and, as mature compensation for the loss of that sensory in-

---

3 Here and elsewhere Wordsworth is cited from Thomas Hutchinson's handy one-volume edition (London: Oxford University Press, 1926).

tensity, sympathy with man, "the still, sad music of hu-
manity." But there are significant differences. Keats, though
he feels the mystery in nature and life, has no clear equiva-
lent of the metaphysical and moral part of Wordsworth's final
stage, the sense of "a spirit, that . . . rolls through all things"
and makes nature

> the nurse,
> The guide, the guardian of my heart, and soul
> Of all my moral being.

Moreover, while Wordsworth is now secure in his final stage
and recalling the past, the young Keats is happy in the earlier
sensuous phase and looking, indeed driving himself, ahead
toward the Wordsworthian poetry of the human heart. It is
likewise apparent that Keats is here anticipating his famous
letter to Reynolds of May 3, 1818, on the mansion of life,
the progression from thoughtless enjoyment of "pleasant
wonders" to sober comprehension of the heart and the misery
of man.

Lines 125–162 of *Sleep and Poetry* bring the somewhat
Shelleyan image of a charioteer, the symbol of poetic im-
agination, followed by "Shapes of delight, of mystery, and
fear"; Keats may have remembered the charioteer Apollo,
and Flora, the nymphs, and the garden, from Poussin's
L'Empire de Flore, and perhaps Shelley's *Daemon of the
World* (published with *Alastor* in February, 1816). But—as
often in *Endymion*—the ideal vision fades into a disillu-
sioned, muddy "sense of real things," which must be fought
against. Then, with the usual intolerance of young rebels,
Keats goes beyond the relatively mild utterances of his ro-
mantic elders and launches (162–206) an attack on what
Hunt and others called "the French school" of Boileau and
Pope. The mechanical snip-snap of the Popian couplet re-
flects a mechanistic view of both poetry and the world. The
image of the infant on a rocking-horse Pegasus comes from
Hazlitt's essay *On Milton's Versification;* "The blue/Bared
its eternal bosom" echoes Wordsworth's "The world is too

much with us." The whole passage was to infuriate Byron, the champion of Pope and scorner of the Lake Poets.

Keats turns to the modern world to salute some truly poetic souls: Chatterton (218–219), Wordsworth (224–226), and presumably Hunt (226–229). But in the next paragraph (230–247) he is bold enough—though the writing is vague and awkward—to note "ugly" defects as well as virtues in the leaders of the new poetry. Hunt, whose esteem for Wordsworth was qualified by dislike of grim tales and trivialities, in his review of Keats's *Poems* took the lines as censure of "the morbidity that taints the productions of the Lake Poets" (*Examiner*, July 13, 1817). Keats was doubtless reflecting Hunt—and Hazlitt—and anticipating his own later condemnation of Wordsworth's didacticism and excessive introspection, the "egotistical sublime." Against such perversions he sets up the conception of poetry as "A drainless shower/Of light," "might half slumb'ring on its own right arm," "a friend/To sooth the cares, and lift the thoughts of man." With an apology for youthful presumption, he reaffirms his vision of "A vast idea," "The end and aim of Poesy," "An ocean dim" that "Spreads awfully before me." In the last hundred lines he comes down to the pleasures of friendship, the "store/Of luxuries" there are to enjoy, and the poets' busts and mythological pictures in Hunt's study, where he has been given a bed for the night.

The vast, remote, but compelling "idea" of poetry and the calm serenity of true power were soon presented to Keats in terms of another art. On March 1 or 3, 1817, with Reynolds and with Haydon as the predestined guide, he viewed the Elgin Marbles, and he gave a half-inarticulate sonnet to their overwhelming effect on his senses and imagination. In the same month two examples of much less massive art inspired two more sonnets, *On a Leander Gem* and *On 'The Story of Rimini.'* If these suggest the earlier Keats, a sonnet of January 31, "After dark vapours have oppress'd our plains," was a foretaste of the future in its quietly happy feeling for nature's processes and in some phrases of fresh simplicity.

Impatient youth, even when endowed with real artistic genius, often seeks to proclaim outwardly a high vocation before admission has been earned, and Keats had taken to a mode of dress that struck some beholders as less poetical than nautical. In the late winter he was guilty of a small freak for which he soon apologized in an *Ode to Apollo:* he and Hunt, dining together, gave each other crowns of laurel and ivy, and, when surprised by callers, Hunt snatched his off but Keats defiantly kept his on without explanation.

On March 3, 1817, he had a more authentic coronation with the publishing of his *Poems,* which in a prefatory sonnet he dedicated to Hunt. During the several months since he had become legally entitled to practice his medical profession, he had carried on some work as a dresser at the Hospital but had not committed himself further. According to his Hospital friend, Henry Stephens, Hunt's article on *Young Poets* (December 1) "sealed his fate." In the course of this winter, when Richard Abbey urged Keats to hang out his shingle, the young man said that he did not intend to be a surgeon, that he was going to rely on his poetic abilities. That resolve would have been finally confirmed by the appearance of his book; Keats gave a copy to Abbey, whose response was characteristically crude. Reynolds promptly published a laudatory review in the paper he was attached to, *The Champion* (March 9); but, since other reviews came later, the story of the book's reception may be postponed.

3

Endymion and Other Poems
(April, 1817–February, 1818)

IN MARCH, 1817, Keats and—then or soon—his brothers
moved from Cheapside to 1 Well Walk in Hampstead;
they lodged with a friendly postman whose children's noise
and smelly stockings could be oppressive. Keats's circle of
friends was widening. In his first year at Guy's Hospital,
1815–1816, he had met a young solicitor, William Haslam,
who was to prove actively and unfailingly loyal, kind, and
helpful, and the aspiring painter, Joseph Severn, who did
not become a central figure in Keats's life until the end. In
the autumn and winter of 1816–1817, as we have seen, came
intimacy with Hunt, Haydon, and the younger Reynolds,
and some acquaintance with Shelley. The spring and summer
of 1817 brought in—mainly through Reynolds—others who
during the next few years were to be, along with Reynolds
(and of course Keats's brothers and sister and Fanny Brawne),
his chief associates and correspondents: James Rice, an at-
torney, whose gaiety and goodness were not soured by pro-
longed disease; Benjamin Bailey, an Oxonian candidate for
holy orders, for whom Keats had a strong liking and respect;
the admiring publisher and friend John Taylor, who, with
his partner James Hessey, took over from the Olliers the un-
sold copies of *Poems* and issued Keats's second and third vol-
umes, and who lent him books and advanced money; Charles
Dilke, a literary and scholarly employee of the Navy Pay

Office (where Dickens' luckless father had worked for a time);
Charles Brown, who had quitted business on inheriting a
legacy and had had a comic opera produced at Drury Lane;
and, now or later, Richard Woodhouse, a conveyancer and
legal and literary adviser to Taylor and Hessey, who was to
be a devoted and important collector and transcriber of
Keats's manuscripts. All these friends, except Haslam, were
from one to fourteen years older than Keats.

Before we come to *Endymion,* we may take account of the
reception of the *Poems* of March, 1817. The high hopes that
Keats's brothers and friends had built on that first book—his
own may have been dimmed by maturing judgment—were
disappointed by general lack of interest and a meager sale.
The amiable Charles Ollier, the publisher, had contrived a
sonnet to celebrate the publication (March 3), but eight
weeks later his brother James replied with anger to a broth-
erly though unwarranted complaint from George Keats.
There were six reviews in eight months. Reynolds, as we
noted, had written a prompt eulogy for his paper, the *Cham-
pion* (March 9); quoting abundantly, he praised Keats's
freshness and naturalness, and predicted his immortality. In
the *European Magazine* (May) Keats's former friend, George
Felton Mathew, rebuked Reynolds' extravagance and was
condescendingly self-assured both in his praise of the young
poet's luxuriant imagination and in his censure of a Huntian
mixture of foppish affectation and puerile sentiments. Hunt,
who doubtless knew that association with him might be the
kiss of death (as it proved to be), had a three-part review in
the *Examiner* (June 1, July 6 and 13), in which judicious
commendation was supported by judicious extracts. There
were three reviews by strangers. The *Monthly Magazine*
(April) had a brief but favorable notice. The *Eclectic Review*
(September) and the *Scots Magazine* (October), while regret-
ting the manifest influence of Hunt, were friendly. The
former saw many faults of immaturity but also "vivid imag-
ination and fine talents" and promise of possible excellence.
The *Scots Magazine* was decidedly cordial in praising Keats's

Spenserian and picturesque quality, his deep tone of moral energy, and "such a glorious and Virgilian conception" as the lines on the moon in "I stood tip-toe" (113–115). Though this review quoted three sonnets and the *Eclectic* two, neither mentioned the great one. Nowadays we know what Keats was to become, and we recognize the utter dedication to poetry that burns through the actual weakness of most of this first volume, but, if faced with it in 1817, we might have discerned few signs of power. At any rate, whatever small cheer these items may have given Keats, who was now approaching the end of *Endymion*, the penalties of a connection with Hunt became more ominously apparent in the October number of *Blackwood's Edinburgh Magazine:* Lockhart's first article *On the Cockney School of Poetry* included a contemptuous reference to Keats, who saw himself as probably the next victim.

To return to the spring of 1817, just after Keats and his brothers moved to Hampstead, Hunt and his family left, to visit Shelley at Marlow; after that they settled in another part of London. This external separation attended or slightly anticipated an internal one. Keats had owed much to Hunt, both privately and publicly (and late in March he wrote a poor sonnet in honor of the second edition of *The Story of Rimini*), but he was beginning to grow restive under his mentor's patronage. When in April and May he was unable to get *Endymion* properly started, he could even go along with Haydon's unjust charge that Hunt deluded himself in regard to his own poetical stature (I, 135, 143). However, Hunt's influence—or what can hardly be distinguished from that, the similar conventional qualities in his protégé—continued to operate in Keats's next and longest poem, though his individual voice was gaining strength. He had been invited to visit Shelley, but he wanted solitude and his own "unfetterd scope" (I, 170).

The theme of *Endymion*, at which "I stood tip-toe" had been an abortive attempt, Keats was now resolved to carry through, and it was to be his main occupation from the end of April to the end of November (as he said, more amply, in the prelude). Urged by his brothers, he sought stimulus for the new and formidable project in a change of scene. On April 14 he set off, with a set of Shakespeare just acquired, for the Isle of Wight. He spent a week at Carisbrooke. In the hallway of his lodging was a portrait of Shakespeare that he greatly liked, and he took as a good omen his landlady's bestowing it upon him when he left; he still had it in 1820. Haunted by a phrase (misquoted) from *King Lear,* he wrote the sonnet *On the Sea,* which in its opening lines has a massiveness not unworthy of its subject and inspiration. Before the end of April he had moved to the familiar Margate (where Tom joined him) and had begun *Endymion.* On May 16 he went with Tom to Canterbury. He made a short visit to a seaside village Haydon was acquainted with, Bo-Peep, near Hastings, where he met a Mrs. Jones who will turn up again. By June 10 Keats was back in Hampstead, working and looking up friends. Late in August he finished the second book of the poem. From early September to early October, Keats stayed with Bailey at Oxford, writing regularly and walking and boating on the Isis; at Oxford, on September 26, he finished the third book. During most of October and November he was in Hampstead. On November 28, at Burford Bridge under Box Hill, he completed the fourth and last book. Here he wrote that strangely moving lyric, "In drearnighted December." About December 5 he returned to Hampstead.

Keats had determined, understandably if perhaps unwisely, to write a very ambitious poem, to make, as he put it, four thousand lines of one bare circumstance, the love of Cynthia (Diana) for the mortal Endymion. Such a mythic "romance" would—in a heroic spirit akin to Haydon's—have a scope far beyond anything in the *Poems* (or *The Story of Rimini*); it would test his powers of invention; and it would give lovers of poetry a spacious field in which to wander and enjoy variety and surprise (I, 169–170). Not only did Keats find much difficulty in starting, but before he was done he realized that, while he had learned much from the effort, the poem was not what he had hoped to make it. When in August, 1820, he wrote to Shelley that his mind at the time had been like a pack of scattered cards, he was presumably indulging somewhat in retrospective exaggeration. We do not know how far, when he began, he had formulated a viable conception of the myth, though he could not have begun at all without something of the sort; nor do we know how far his initial conception was developed or modified as he went along. But, for all its lack of firm control and often of clarity, *Endymion* does have a fairly coherent theme and direction. The few modern critics who have denied this, who have seen only a celebration of sexual love, are able to hold such a view by ignoring or slighting the many parts of the poem that are manifestly allegorical or symbolic and that make no sense in merely erotic terms. The argument that an allegorical theme was not spoken of by Keats and was never suspected until Mrs. Owen's book of 1880 is hardly valid. Keats did not speak of the "meaning" of either *Hyperion* or of the great odes or of *Lamia;* and the accepted reading of all his major poems is largely a product of our century, since previous criticism contributed very little in the way of specific interpretation. Moreover, the allegorical *Endymion* is a logical and necessary link in Keats's whole evolution; it is in fact a seedbed of Keatsian ideas, and critics have continually cited from it embryonic illustrations of the most mature poems.

The fable was a quite natural sequel to Keats's earlier pieces. We have observed his complete devotion to poetry, and his conspicuous linking of poetry with nature and myth. Intensely sensuous apprehension of natural beauty was not only precious in itself but a means of imaginative intuition; most significantly in "I stood tip-toe," the creator of the myth of Endymion and Cynthia "had burst our mortal bars," had transcended the limits of ordinary human knowledge and understanding. In Lempriere's *Classical Dictionary* and elsewhere Keats would have met the allegorical tradition of many centuries, that the lover of the moon was a student of astronomy; and it was no long step to translate contemplation of the heavens into the poet's quest of beauty and truth, of poetic fulfillment.

Such instinctive idealism, however meager Keats's literary and scholarly sophistication, belonged to the broad stream of European romanticism; and his instinctive use of a myth was no less in the particular current of romantic Hellenism. Renaissance poets, from Spenser to Milton, had—with aid or sanction from allegorical mythographers—given ancient myth both a rich costume and rich symbolic value; and the old poets, major and minor, had already done much for Keats's general nourishment and for his imaginative approach to myth (if not for his undisciplined view of storytelling). In the Augustan age that fertilizing stream had been largely dried up, or rather driven underground, by the dominant rationalism, but it was now flowing freely again through the romantic revival of feeling and imagination and all things natural and primitive. Hunt and Hazlitt were two such re-interpreters. Coleridge had a nostalgic statement of the irresistible claims of myth in his translation of the second part of Schiller's *Wallenstein* (*The Piccolomini*, II.iv.123f.):

> The intelligible forms of ancient poets,
> The fair humanities of old religion,
> The Power, the Beauty, and the Majesty,
> That had their haunts in dale, or piny mountain,
> Or forest by slow stream, or pebbly spring,
> Or chasms and wat'ry depths; all these have vanished.
> They live no longer in the faith of reason!
> But still the heart doth need a language, still
> Doth the old instinct bring back the old names. . . .

Wordsworth, who at first thought might seem a foreordained enemy, and who in some measure shared eighteenth-century disgust, came to see ancient myth as the imaginative and vital flowering of the Greek religion of nature, a religion—on a lower pagan level—akin to his own in its intimations of continuity, unity, and infinity. The extended passages on Greek myth in *The Excursion* (iv.717f., 847f., and also vi.538f.) were, we may assume, among the reasons for Keats's naming that much abused poem, along with Haydon's paintings and Hazlitt's depth of taste, as "three things to rejoice at in this Age" (letter to Haydon, January 10, 1818: I, 203; also, I, 204–205).

Keats's conscious development of a parable in *Endymion* can be made clear only through an outline that pays due regard to unmistakably "philosophic" themes and motives, which may at times be obscured by fumbling expression, wayward narrative, and lush description. The familiar first line, "A thing of beauty is a joy for ever," proclaims its author's concrete particularity of apprehension, so distinct from Shelley's vein of abstraction; and he is not yet troubled by the idea of impermanence. In the manner of his earlier long poems, but with a more evident philosophic purpose, Keats joins beautiful objects of nature, from the sun to flowers, with those of art; and the moon is joined or identified with "The passion poesy." All such things, enduring or transient, are primary "essences" that supply "An endless fountain of immortal drink," the essential sustenance of the human spirit (which is itself an "essence," a distinct portion of being); with the Keatsian addition of art, these correspond in effect to Wordsworth's moments of sensory experience and vision, "spots of time." Another significant word in the earlier Keatsian vocabulary is "ethereal," which will appear in some extracts as we go on. Beautiful objects and the immediate responses they evoke may, through the creative insight of the imagination, be transposed into a higher "ethereal" key. One gloss on this word might be taken from the letter to Haydon of May 10–11, 1817 (I, 143): "the looking upon the Sun the Moon the Stars, the Earth and its contents as materials to form greater things—that is to say ethereal things—but here I am talking like a Madman greater things that [*for* than] our Creator himself made!" Thus, launching upon his story, Keats prays for "a portion of ethereal dew" (i.131).

The elaborate picture of the feast of Pan (i.89f.), perhaps suggested by the opening of Michael Drayton's *The Man in*

the Moon, includes a glimpse of Endymion as the local chief-
tain, a young man of action now disturbed by some inward
anxiety. The choric hymn to Pan may be called the first of
Keats's great odes; it was, in spite of some faults of diction
due to the exigencies of rhyme, the finest sustained writing
he had yet done. The specific attributes and services of the
shepherd-god, gathered mainly from a number of Elizabethan
poets, are organized toward a grand crescendo of both mean-
ing and sound. Pan—who had long filled many allegorical
roles, from Christ to "Universal Nature"—rises above his
crude mythological self to become a

> Dread opener of the mysterious doors
> Leading to universal knowledge,

the symbol of the romantic imagination:

> Be still the unimaginable lodge
> For solitary thinkings; such as dodge
> Conception to the very bourne of heaven,
> Then leave the naked brain: be still the leaven
> That spreading in this dull and clodded earth
> Gives it a touch ethereal—a new birth:
> Be still a symbol of immensity;
> A firmament reflected in a sea;
> An element filling the space between;
> An unknown. . . .

It is regrettable, if understandable, that Wordsworth, when
he heard Keats recite this hymn, could label as "A very pretty
piece of paganism" an interpretation of Greek myth so close
to his own; Keats had none of Wordsworth's Christian res-
ervations.

The theme of suprahuman aspiration is carried on in a
quiet passage (i.355f.) in which the priest and sober elders,
with young Endymion,

> discours'd upon the fragile bar
> That keeps us from our homes ethereal.

The various hopes and visions of immortality are in accord
with Keats's idea, expressed in the notable letter to Bailey

of November 22, when he was just finishing the poem, "that we shall enjoy ourselves here after by having what we called happiness on Earth repeated in a finer tone. . . ."[1] The summary of conversation and the hymn to Pan prepare for the vision and quest of the poet-hero.

Endymion, going apart with his sister Peona, has a refreshing sleep (a state identified with visionary power) and then explains why he, the active leader of his people, has been so troubled and listless. In a dream he had seen a dazzling moon, then a dazzling goddess who had carried him through the skies and brought him down to earth; the return to actuality had blighted all lovely things around him (i 691f). Peona, the voice of common sense, reproaches him for sullying "high and noble life with thoughts so sick." But Endymion declares that, though he has cherished ambitions of public service, his distracting vision was no sick fancy. Then comes the revised passage (i.777f.) that Keats wrote of so urgently to his publisher, "a consequitive Man" (like Peona), as not "mere words" but

a regular stepping of the Imagination towards a Truth. My having written that Argument will perhaps be of the greatest Service to me of any thing I ever did—It set before me at once the gradations of Happiness even like a kind of Pleasure Thermometer— and is my first Step towards the chief Attempt in the Drama—the playing of different Natures with Joy and Sorrow. (January 30, 1818: I, 218–219)

Since Keats had only an improvised philosophical vocabulary, and since he was as yet imperfectly articulate, the lines in the poem are somewhat cloudy. Yet the main points seem clear. The first stage of happiness, "fellowship with essence," is set forth in terms similar to those of the opening paragraph: it is sensuous and imaginative response to things of nature ("The clear religion of heaven"), music, and poetry.

1 I, 185. Is the last phrase an echo of Wordsworth's "Music of finer tone" (*Excursion*, ii.710), with which might be linked lines 101–108 of *Laodamia?* The idea appears in Hunt and such other minor poets as Rogers and Campbell [Newell F. Ford, *The Prefigurative Imagination of John Keats* (Stanford, Calif.: Stanford University Press, 1951), pp. 100–111].

Through such feelings we step into "a sort of oneness" with
the universe and man (the names of Apollo and Orpheus go
along with the favorite romantic image of the Aeolian harp).

>   But there are
>   Richer entanglements, enthralments far
>   More self-destroying, leading, by degrees,
>   To the chief intensity: the crown of these
>   Is made of love and friendship, and sits high
>   Upon the forehead of humanity.

The second stage of happiness is friendship, the brotherly
and beneficent love of man as well as men, a steady and sub-
stantial quality of heart and mind. The third and topmost
stage is love, the very "pith" of experience, for which men
have been content to lose the world, and which is indeed the
vital force of nature. (At the end of his letter to Reynolds of
May 3, 1818, Keats looked beyond the painful "Chamber of
Maiden-Thought" to a "third Chamber of Life . . . stored
with the wine of love—and the Bread of Friendship.") But if
earthly love can thus make mortal men immortal, what is to
be said of the immortal love that has laid hold upon En-
dymion? Here, as elsewhere, "immortal" partakes of the lit-
eral sense already noted, but clearly and mainly signifies
"endowed with suprarational insight"; Keats's concern is
with human experience raised to the imaginative "sublime."
Three times Endymion has seen his "fair enchantment," and
his love, his feeling of "renewed life," remains intense, tor-
tured, and baffling; it seems as if he must go back to his old
uninspired round. All this is far from mere eroticism.

The prelude to the second book glorifies love and lovers
in contrast with the "gilded cheat" of war and history. Then
the troubled Endymion is led into a quest for his dream
goddess. It is to take him successively, in books two, three,
and four, through the bowels of the earth, under the sea, and
through the sky.[2] The second book is the least clear of the

---

2 Along with a desire for variety, Keats may have thought of the parallel
journeyings in Southey's *Curse of Kehama* (a poem he echoed in *Isabella*)
and of Cynthia's triple role as—in the words of his own sonnet *To Homer*—

four in its functional contribution to the total plan. It follows logically upon book one in its reminders (ii.123–125, 185–186, 211–212, 310f., 438, 686) that from the start Endymion is leaving the mortal world in search of what Keats calls immortality. It is psychologically sound—as it was in *Sleep and Poetry* after the chariot of imagination had fled—that ideal aspirations should be followed by moments of realistic frustration and despair (*e.g.,* i.620–622, 691f.). Such a passage as this carries its own sober warrant of authenticity (ii.153f.):

> But this is human life: the war, the deeds,
> The disappointment, the anxiety,
> Imagination's struggles, far and nigh,
> All human; bearing in themselves this good,
> That they are still the air, the subtle food,
> To make us feel existence, and to show
> How quiet death is. Where soil is men grow,
> Whether to weeds or flowers; but for me,
> There is no depth to strike in. . . .

This is a partial anticipation of "The vale of Soul-making" and of the end of *Hyperion*. There is also this significant bit (ii.275–276):

> And thoughts of self came on, how crude and sore
> The journey homeward to habitual self!

It may seem less logical that a "Platonic" pilgrimage should, in this second book, put stress on erotic passion—first, Endymion's envious witnessing of the warm reunion between Venus and Adonis, and then his own sexual consummation with his goddess (whose identity, we may remember, he does not know); this last incident (ii.707f.), which Keats wants to treat with high intensity, occasions some of the worst writing in the whole poem. He was a half-disciplined poet

---

"Queen of Earth, and Heaven, and Hell." There is also his reference in *Endymion* (iii.31) to the Powers "In water, fiery realm, and airy bourne," although the poem has no fiery realm. Among many suggested "sources," Keats apparently owed more or less to George Sandys' translation of Ovid's *Metamorphoses* with an allegorical commentary—which, in the 1640 edition, he was to cite in working on *Hyperion*.

composing his first long narrative, a visionary narrative, and he was also a young man of rarely potent senses, so that it is no wonder if eroticism, or erotic language, was sometimes obtrusive—though anti-allegorical critics greatly exaggerate its prominence in relation to the whole. Further, "elemental passion," while doubtless intended to be one of the "gradations of Happiness," is clearly an initial and not a final phase, as books three and four make plain; Keats somewhat confused the issue by making the dream goddess the willing sharer of this first physical rapture and by turning the "immortality" of suprahuman knowledge into an immortality of passion. But to say that he largely failed here to transmute erotic action into ideal symbol is not at all to say that *Endymion,* or even this passage, is mainly about sex. Endymion recalls his old ambition to be the friend of his people, and—in keeping with the main line of books one, three, and four—what had been presented as love's madness is taken, not as an end, but as a means or symbol of exalted vision (ii.904f.):

> Now I have tasted her sweet soul to the core
> All other depths are shallow: essences,
> Once spiritual, are like muddy lees,
> Meant but to fertilize my earthly root,
> And make my branches lift a golden fruit
> Into the bloom of heaven.

The next incident shows Endymion's enlarged sympathies and provides a link between the second book and the third. He hears the river-god Alpheus pleading with Arethusa to grant him her love; whereas before, as a self-centered and ungratified lover, Endymion had envied Venus and Adonis, now, after full experience with his own goddess, he can forget himself and pray to her to make this pair happy. We remember that, above "fellowship with essence," are

> Richer entanglements, enthralments far
> More self-destroying. . . .

Book three opens with the badly written blast of a young liberal against the Establishment and spurious public values;

in contrast is set the genuine regality of contemplation of "ethereal things." Keats goes on to apostrophize the moon as the symbol of beauty and love, and this theme is developed in a soliloquy by Endymion—a reminder, if any were needed, that poet and *persona* are one. From his boyhood the moon had represented and consecrated all that Endymion loved and aspired to—nature, wisdom, poetry, friends, great deeds, the charm of women:

> On some bright essence could I lean, and lull
> Myself to immortality.

Then, with the appearance of his dream goddess, the moon's spell had partly faded, though now it is reviving and imperils his "sovereign vision." The whole passage is an explicit statement of the poet's allegorical intention.

There follows the episode of Glaucus, which occupies the third book and which is meaningless unless it constitutes an important stage in Keats's "gradations of Happiness." The story of Glaucus' life, from concern for self to concern for others, turns out to be partly a parallel, partly a contrast, with Endymion's experience. At first a solitary quietly content with nature and man, he had felt "distemper'd longings" and had been granted his wish to be a sea-god; falling vainly in love with Scylla, he had been seduced by Circe, had fled from her sensual bondage and cruelty, and had had a thousand-year curse pronounced upon him by the angry witch. Now he hails Endymion as the destined agent of his deliverance, and Endymion's sudden fear soon gives place to pity. Glaucus' release from thralldom and death involves two obligations. He must search for knowledge, explore

> The meanings of all motions, shapes, and sounds;
> . . . all forms and substances
> Straight homeward to their symbol-essences;

and especially he must collect and, with Endymion's aid, restore to life the bodies of lovers drowned at sea (a motif perhaps derived from Ben Jonson's *Masque of Lethe*). This magical act, carrying on from Endymion's sympathy with

Alpheus and Arethusa and with Glaucus, manifests his growth in "friendship," humanitarian service; and the revival of the dead lovers brings to both Endymion and Glaucus the taste of "a pure wine/Of happiness." (This metaphor and the theme of universal knowledge come together in one sentence in Keats's letter of November 22 to Bailey, where he speaks of "this old Wine of Heaven" as "the redigestion of our most ethereal Musings on Earth.") The concluding and over-decorated celebration at Neptune's palace reiterates the theme of Endymion's approaching release "from dull mortality's harsh net."

The fourth book begins with a sketch of the historical movement of poetry from the East to the West. Then, abruptly, we hear the lamenting voice of a woman who proves to be an Indian left behind Bacchus' triumphal westward march. Endymion is horrified to find himself in love with this new being; the lover of the moon, of the dream goddess, and now of the girl before him, he has "a triple soul." The Indian maid sings a lyric to Sorrow which frames the very different Bacchic processional, and both illustrate Keats's frequent failure to control his invention and to render his theme. The description of Bacchus and his throng of people and animals (inspired, no doubt, by Titian's painting and drawing details from many sources) is in itself a remarkable bravura piece both in exotic picture-making and in orchestration of sound, but it has no apparent function; if it is a graphic illustration of the westward movement of poetry, that idea does not come through. And the enveloping ode to Sorrow is a lilting ditty that makes no serious impact at all as an exposition of Keats's prolonged concern with the mixture of joy and sorrow and the sorrow that is wisdom—although he evidently thought the lyric had weight, since, in that letter of November 22, expounding his central and passionate faith in the imagination and beauty, he said: "In a Word, you may know my favorite Speculation by my first Book and the little song I sent in my last—which is a repre-

sentation from the fancy of the probable mode of operating
in these Matters. . . ."

The remaining seven hundred lines of the poem describe
Endymion's painful vacillation between his celestial and his
earthly love. At lines 429–431, in a dream of heaven, he
recognizes for the first time that his goddess is Diana, so that
his three attachments are reduced to two. Torn between
them, he wonders

> What is this soul then? Whence
> Came it? It does not seem to be my own, and I
> Have no self-passion or identity.

Again we remember the "enthralments far/More self-destroy-
ing" and Keats's concern in the letters with "identity." A
deeply felt and impressively written passage (512f.) tells of
Endymion's suffering when he finds himself alone in a "Cave
of Quietude," a "native hell" where he feels the apathetic
content of complete despair—"self spiritualized into a kind
of sublime Misery" (to use words from a letter to Bailey of
October 29, 1817). He does not heed a celestial song in
honor of "Cynthia's wedding." He condemns himself bitterly
for having

> clung
> To nothing, lov'd a nothing, nothing seen
> Or felt but a great dream!

In pursuing a heavenly ideal he has sinned against all natural
earthly ties:

> There never liv'd a mortal man, who bent
> His appetite beyond his natural sphere,
> But starv'd and died.

Although he still loves his goddess, he will be cheated no
more by airy voices; the Indian maid has redeemed his life
"from too thin breathing" (an echo of Peona's phrase at
i.751). One human kiss is better than celestial dreams.

So far the idea is clear, but some further steps are less so.
The Indian maid avows that she is forbidden to be En-
dymion's love. The unhappy pair meet Peona, who says that

festive hymns are being sung to Diana. Endymion tells the Indian maid that there are pleasures, higher than those of earth, which he may not see "If impiously an earthly realm I take"; with her for a friend only, he will live as a hermit, serving his people. If this resolution represents Endymion's conquest of "self," it is left uncertain, especially as he goes on to complain of his undeserved lot, since he has wedded himself "to things of light from infancy" (957–958). He asks Peona to pronounce, if it is heaven's will, on their sad fate— perhaps a final renunciation of self. Then, before his eyes, the Indian maid is revealed as the goddess of his pilgrimage; she explains that he needed "from this mortal state" to be "spiritualiz'd" before his love could be fulfilled.[3]

Even a meager outline, whatever obscurities appear, rules out the notion that Keats was devoting four thousand lines to glorifying romantic eroticism. There is abundant evidence that he was grappling with what had hitherto been and was to remain his prime concern, the nature of poetry and the poet, even if here his conception and execution were immature and often ineffectual. *Endymion* has two interwoven main themes. One is "the gradations of Happiness," from responsiveness to nature and art through beneficent service to love; and, while love includes ordinary sexual love, it means chiefly—the fable being a poet's progress—the all-embracing power of the imagination. Keats is groping toward a unified consciousness. A second main theme, possibly the result of a late change of plan, is defined through Endymion's wavering between his dream goddess and the Indian maid, his final cleaving to the latter, and the revelation that the two are one: that is, the poet cannot directly realize an abstract ideal but must come at it by way of common, concrete experience. (Whether or not Keats had Shelley's *Alastor* in mind, the

[3] This device—Diana, as a nymph, winning Endymion's love away from her divine self and then disclosing her identity—had been the plot of Drayton's *Endimion and Phoebe* (it was not retained in his revised version, *The Man in the Moon*). Keats might have read it, since one of the several surviving copies was in the library of Westminster Abbey. But no source has been found for Drayton's Platonic parable, and to assume that Keats must have read it is to assume that Drayton could invent what Keats could not.

basic contrast between the two poems—not to mention many lesser contrasts—is characteristic of their authors: Shelley's conception—summarized in the first half of his preface and developed in the poem, though partly undercut in the second half of the preface—is of a poet who, seeking the realization of his ideal vision, ends his vain quest with death, not with the Keatsian discovery that the way to the ideal lies through the actual.) There are also subsidiary themes. One, which was later to become central for Keats, is the rival claims of poetic contemplation and humanitarian action. Another, apparently, is "Negative Capability," but this may be postponed for a bit.

While the earlier poems, especially the longer ones, lead us toward *Endymion*, the letters written during the period of its composition tell us of Keats's states of mind but, until the end, not much about the poem itself. At the start he "cannot exist without poetry—without eternal poetry" (April 18, 1817: I, 133); and, if he dared, he would like to think of Shakespeare—whom he is always quoting—as his "Presider" (I, 142). Yet he sees in himself, as the worst enemy of his writing, a horrid morbidity of temperament (*ibid.*), and he is the victim of both dormant, sterile seasons and recurrent fear about his capacity and the magnitude of his enterprise; at times he feels "anxiety to go on without the Power to do so" (I, 146). By the end of September he is tired of *Endymion* but he cannot rewrite it; he would rather think of "a new Romance" for the next summer (I, 168). Yet Hunt's reported comment on the diffuseness of the poem prompts a defense and an assertion of his effort to write independently (I, 169–170). On October 29, in a letter to Bailey, Keats makes his first really critical comment on Wordsworth (apart from summer talks with Bailey), an acute one on a too "comfortable" poem, *Gipsies*. On November 3, ecclesiastical ill usage of Bailey inspires a wish "for a recourse somewhat human independant of the great Consolations of Religion and undepraved Sensations. of the Beautiful. the poetical in all things" (I, 179).

The most important letter, that written to Bailey on November 22, when *Endymion* is almost done, one would like to quote in full (I, 183–187). Since parts of it grew out of Bailey's troubles, they may not directly concern *Endymion,* but we have here early formulations of some of Keats's leading ideas. One is his instinctive version of that doctrine of European romanticism, "the beautiful soul":

I am certain of nothing but of the holiness of the Heart's affections and the truth of Imagination—What the imagination seizes as Beauty must be truth—whether it existed before or not—for I have the same Idea of all our Passions as of Love they are all in their sublime, creative of essential Beauty. . . . The Imagination may be compared to Adam's dream—he awoke and found it truth.[4] I am the more zealous in this affair, because I have never yet been able to perceive how any thing can be known for truth by consequitive reasoning—and yet it must be. . . . However it may be, O for a Life of Sensations rather than of Thoughts! It is 'a Vision in the form of Youth' a Shadow of reality to come. . . .

The exclamation means "O for the sensuous, imaginative, and intuitive life of the artist rather than that of analytical reason!" Then Keats develops the idea we met before, that life in the hereafter must be that of earth repeated in a finer tone—yet this can be the lot only of those who delight in sensation rather than hunger, like Bailey, after truth. A complex mind, he proceeds, exists "partly on sensation partly on thought" and grows with years and study and knowledge.

Keats goes on to say that he scarcely remembers counting upon any happiness; nothing startles him beyond the moment. "The setting sun will always set me to rights—or if a Sparrow come before my Window I take part in its existince and pick about the Gravel." Keats's empathy with the sparrow exemplifies his doctrine of "Negative Capability," which is first enunciated—though not named—in this letter:

Men of Genius are great as certain ethereal Chemicals operating on the Mass of neutral intellect—by [*for* but] they have not any individuality, any determined Character. I would call the top and head of those who have a proper self Men of Power.

[4] *Paradise Lost,* viii.452–490.

In Keats's letter to his brothers of late December, 1817 (I, 193–194), his definition has a somewhat different emphasis. Negative capability is here said to distinguish a man who, like Shakespeare above all,

is capable of being in uncertainties, Mysteries, doubts, without any irritable reaching after fact & reason—Coleridge, for instance, would let go by a fine isolated verisimilitude caught from the Penetralium of mystery, from being incapable of remaining content with half knowledge. This pursued through Volumes would perhaps take us no further than this, that with a great poet the sense of Beauty overcomes every other consideration, or rather obliterates all consideration.

In a letter to Woodhouse of nearly a year later (October 27, 1818: I, 387), Keats returned to his original emphasis. In contrast with "the wordsworthian or egotistical sublime" he sets up the truest kind of poet, who has no cramping or warping sense of personal identity and hence no doctrinal message but is wholly impersonal, unbiased creativity:

it is not itself—it has no self—it is every thing and nothing—It has no character—it enjoys light and shade; it lives in gusto, be it foul or fair, high or low, rich or poor, mean or elevated—It has as much delight in conceiving an Iago as an Imogen. What shocks the virtuous philosop[h]er, delights the camelion Poet. It does no harm from its relish of the dark side of things any more than from its taste for the bright one; because they both end in speculation. A Poet is the most unpoetical of any thing in existence; because he has no Identity. . . .

This conception of the poet as a purely creative being, without individual character or identity, Keats took over from a prime source of his ideas, Hazlitt, and made very much his own. His early misgivings about his poetic elders' obtrusive subjectivity had found vague utterance in *Sleep and Poetry* (230f.), and were to become very explicit in regard to Wordsworth (and sometimes Byron). But Hazlitt made Keats's understanding larger and more positive. In the essay *On Posthumous Fame* in *The Round Table,* which Keats had read at Oxford, Hazlitt had described Shakespeare as a poet who seemed scarcely to have an individual existence of his own, but to borrow that of others at will, and to pass successively through 'every variety of untried being,'—to be now *Hamlet,* now *Othello,* now *Lear,* now *Falstaff,* now *Ariel.*

His essay *On Gusto* had opened with the succinct definition "power or passion defining any object"—an idea akin to Hopkins' "inscape." Keats also read—on Bailey's recommendation, it seems—Hazlitt's first and much-ruminated book, *An Essay on the Principles of Human Action* (1805), in which, opposing old crude views of self-interest, Hazlitt had argued for "the natural disinterestedness of the human mind," a potentiality that needed the work of the imagination for its fulfillment. In the third of his current lectures on *The English Poets* (January 27, 1818), Hazlitt exalted Shakespeare as an impersonal creative power and contrasted his and Milton's objectivity and range with the morbid and devouring subjectivity of "a modern school of poetry" (that is, Wordsworth in particular).

As Keats at this stage assimilated these ideas of gusto and disinterestedness, they were almost wholly aesthetic and sensuous. The poet suppresses his own personality in order to become, and thereby render most vividly, the essence, the "thisness," of his subject. Such a theory philosophized and stimulated Keats's native genius for empathy, although in his poetry this power was mainly limited to levels below that of human character; in his living experience it was not, as his letters show. Joseph Severn, when they walked together, noted his companion's penetrating observation:

even the features and gestures of passing tramps, the colour of one woman's hair, the smile on one child's face, the furtive animalism below the deceptive humanity in many of the vagrants, even the hats, clothes, shoes, wherever these conveyed the remotest hint as to the real self of the wearer.

It might be remarked also that the theory was to prove inadequate for Keats's more mature recognition of the poet's need for ethical identity and stability—qualities which modern critics, more than the romantics, are given to finding in

Shakespeare. To come back to *Endymion*, it would appear that the hero's continuing concern with self and self-destroying enthrallments, up through his final submission to Peona's command, represents, however unclearly, Keats's conscious effort to depict a progressive extinction of personality as part of the process of artistic growth.

If the Indian maid's identification with Cynthia is in itself an unrealized bit of Platonic sleight of hand, it none the less puts a theoretical seal not only upon "the holiness of the Heart's affections" but upon the concreteness of apprehension that was announced in the first line of the poem. For all the romantic strangeness of the various scenes, the details, whether they belong to nature or art, are predominantly realistic and substantial—and far removed from the panoramic phantasmagoria of *Alastor*. Much of Keats's best writing is the result of direct "sensations" of either nature or myth. Examples of the former are these:

>   . . . rain-scented eglantine
> Gave temperate sweets to that well-wooing sun;
> The lark was lost in him; cold springs had run
> To warm their chilliest bubbles in the grass;
> Man's voice was on the mountains; and the mass
> Of nature's lives and wonders puls'd tenfold,
> To feel this sun-rise and its glories old. (i.100f.)

> And like a new-born spirit did he pass
> Through the green evening quiet in the sun,
> O'er many a heath, through many a woodland dun,
> Through buried paths, where sleepy twilight dreams
> The summer time away. (ii.71f.)

>   Cold, O cold indeed
> Were her fair limbs, and like a common weed
> The sea-swell took her hair. (iii.623f.)

Allusions to myth may attain a similar felicity through association with human feeling or natural beauty:

> Than Dryope's lone lulling of her child (i.495)

> Or blind Orion hungry for the morn (ii.198)

> Æa's isle was wondering at the moon (iii.415)

Or one might quote the massive—and much revised—picture of Cybele (ii.639f.), which owed something to George Sandys' translation of Ovid. Since every page of *Endymion* is uneven in quality and exhibits diffuseness, bad poetical diction, and slack versification, we cannot say that Keats has achieved a style or rhythm; but he is on the way. Though his total parable is deeply sincere, it is a theory he is groping toward rather than a digested experience, and his emergent style appears chiefly in lines or passages that tell of happy or—as in that on the Cave of Quietude—gloomy moods that he has felt. Such generalities must no doubt be qualified. If, for instance, Endymion's sexual passion represents Keats's own, actuality did not secure him against distressing mawkishness (and the Indian maid, despite her symbolic function, is something of a coquette).

This last sentence brings up a biographical matter that seems to demand more space than a gratuitous and nebulous notion deserves. While some letters indicate clearly enough that Keats's years of maturity included sexual experience, there are no valid grounds whatever for the idea that he had contracted syphilis during his visit with Bailey at Oxford. In a letter of October 8 to that strictly virtuous cleric, Keats urged him to slacken his hard reading and thereby relieve his physical disorders, and he added:

The little Mercury I have taken has corrected the Poison and improved my Health—though I feel from my employment that I shall never be again secure in Robustness—would that you were as well as your sincere friend & brother, John Keats (I, 171).

On the strength of this, apparently (he gave no evidence at all), Dr. (later Sir) Benjamin Richardson said that at Oxford Keats "runs loose, and pays a forfeit for his indiscretion, which ever afterwards physically and morally embarrasses him."[5] W. M. Rossetti, in his *Life of John Keats* (1887),

---

[5] *The Asclepiad* (1884), p. 143. Richardson was a friend of Keats's fellow student Henry Stephens, but, so far as we know, Stephens and Keats did not meet or communicate after March, 1817, except briefly in June, 1818; and anyhow Stephens declared in 1847 that Keats's "absolute devotion to Poetry prevented . . . his indulging in any vice" (*K.C.*, II, 210).

picked up the notion from Richardson and cited the allusion to mercury. The chief and sufficient refutation of the inference is the fact that, as Amy Lowell was at special pains to show, in Keats's time mercury was used for various ailments, including indigestion and any kind of inflammation, whereas by the 1880's its functions had been narrowed down to virtually one, so that Richardson and Rossetti were much too easily misled. A modern medical authority, Sir William Hale-White, said in his book on Keats (1938) that, when used for syphilis, mercury was always required "in considerable doses for a long period," that no doctor in his senses would prescribe a "little," and that Keats certainly "did not take it for this malady." The rest of Keats's sentence, as Hale-White observes, "merely means that he had dedicated himself to a sedentary occupation," and he wishes the studious Bailey were faring as well.

Further, the substance and tone of the current letters (October 8 and 28–30, November 22) do not warrant the idea that their author is suffering from such a disease. On October 28–30, after philosophizing about illness and uncomfortable activity of mind, Keats replies, avowedly in the same vein, to Bailey's inquiry about his health and spirits:

Health and Spirits can only belong unalloyed to the selfish Man —the Man who thinks much of his fellows can never be in Spirits —when I am not suffering for vicious beastliness I am the greater part of the week in spirits (I, 175).

The words seem to describe a mental and variable rather than a physical state. If Keats's thoughts have a logical sequence, "vicious beastliness"—which has been taken as evidence of syphilis—should mean that he is afflicted by man's inhumanity to man (in this letter he had blamed himself for being "neglectful" of Bailey's worries). If the words have a sexual meaning (which nothing in the letter suggests), they might refer to regrets for indulgence (witness the hope expressed in the letter to Tom of July 26, 1818: I, 351). Finally, in the famous letter of November 22 on "the holiness of the Heart's

affections" and other prime articles of faith, Keats says that
he is not pestered with many of the troubles the world is full
of:

I think Jane or Marianne [Reynolds] has a better opinion of me
than I deserve—for really and truly I do not think my Brothers
illness connected with mine—you know more of the real Cause
than they do—nor have I any chance of being rack'd as you have
been (I, 186).

The Reynolds sisters have apparently been worried about
Keats's having consumption and have given him too much
credit for courage. If Bailey knew that "the real Cause" was
syphilis, he would surely, on his own account as well as
Keats's, not have allowed Lord Houghton to reprint this bit
and the reference to mercury;[6] moreover, in the very admir-
ing reminiscences of Keats that he sent to the biographer, he
did not give the slightest hint of such a thing. In short, there
is no evidence for the idea and there is much against it.

Soon after Keats's return from Burford Bridge to Hamp-
stead, George went with Tom to stay at Teignmouth on the
coast of Devonshire, in the hope that Tom's failing health
might improve. For Keats himself the writing of *Endymion*—
the anxious spells of dryness, the spurts of high activity, and
the ebbing of his original hopes for the poem—had been,
despite moments of buoyancy, a heavy strain. During the
winter months of 1817–1818 he was engaged in his normal
round of occupations, social and literary; at times he was, he
could confess, going about too much. In the middle of De-
cember, Keats witnessed two performances by the celebrated
Edmund Kean; and, as a substitute for Reynolds, he wrote
three theatrical reviews, one of them on Kean, for the *Cham-
pion* (December 21, January 4). Dining with a group of men
who belonged mostly to the upper literary world—among
them Horace Smith, the host, and his brother James, co-
authors of the famous parodies, *Rejected Addresses*—Keats

6 Dorothy Hewlett, *A Life of John Keats,* second edition, revised and en-
larged (New York: Barnes & Noble, Inc., 1950), p. 121.

disliked their modish wit and affectations and condescending talk about Kean and his low company. He was taken by Haydon to meet Wordsworth, who was on one of his visits to London; Keats's reciting of his "Hymn to Pan," at Haydon's entreaty, drew the chilly response recorded above ("A very pretty piece of paganism"). On December 28 was held what Haydon, the exuberant host, called his "immortal dinner." The guests were Wordsworth (in genial mood), his London relative Thomas Monkhouse, Charles Lamb, Keats, and others who came in later. Talk began with Homer, Shakespeare, Milton, and Virgil, but descended to more convivial levels. A Deputy Comptroller of Stamps named Kingston (who had been at the Smith dinner), a pushing admirer of Wordsworth, made such solemnly naïve efforts at intellectual conversation that the tipsy Lamb behaved rudely, and Keats helped Haydon to bundle the irrepressible offender into another room.

Keats had other meetings with Wordsworth, alone or in company. In letters of February 21 and April 8 he remarked that Wordsworth had left a bad impression in town and had gone away "rather huff'd," having received less complete deference at "his fireside Divan" than he expected. But, notwithstanding personal and critical reservations, and even times of revulsion, Keats reverenced Wordsworth as the great poet of the age; whenever he brooded on the human condition, he was likely to quote *Tintern Abbey* or *Intimations of Immortality*. And if Shakespeare, the supreme creator, was beyond emulation, Wordsworth, the compassionate poet of the human heart, had shown the way modern poetry should take. In January and later, Keats was also seeing something of Hazlitt, whom he had met before and to whose ideas, as we have observed, he owed much. He arrived too late for the second of Hazlitt's lectures on *The English Poets* (January 20) at the Surrey Institution, but he seems to have attended the other seven. Phrases from the lectures were to be echoed in Keats's odes of 1819. Writing on February 14(?) to George

c

and Tom in Devon, Keats reported with amusement that he himself was increasingly recognized: among the signs was a call from Crabb Robinson, who liked to know everyone of account in the literary world—though he did not record this visit in his diary.

During these early weeks of 1818, Keats was not finding Hazlitt's ideal of "disinterestedness" in operation among several friends: Haydon was having angry quarrels with both Reynolds and Hunt and rights and wrongs were hard to assess. "Men should bear with each other," Keats wrote to Bailey on January 23: "there lives not the Man who may not be cut up, aye hashed to pieces on his weakest side. The best of Men have but a portion of good in them—a kind of spiritual yeast in their frames which creates the ferment of existence—by which a Man is propell'd to act and strive and buffet with Circumstance" (I, 210). A few days earlier, writing to his brothers about the feuds going on, Keats had made a distinction which was to recur in his letters and was to come up in the *Fall of Hyperion*. Works of genius, he says, are not the first things in life. "No! for that sort of probity & disinterestedness which such men as Bailey possess, does hold & grasp the tip top of any spiritual honours, that can be paid to any thing in this world" (I, 205). Although Keats was, less than three weeks later, to write to his publisher about his "Pleasure Thermometer" in *Endymion*, he has already, at least for the moment, moved beyond it.

Endymion was undergoing revision for the press from early January until the middle of March. Also, a renewal of poetic energy manifested itself in half a dozen short pieces; four of them touch, with varying focus, on the problems of the poet and "the burthen of the mystery." Keats took the first book of *Endymion* to show Hunt, who vexed him by objecting, as he skimmed over it, to the unnaturalness of the talk and other things. Hunt proudly displayed "a real authenticated Lock of Milton's Hair" and asked Keats to respond forthwith to such an inspiration, which, with natural misgivings, he did,

in the rather forced little ode, "Chief of organic numbers!"
The most significant note in it—in view of the prolonged
oscillation in subsequent letters over the place of knowledge
in the poet's equipment—is Keats's declaration, his first of
the kind, that present burning and strife are vain, that he
must "grow high-rife/With old Philosophy" (I, 210–212).

In the next few days Keats wrote two sonnets, *On Sitting
Down to Read King Lear Once Again* and "When I have fears
that I may cease to be." Neither has the massive simplicity of
the early sonnet on Chapman; indeed, though the main drift
of the first is clear, some details are not, and the total import
of the second has been disputed. In late December, in report-
ing to his brothers his opinion of Benjamin West's painting,
Death on the Pale Horse, Keats had enunciated what was to
be a main principle of his mature poetry (I, 192):

. . . the excellence of every Art is its intensity, capable of making
all disagreeables evaporate, from their being in close relationship
with Beauty & Truth—Examine King Lear & you will find this
examplified throughout; but in this picture we have unpleasant-
ness without any momentous depth of speculation excited, in
which to bury its repulsiveness.

(Keats's "disagreeables," as W. J. Bate says, are the irrelevant
and discordant, whatever interferes with the unified intensity
and reality of the work and of the human spirit's response to
it.) On January 20 Keats handed in to his publisher the re-
vised first book of *Endymion;* on the twenty-first he wrote the
Miltonic ode, avowing the vanity of burning and strife until
he could grasp "old Philosophy"; on the twenty-second he
wrote the sonnet on *King Lear;* and the next day he began
the revision of the second book of *Endymion.* Thus when in
the sonnet he dismisses "golden tongued Romance, with
serene lute," and braces himself to "burn through" again

> the fierce dispute
> Betwixt damnation[7] and impassion'd clay,

7 Originally "Hell torment" (I, 215).

he is turning away from *Endymion*—and, by implication, from all inferior kinds of romantic idealism—to face the soul-searing ordeals of the highest tragedy (I, 214–215). And his concluding hope is:

> But, when I am consumed in the fire
> Give me new Phoenix wings to fly at my desire.

"When I have fears" was Keats's first sonnet in the Shakespearian form of three quatrains and a couplet, and the style has a Shakespearian coloring. Both the sense of the words and the melancholy tone seem to express, not so much the ostensible theme, Keats's fear of being cut off before fulfillment, but rather, as W. J. Bate perceived, a more realistic fear of poetic failure hiding behind the thought of early death.

A letter of January 31 to Reynolds (at the end of which Keats copied the preceding sonnet) was composed mainly of impromptu verses: a ditty about "Maidenheads . . . going"; then a lighthearted banishment of common drinks in favor of the brighter wine of nature, poetry, and Apollo; and then the very serious appeal to the "God of the Meridian." This last develops, with urgent intensity, the problem touched in the ode to Milton, the "terrible division" between soaring imagination and earthbound body, the conflicting claims of "sensation" and "thought"; and here, as before, Keats prays for the moderating power of "staid Philosophy." When this question comes up, as it is to do more and more insistently, Keats sometimes means intellectual knowledge but more often ethical insight and wisdom.

The "fair creature of an hour" of "When I have fears" may have been the woman seen briefly at Vauxhall long before and celebrated in "Time's sea hath been five years at its slow ebb" (February 4). This sonnet is notable chiefly for the degree to which Keats was able to imitate Shakespeare's manner —not that the poem could be taken for his. On the same day, or perhaps on February 6, Shelley, Keats, and Hunt had a competition in writing sonnets on the Nile, and for once the

least of the three triumphed; the poet of the sentimental
chirp rose to the heroic line on Cleopatra, "The laughing
queen that caught the world's great hands." Keats's contribu-
tion was "Son of the old moon-mountains African."

Several other poems of February record in varying tones
one of Keats's revulsions against Wordsworthian subjectivity
and didacticism—qualities which he, like Hazlitt, contrasted
with Elizabethan virtues. Reynolds had sent him two sonnets
on Robin Hood and these helped to set him off, in his letter
of February 3:

. . . for the sake of a few fine imaginative or domestic passages,
are we to be bullied into a certain Philosophy engendered in the
whims of an Egotist. . . . We hate poetry that has a palpable de-
sign upon us. . . . Poetry should be great & unobtrusive, a thing
which enters into one's soul, and does not startle it or amaze it
with itself but with its subject.

After a glance at the large-minded Elizabethans, he goes on:

I will have no more of Wordsworth or Hunt in particular. . . . I
don't mean to deny Wordsworth's grandeur & Hunt's merit, but
I mean to say we need not be teazed with grandeur & merit—
when we can have them uncontaminated & unobtrusive. Let us
have the old Poets, & robin Hood. (I, 223–225)

Thereupon Keats throws in two pieces "written in the Spirit
of Outlawry," *Robin Hood* and "the Mermaid lines" ad-
dressed to "Souls of Poets dead and gone." These, by the way,
were, along with *Isabella,* the only poems written between
Endymion and *Hyperion* that Keats chose to print in his
third and last volume; even the best among his many sonnets
were left out.

A couple of weeks later the question assumed its more
general and Keatsian form of sensation versus knowledge.
The letter to Reynolds of February 19 is a plea for quiet
contemplation, for the spider's spinning "from his own in-
wards his own airy Citadel," as against the acquisitive bee's
restless hurrying about. Keats has been led into these thoughts

by the beauty of the morning operating on a sense of Idleness—I have not read any Books—the Morning said I was right—I had no Idea but of the Morning and the Thrush said I was right.

Then follow the fourteen unrhymed lines supposedly sung by the bird to sustain a poet's anti-intellectual mood:

> O fret not after knowledge—I have none,
> And yet my song comes native with the warmth. . . .

Keats's usual good sense tells him that "all this is a mere sophistication, however it may neighbour to any truths, to excuse my own indolence." Two days later he reported to his brothers that he was reading Voltaire (whom Hazlitt had lately touched in a lecture) and Gibbon, although, he adds, he had written to Reynolds the other day to prove reading of no use. Such shifts of mood were to continue; active assimilation of knowledge and ideas and passive receptivity to "sensation" were both valuable and nourished each other.

On February 27, sending some corrections to Taylor, Keats remarked that in *Endymion* he had "most likely but moved into the Go-cart from the leading strings," and added a description of the kind of writing he was in time to achieve:

In Poetry I have a few Axioms, and you will see how far I am from their Centre. 1st I think Poetry should surprise by a fine excess and not by Singularity—it should strike the Reader as a wording of his own highest thoughts, and appear almost a Remembrance—2nd Its touches of Beauty should never be half way therby making the reader breathless instead of content: the rise, the progress, the setting of imagery should like the Sun come natural natural too him—shine over him and set soberly although in magnificence leaving him in the Luxury of twilight—but it is easier to think what Poetry should be than to write it—and this leads me on to another axiom. That if Poetry comes not as naturally as the Leaves to a tree it had better not come at all. However it may be with me I cannot help looking into new countries with 'O for a Muse of fire to ascend!'—If Endymion serves me as a Pioneer perhaps I ought to be content. I have great reason to be content, for thank God I can read and perhaps understand Shakespeare to his depths, and I have I am sure many friends, who, if I fail, will attribute any change in my Life and Temper to Humbleness rather than to Pride—to a cowering under the

Wings of great Poets rather than to a Bitterness that I am not appreciated.[8]

M. H. Abrams remarks, in *The Mirror and the Lamp,* that, although Keats probably did not know "Longinus" at first hand, his three poetic axioms "read like a gloss upon some doctrines of *Peri Hypsous."*

[8] I, 238–239. For the idea that poetry should come naturally Rollins cites Hazlitt, *Works,* ed. Howe, IV, 24.

4

Poems, the Northern Tour, and Reviews
(March–September, 1818)

SINCE EARLY DECEMBER, George Keats had been looking after Tom in Devon, and he was concerned about his own present and future; he became twenty-one on February 28. Within the next few days he returned to London, talked with John, and proceeded with arrangements to marry Georgiana Wylie and emigrate to the United States; he hoped to establish himself in the Middle West. On March 4, the night of a great storm, John set off, as an outside passenger, for Devonshire. He and Tom stayed at Teignmouth, where it rained almost incessantly, for two months.

During the first weeks in Devon Keats wrote (along with lighter verses) the sonnet, "Four seasons fill the measure of the year," a mild acceptance of man's stages of ripening and decay; the seasonal pattern had diverse precedents in the *Excursion* (v. 390f.) and Sandys' translation of Ovid (xv. 199–213). In a letter to Bailey of March 13, in which he copied the sonnet, Keats's mind played around some characteristic ideas. Starting from a lack of relish for both the people and the landscape, he declared that scenery was fine but human nature finer. Apropos of his inability to share the religious side of Bailey's life and thoughts, he could say that he was sometimes so very skeptical as to think poetry itself "a mere Jack a lanthern to amuse whoever may chance to be struck with its brilliance." That leads to another definition of his old word "ethereal." Ethereal things are of three kinds: "Things real" (the sun, moon, stars, and passages of Shakespeare); "Things semireal such as Love, the Clouds &c which require a greeting of the Spirit to make them wholly exist"; and "Nothings which are made Great and dignified by an ardent pursuit." After the sonnet comes Keats's "old maxim" that every point of thought "is the centre of an intellectual world. . . . We take but three steps from feathers to iron." And he adds at once that he has no idea of the truth of any of his speculations, that he will never be a reasoner because he does not care to be in the right.

He did care, of course, though not in the way of argument. On March 25 he wrote to Reynolds, who had been ill, that epistle in verse which, if a sometimes ragged and sometimes cloudy impromptu, becomes a significant stocktaking of life and himself. After a half-playful prelude on last night's incongruous dreams, Keats describes Claude's paintings, *The Sacrifice to Apollo* and *The Enchanted Castle*. But from those serene visions of a remote ideal world he turns—somewhat like Wordsworth in *Elegiac Stanzas*—to anxieties and gropings that had appeared in poems and letters of the past year or more:

> O that our dreamings all of sleep or wake
> Would all their colours from the Sunset take:
> From something of material sublime,
> Rather than shadow our own Soul's daytime
> In the dark void of Night. For in the world
> We jostle—but my flag is not unfurl'd
> On the Admiral staff—and to philosophize
> I dare not yet!—Oh never will the prize,
> High reason, and the lore of good and ill
> Be my award. Things cannot to the will
> Be settled, but they tease us out of thought.
> Or is it that Imagination brought
> Beyond its proper bound, yet still confined,—
> Lost in a sort of Purgatory blind,
> Cannot refer to any standard law
> Of either earth or heaven?—It is a flaw

c*

In happiness to see beyond our bourn—
It forces us in Summer skies to mourn:
It spoils the singing of the Nightingale.

While there are some unclear links or leaps of logic and
association, we seem to have the poet's avowedly illusory wish
for full contentment in "sensation" as against the oppressive
and inescapable problems of life and consciousness; and his
recognition that, though the poetry of knowledge and ethical
thought is beyond him, in a world that affords no absolutes
the imagination alone is a not wholly free and reliable guide.
These perplexing questions end much as they began, but the
wish has become a simple affirmation in the vein of what the
thrush had said and of what Endymion had learned. (Some-
what similar things had got into a fantastical letter written
the previous day to James Rice.) Keats proceeds to picture a
quiet evening by the seashore, but—this comes as a shock—
behind the beauty and apparent happiness of nature is the
hideous fact of "an eternal fierce destruction" going on
among the creatures of sea and earth and air. The idea—
most familiar to us in Tennyson's "Nature, red in tooth and
claw"—had been expressed by many writers, from Goethe
(whose *Werther* Keats may echo) and Erasmus Darwin ("And
one great Slaughter-house the warring world") back through
Milton to Lucretius; and possibly Keats's recent reading in
Voltaire had included *Le Désastre de Lisbonne*. There was,
too, the nearer fact that Tom had lately had a hemorrhage.
Keats continues to be haunted by the horrible vision, though
he tries to push it away and brings his epistle to an end with

Do you get health—and Tom the same—I'll dance,
And from detested moods in new Romance
Take refuge. . . .

The general human problems that thrust themselves into
this epistle would be aggravated by Keats's personal thoughts
and feelings during these rainy and depressing weeks in
Devon. The three brothers and their young sister, left or-
phans at so early an age, had been bound together by special

ties of affection. Now Keats was closely confined with Tom, and his medical knowledge would sharpen his watchful anxiety about the invalid. In a few months George would be leaving to settle in the United States, and his practical mind had made him in some ways the head of the family; as John said later, George had always stood between him and any dealings with the world, and now John would bear full responsibility in addition to losing his "greatest friend." Then, too, *Endymion* was finished, and, since Keats's own earlier confidence had melted away, he could not hope for much public encouragement. There was also the question of his next major enterprise, which would be the real test of his maturing powers.

Endymion was published toward the end of April; reviews of it, which spread out over a long time, may be postponed. On March 19 Keats had written a preface, a mixture of something like petulance and affected jauntiness, which Reynolds and his publishers agreed would not do; it sounded too much like Hunt. Keats was somewhat hurt, but on April 10 he produced the remarkably candid and manly preface that we know. He anticipated the reader's perception of "great inexperience, immaturity, and every error denoting a feverish attempt, rather than a deed accomplished." Yet another year of revision would not set right a work that had such sandy foundations. "It is just that this youngster should die away," however sad a thought for its author; but he hopes that he has learned enough to make "verses fit to live." He does not seek to forestall criticism: "there is not a fiercer hell than the failure in a great object." The conclusion, though it is so familiar, must be quoted in full:

The imagination of a boy is healthy, and the mature imagination of a man is healthy; but there is a space of life between, in which the soul is in a ferment, the character undecided, the way of life uncertain, the ambition thick-sighted: thence proceeds mawkishness, and all the thousand bitters which those men I speak of must necessarily taste in going over the following pages.
I hope I have not in too late a day touched the beautiful

mythology of Greece, and dulled its brightness: for I wish to try once more, before I bid it farewel.

In his letter to Reynolds of April 27, Keats for the first time named *Isabella,* which he had finished; this was presumably the "new Romance" referred to in the verse epistle to Reynolds of March 25. Keats had begun the poem in February, before he went down to Devon, and probably wrote most of it between March 25 and April 27. He and Reynolds had planned a joint volume of tales versified from Boccaccio's *Decameron,* but Reynolds, who was now involved in legal work and had recently been ill, could not do his share and Keats did not go on with the project. Their original impulse may have come from Hazlitt's lecture of January 27 on Dryden and Pope, in which, speaking of the *Fables,* he had suggested a parallel enterprise for modern poets and named "Isabella" among attractive items. Keats was not held back by the feeling he expressed in a letter to Haydon on March 21: "It is a great Pity that People should by associating themselves with the fine[st] things, spoil them—Hunt has damned Hampstead [and] Masks and Sonnets and italian tales" (I, 251–252).

The brief story in the *Decameron* (Day IV, Novel 5) Keats read in the 1684 edition of a translation, perhaps by John Florio, first published in 1620. This version, while it largely preserved Boccaccio's crisp storytelling, changed the liaison between Lorenzo and Isabella into an innocent idyll and made her brothers—now left without a valid motive—more wantonly cruel. The romantic idealizing of the lovers was carried further through Keats's expansion of the opening part and through his whole mode of treatment. His second line, "Lorenzo, a young palmer in Love's eye," suggests—however unhappy in itself—that he had thoughts of *Romeo and Juliet* (I.v.95f.); and there seem to be several echoes and imitations of Chaucer; but such salutary thoughts were not enough to counteract the established manner, the more or less languishing tone, of contemporary romantic narrative as it was practiced from the Spenserian Mrs. Tighe up through Hunt's *Story of Rimini,* Mrs. Hemans, and the slightly later "Barry Cornwall"; even the tales of the severely classical Landor could have their embarrassing moments. Potent as the convention was, we may still wonder that it could lead into sentimental pathos the maturing poet who had lately dismissed romance to welcome, in *King Lear,* "the fierce dispute/Betwixt damnation and impassion'd clay," who had faced grim reality in the *Epistle to Reynolds,* and who had just been feasting on Milton. But—not to mention the praises of Keats's closer friends—Charles Lamb, whose taste was fairly robust, pronounced *Isabella* the finest thing in the volume of 1820. Keats himself, in September, 1819, could not bear what he then saw as mawkish and much inferior to the *Eve of St. Agnes* and especially *Lamia* (II, 162, 174).

It is not surprising that a generation later Matthew Arnold, in his first critical essay, the preface to his *Poems* of 1853, should take *Isabella* as an example of romantic concern with decorative luxuriance and of indifference to action and structure. But it is surprising that so devout and discerning a classicist could, in supporting that judgment, say that *Isabella* "contains, perhaps, a greater number of happy single expressions which one could quote than all the extant tragedies of Sophocles." (*The Eve of St. Agnes* would have served far better for felicities of phrase but not so well for defective structure.) Certainly *Isabella* has many good and some notable things. Everyone since Lamb has spoken of the darkly proleptic phrase,

> So the two brothers and their murder'd man
> Rode past fair Florence. . . .

There is stanza liii, which is all the stronger for its echoes of the opening account of idyllic love:

> And she forgot the stars, the moon, and sun,
> And she forgot the blue above the trees,
> And she forgot the dells where waters run,
> And she forgot the chilly autumn breeze;

> She had no knowledge when the day was done,
>   And the new morn she saw not: but in peace
> Hung over her sweet basil evermore,
> And moisten'd it with tears unto the core.

Above all there is the one piece of sustained strength, Isabella's vision of her dead lover and his speech (xxxv–xli), where Keats's combined power of macabre imagination and expression rises far beyond his simple source; with that may be linked the gruesome explicitness of Isabella's cleansing of her lover's head (li). And other details and phrases could be cited.

But the texture in general is very uneven, sometimes awkward, flat, or obscure, sometimes sugary or turgid. Of the sugary, one familiar example will do:

> So said, his erewhile timid lips grew bold,
>   And poesied with hers in dewy rhyme.

Just before "the two brothers and their murder'd man" we have " 'Good bye! I'll soon be back.'—'Good bye!' said she" —a bit of Huntian chattiness not redeemed by the presumably ironical intention of showing the lovers' untroubled security. In stanza xlvii Isabella, digging, came on a glove

> And put it in her bosom, where it dries
> And freezes utterly unto the bone
>   Those dainties made to still an infant's cries—

lines which for the older modern critics embodied all the poignancy of thwarted motherhood but which for us are spoiled by the amatory falsetto of "dainties." This stanza ends with a finely realistic and dramatic gesture:

> Then 'gan she work again; nor stay'd her care,
>   But to throw back at times her veiling hair.

The ending of the next stanza is one of the victims of rhyme and rhetoric:

> At last they felt the kernel of the grave,
>   And Isabella did not stamp and rave.

POEMS, THE NORTHERN TOUR, AND REVIEWS 79

Since the source left the brothers with no adequate motive for murdering Lorenzo, the young liberal supplied one: the avaricious capitalists wanted their sister to marry a nobleman, not their employee. We remember that Bernard Shaw found potential Marxism in stanzas xiv–xvii. Keats's picture of the toilers, who, in far-flung mines, factories, rivers, and seas, endure harsh oppression and danger to fill the coffers of the wicked pair, seems to combine hints from Dryden's *Annus Mirabilis* (iii), Southey's *Thalaba* (i.239f.), a work already echoed in *Endymion,* and perhaps Robertson's account of the gold-seeking Spaniards in America. But while the idea was good, and some particulars are arresting, stanza xvi—which Scott Fitzgerald in a letter strangely called "great"—was the acme of the repetitive and turgid:

> Why were they proud? . . .
> . . . .
> Why were they proud? again we ask aloud,
> Why in the name of Glory were they proud?

If such fustian recalls the worst bits of *Endymion, Isabella* as a whole does in time tell its story, and the simplicity of the original is given psychological and dramatic as well as decorative elaboration. The *ottava rima,* which Byron could put to such brilliant comic use, was for Keats a dubious advance on the rhymed couplet as a narrative medium; it may have helped to move and control the story, but it also invited padding and forced rhymes. No doubt he chose that form as appropriate for an Italian tale, and no doubt he modeled his handling, however distantly, on the more rapid stanzas of Edward Fairfax's Elizabethan translation of Tasso (of which he owned a copy). He did not, though, follow Fairfax's Spenserian style; and he carried further Fairfax's tendency to make the final couplet a self-contained summary unit (which, through Waller, had had a share in molding the Augustan heroic couplet). Also, as W. J. Bate has pointed out, Keats went against Hunt's critical theory in the plentiful use of antithesis and repetition, and he greatly curbed his youthful (and Huntian) addiction to the chirpy feminine ending.

Earlier we observed Keats's shifting attitudes in regard to the poet's need of intellectual knowledge, and these continue. Writing to his publisher, Taylor, on April 24, he is firmly on the intellectual side:

I was purposing to travel over the north this Summer—there is but one thing to prevent me—I know nothing I have read nothing and I mean to follow Solomon's directions of 'get Wisdom—get understanding'—I find cavalier days are gone by. I find that I can have no enjoyment in the World but continual drinking of Knowledge—I find there is no worthy pursuit but the idea of doing some good for the world.

While people do good in various ways (in view of things to come, it is significant that Keats links intellectual knowledge, beneficent action, and poetry),

there is but one way for me—the road lies th[r]ough application study and thought. I will pursue it and to that end purpose retiring for some years. I have been hovering for some time between an exquisite sense of the luxurious and a love for Philosophy—were I calculated for the former I should be glad—but as I am not I shall turn all my soul to the latter (I, 271).

All this, and especially the last sentence, we may take as one of Keats's conscious steps into maturity—not that the young poet had lacked "Philosophy" or that the later one was to forswear "the luxurious." On April 27 he communicated similar resolutions to Reynolds:

I have written to George for some Books—shall learn Greek, and very likely Italian—and in other ways prepare myself to ask Hazlitt in about a years time the best metaphysical road I can take.—For although I take poetry to be Chief, there is something else wanting to one who passes his life among Books and thoughts on Books—I long to feast upon old Homer as we have upon Shakespeare, and as I have lately upon Milton (I, 274).

We remember Keats's early resolution to move from the realm of Flora and old Pan to "the agonies, the strife/Of human hearts." Now the senses must give place to intellectual knowledge, and knowledge is to be the means of doing some good for the world. Yet this conflict, though it points toward the *Fall of Hyperion,* is at the moment not at all painful; and doing good seems to imply only more philosophical poetry, not a setting of poetry below humanitarian service.

Perhaps about this time Keats wrote the sonnet *To Homer,* which appears to take the non-intellectual side of the question. In thinking of the "triple sight" possessed by the blind Homer, Keats was doubtless thinking also of the blind (though immensely learned) Milton and his compensating inner light. In a more general way, Homer is seen as having —to use a key phrase from *Endymion*—"A fellowship with essence." And Keats may be recalling his belief in "a very gradual ripening of the intellectual powers" (I, 214. For the poetic sensibility, apparent ignorance and passiveness may yield true knowledge:

> Aye, on the shores of darkness there is light,
>   And precipices show untrodden green;
> There is a budding morrow in midnight;
>   There is a triple sight in blindness keen. . . .

Although Keats's letter to Reynolds of May 3, 1818, is one of the most familiar, it is so important a stocktaking that we must remind ourselves of its contents. Every department of knowledge he sees as "excellent and calculated towards a great whole"; he is glad that he still has his medical books to review. Sensations are not enough: "An extensive knowledge is needful to thinking people—it takes away the heat and fever; and helps, by widening speculation, to ease the Burden of the Mystery" (I, 277). Yet "it is impossible to know how far knowledge will console us for the death of a friend and the ill 'that flesh is heir to.' " With respect to the affections and poetry, his friend knows Keats's thoughts by sympathy, and as "a ratification" of these he copies the fragment, "Mother of Hermes! and still youthful Maia!", which he had written on May Day. This simple, mellow utterance, one part Greek and three parts romantic, seems to be on the side of sensation rather than knowledge, another version of the sonnet on the thrush's song; there is no agonized straining after

"Philosophy," only rich content with finitude, and that feeling is confirmed by a rightness of style that is wholly free from the faults of *Isabella*.

Then comes the question "whether Miltons apparently less anxiety for Humanity proceeds from his seeing further or no than Wordsworth." So far as our experience goes, we find Wordsworth true, and "axioms in philosophy are not axioms until they are proved upon our pulses"; "Until we are sick, we understand not;—in fine, as Byron says, 'Knowledge is Sorrow'; and I go on to say that 'Sorrow is Wisdom'—and further for aught we can know for certainty! 'Wisdom is folly.'" Keats proceeds to elaborate the simile of human life as "a large Mansion of Many Apartments," of which he, as yet, knows only two, first "the infant or thoughtless Chamber," then "the Chamber of Maiden-Thought," in which we move from intoxication with pleasant wonders into a darkened and complex vision of "the heart and nature of Man," of a world "full of Misery and Heartbreak, Pain, Sickness and oppression," in which "We see not the ballance of good and evil. We are in a Mist"—the point Wordsworth had reached when he wrote *Tintern Abbey*. Returning to his comparison, Keats, with some apology for presuming, remarks that Milton's "Philosophy, human and divine, may be tolerably understood by one not much advanced in years." (Here, as in this whole comment, Keats shows, like most of his contemporaries except Coleridge, and like many of his successors in the century, a decidedly immature notion of Milton's beliefs and principles.) Yet Wordsworth's deeper exploration of the human heart is due not to individual superiority but to a general advance, "a grand march of intellect," which "proves that a mighty providence subdues the mightiest Minds to the service of the time being, whether it be in human Knowledge or Religion." The third Chamber, Keats winds up, lies still beyond him and Reynolds, but it "shall be a lucky and a gentle one—stored with the wine of love—and the Bread of Friendship"—phrases which, as we noted, recall the two highest levels of the "Pleasure Thermometer" of *Endymion*.

On May 8–9 John and Tom got back to Hampstead; they had stopped on the way home from Devon because Tom had a hemorrhage, but he seemed to make a good recovery. On May 28 George Keats and Georgiana Wylie were married. Keats had come to like Georgiana more and more; in a letter to Bailey on June 10 he declared her the most disinterested woman he ever knew, and, in admiring puzzlement, decided that her and other women's happiness must spring from a blessed lack of imagination. In the same letter he summed up the experience and relations of his brothers and sister and himself: one driven to America for a livelihood, the other, "with an exquisite love of Life, . . . in a lingering state." Both of his brothers he had often vexed, yet his love for them had stifled the impression any woman might otherwise have made upon him.

On June 22–23 Keats and Charles Brown accompanied the married pair to Liverpool, where the latter were to embark for America, and then set off on the long-planned walking tour of northern England and Scotland (which included a glimpse of Ireland). We cannot follow the course of the tour —of which some stages were made by coach or boat—but a partial list of names will outline the itinerary: Lancaster, Windermere, Rydal (Wordsworth was away on political— Tory—business), Keswick, Carlisle, Dumfries, Kirkcudbright, Portpatrick, Belfast, Ballantrae, Ayr, Glasgow, Inveraray, Oban, Iona and Staffa, Ben Nevis, Inverness. Hitherto Keats had never been north of Stratford and had known only the green levels and gentle slopes of southern England, and a main reason for the tour was a desire to see novel and more rugged country. As he wrote to Bailey on July 22, he thought it would give him more experience, rub off more prejudice, inure him to more hardship, introduce him to finer scenes and grander mountains, and strengthen his reach in poetry more than staying at home, even though he should read Homer (I, 342). The visual result was to show itself in the grandeurs of the landscape of *Hyperion* as contrasted with the lush background of *Endymion,* and in such particulars as

"natural sculpture in cathedral cavern," a recollection of
Fingal's Cave (*Hyperion*, i.86; *Letters*, I, 348–349), and the
"dismal cirque/Of Druid stones" seen at Keswick (*Hyperion*,
ii.34–35; I, 306). Although sometimes depressed by rain, poor
food, glimpses of squalor, and thoughts of the Kirk's war on
natural instincts and of the life Burns was condemned to,
Keats responded eagerly to the changing beauties of the scene.
He and Brown became "mere creatures of Rivers, Lakes, &
mountains," and fourteen miles in such country seemed less
than the four from Hampstead to London. Of the travelogue
Keats put into letters, perhaps the most striking utterances
are in his first letter to Tom (June 25–27: I, 299, 301):

. . . the two views we have had of it [Lake Windermere] are of
the most noble tenderness—they can never fade away—they make
one forget the divisions of life; age, youth, poverty and riches;
and refine one's sensual vision into a sort of north star which can
never cease to be open lidded and stedfast over the wonders of
the great Power. . . .
    I shall learn poetry here and shall henceforth write more than
ever, for the abstract endeavor of being able to add a mite to that
mass of beauty which is harvested from these grand materials, by
the finest spirits, and put into etherial existence for the relish of
one's fellows. I cannot think with Hazlitt that these scenes make
man appear little. I never forgot my stature so completely—I live
in the eye; and my imagination, surpassed, is at rest.

During the tour Keats scribbled impromptu verses in
letters to Tom and George and his sister Fanny and, among
serious pieces, wrote two or three that are significant self-
revelations. The sonnet *On Visiting the Tomb of Burns* (July
1) offers difficulties of interpretation which are complicated
by textual problems and are not much eased by Keats's re-
mark that he had written it in a strange mood, half asleep:
"I know not how it is, the Clouds, the sky, the Houses, all
seem anti Grecian & anti Charlemagnish . . ." (I, 309). Some-
what like Coleridge in *Dejection*, Keats can see but cannot
feel the cold, remote beauty around him; it seems that beauty,
the beauty of painful truth, cannot be perceived in absolute
purity by an absolute judge, that it is always discolored by the

mind of the mortal beholder. We may remember the "horrid moods,/Moods of one's mind," that perplexed and darkened the *Epistle to Reynolds*.

The next day he and Brown traversed the country of *Guy Mannering*. Keats, who had read other novels of Scott's but not this one, was diverted by Brown's talk about it, and composed the carefree and charmingly robust ballad, *Meg Merrilies*, in a vein akin to his earlier "Spirit of Outlawry." Meg is at once a real gypsy and a figure of myth.

In *Lines Written in the Highlands after a Visit to Burns's Country* (included in a letter to Bailey, July 18–22), Keats is somewhat diffuse and awkward, but he is again concerned with that teasing problem of the imagination and actuality. Beginning with the theme of ground enriched by historical associations, particularly by the life of such a poet as Burns, he thinks of the short distance between "the sweet and bitter world" and the world of imagination, of the horror of imagining that forgets man's mortal limits and beloved human beings and threatens clarity, even sanity, of vision. Something like this fear had given brief intensity to *God of the Meridian*. A few days later Staffa and the wonders of Fingal's Cave inspired "Not Aladdin magian," into which Keats brought the spirit of Lycidas as priest of "This Cathedral of the Sea." In the soberly reflective sonnet written on the top of Ben Nevis (August 2), he returned to the theme of *Lines Written in the Highlands*: the mist that envelops the peak suggests man's ignorance of hell and heaven and even of himself.

On the Isle of Mull (July 23), after a month that had brought some fatigue as well as novel enjoyments, Keats had caught a cold and developed "a bad sore throat," which led him to break off the tour and return home (the methodical and practical Brown went on). He sailed in a smack from Cromarty on August 8 and reached London on the eighteenth. Apart from the pleasure of seeing friends again, troubles of various kinds now beset him. Tom's condition had lately taken a decided turn for the worse. Keats's own sore throat persisted through September. And in the course of this month there appeared crushing attacks on himself and his poetry in two of the three most powerful periodicals, *Blackwood's Edinburgh Magazine* and the *Quarterly Review,* and another attack in a lesser one.

We may go back some months and pick up the story of Keats's public reputation. Benjamin Bailey, in writing of *Endymion* to the publisher John Taylor on August 29, could deplore what he saw as Keats's unconscious inclination "to that abominable principle of *Shelley's*—that *Sensual Love* is the principle of *things*" (*K.C.,* I, 34–35), but he was none the less a fervently loyal admirer and he sent two rather naïvely eulogistic letters about the *Poems* and especially *Endymion* to the *Oxford University & City Herald* (May 30, June 6, 1818). Reynolds' paper, the *Champion* (June 7, 14), had a judiciously laudatory review by "J.S.," probably the former editor, John Scott, whom Hunt, Keats, and others had wrongly suspected of writing the *Blackwood's* articles on the "Cockney School" and who in 1820–1821 was to make the *London Magazine* illustrious (in 1821 he died of a wound received in a duel occasioned by his attacks on *Blackwood's Magazine*). *Blackwood's* in its May number had ominous slurs and the August issue (published about September 1) devoted its whole fourth article on the "Cockney School" to malignant abuse of Keats and his two volumes. The writer, or principal writer, John Gibson Lockhart (later the son-in-law and later still the biographer of Sir Walter Scott), took unscrupulous advantage of information that had been given to him by the anxious and well-meaning Bailey in an effort to ward off or soften the scorpion's sting. Lockhart made satirical capital out of Keats's medical training and poetical "disease"; fell upon his association with the disreputable Hunt and his tirade in *Sleep and Poetry* against the Popian tradition; poured snobbish scorn on an ignorant Cockney's presuming to deal with mythology in *Endymion,* a work of "calm, settled, imperturbable drivelling idiocy"; and wound up thus:

It is a better and a wiser thing to be a starved apothecary than a starved poet; so back to the shop Mr John, back to "plasters, pills, and ointment boxes," &c. But, for Heaven's sake, young Sangrado, be a little more sparing of extenuatives and soporifics in your practice than you have been in your poetry.

Lockhart, a cultivated and able man, had been brought in to help raise the magazine's circulation, and his methods succeeded; his later remorse may have been sincere, though he could not very justly plead that he had been "a raw boy," since he was a year and a quarter older than his victim.

Some time in September came the June issue of the *British Critic* with another crude and vicious onslaught. Toward the end of the month the belated April number of the far more important *Quarterly Review*, the Tory bible, brought John Wilson Croker's review of *Endymion*. (Keats, Reynolds, Woodhouse, Shelley, and others took the review to be the work of the editor, William Gifford.) Croker was better than Lockhart in that he wrote as a critic, judging the poems (and preface) by the canons of conservative orthodoxy; but he tossed and gored with his own harsh rigor and—in Woodhouse's words—"undiscriminating stupidity." He was of course unable to discern any theme, having avowedly been unable to struggle beyond the first book, but he did acknowledge "powers of language, rays of fancy, and gleams of genius," though these gifts were stifled by the Cockney principle of "the most incongruous ideas in the most uncouth language." Croker pounced, with some justice, on passages in which sense was led by rhyme and on Huntian diction and, more unjustly, on irregular versification; but he quoted nothing except to illustrate faults, although these very passages, as Reynolds and Woodhouse soon said, would have stirred anyone with a spark of poetic feeling.

Against verdicts from such hanging judges not much could be done. "J.S." (John Scott, James Smith, or someone else?) and "R.B." wrote letters in defense of *Endymion* to the *Morning Chronicle* (October 3 and 8); and in the *Alfred, West of England Journal* (October 6) Reynolds, then in Dev-

onshire, published a vigorous reply which, somewhat short-
ened, was reprinted in the *Examiner* (October 11). Reynolds
and Woodhouse sent Keats cheering letters (*K.C.*, I, 43–52).
As Woodhouse said, and as Keats wrote to George on October
14, the *Quarterly*'s violence recoiled on itself and worked in
Keats's favor, among intelligent readers; however, he had
long agreed with Hazlitt that the commonplace majority
"read the Edinburgh and Quarterly and think as they do" (I,
173). Apropos of the letters in the *Morning Chronicle*, Keats
wrote with courage and wisdom to Hessey, John Taylor's
partner, on October 8. He was, he said, much less affected by
others' praise or blame than by his own inward judge. *En-
dymion*, he knew, had many defects, but it was as good as he
had had the power to make it:

I have written independently *without Judgment*—I may write
independently *& with judgment* hereafter.—The Genius of Poetry
must work out its own salvation in a man: It cannot be matured
by law & precept, but by sensation & watchfulness in itself—That
which is creative must create itself—In Endymion, I leaped head-
long into the Sea, and thereby have become better acquainted
with the Soundings, the quicksands, & the rocks, than if I had
stayed upon the green shore, and piped a silly pipe, and took tea
& comfortable advice.—I was never afraid of failure; for I would
sooner fail than not be among the greatest—But I am nigh get-
ting into a rant. . . . (I, 374)

In writing to George and Georgiana on October 14—when
he had got well into *Hyperion*—Keats referred briefly to the
attacks in *Blackwood's* and the *Quarterly* and to his several
defenders, and he could cheer both his brother and himself
with the quiet assurance: "This is a mere matter of the mo-
ment—I think I shall be among the English Poets after my
death" (I, 393–394). But later allusions to the reviews were
to show how deep the wound had gone.

5

The Great Year: I
(September, 1818–February, 1819)

DURING THIS AUTUMN and early winter Keats was
under stresses of various kinds and degrees, some of
them temporary, some destined to continue and grow heavier.
With however brave a front he disdained the reviewers' at-
tacks, these could not be easily brushed off, even in regard to
the practical problem of making a living by poetry. Keats's
sore throat—no light matter for him—was more or less trouble-
some up into February. In almost every letter of these months
he reported that Tom was worse, and he hardly needed his
medical knowledge to see that the end was not far off. In
addition to watching Tom wither away, and nursing him,
Keats was worried about getting Richard Abbey's permission
for their sister to come to see him and about the ill as well as
good effects of such meetings. In September he began to com-
pose *Hyperion*, partly as an escape from wearing anxieties.
During several weeks, apparently, he could be disturbed by
the beauty ("the Beauty of a Leopardess"), the voice, and the
personality of one Jane Cox, a cousin of the Reynoldses, who,
if not a Cleopatra, was at least a Charmian (I, 395). In a
letter to Reynolds (of September 22?) several of these emo-
tional strains came together. Urging Reynolds—who was
visiting his fiancée and her family—to gorge the honey of
life while it lasts, he speaks of his own present drinking of
bitters, and goes on (I, 370):

I never was in love—Yet the voice and the shape of a woman has haunted me these two days—at such a time when the relief, the feverous relief of Poetry seems a much less crime—This morning Poetry has conquered—I have relapsed into those abstractions[1] which are my only life—I feel escaped from a new strange and threatening sorrow.—And I am thankful for it—There is an awful warmth about my heart like a load of Immortality.

Poor Tom—that woman—and Poetry were ringing changes in my senses—now I am in comparison happy. . . .

On September 21 he wrote in a similar vein to Dilke (I, 368–369):

I wish I could say Tom was any better. His identity presses upon me so all day that I am obliged to go out—and although I intended to have given some time to study alone I am obliged to write, and plunge into abstract images to ease myself of his countenance his voice and feebleness—so that I live now in a continual fever—it must be poisonous to life although I feel well. Imagine 'the hateful siege of contraries'—if I think of fame of poetry it seems a crime to me, and yet I must do so or suffer. . . .

During these troubled months Keats's letters had little to say about poetry, but two passages are important. In his first long letter to George and Georgiana he spoke, among many topics, of "Charmian" and of a chance encounter with the Isabella Jones whom he had met before,[2] and then declared

---

1 Keats seems to use "abstractions" and "abstract" not so much in our sense of philosophized generality but in the sense of "imaginative," "divorced from the actual."

Some scholars have taken the woman to be Fanny Brawne, but general probabilities seem to be against that (see a few pages below); and Keats's words here accord with his later detailed account of Jane Cox (I, 395–396) but hardly with his account of Fanny (II, 13).

2 Since a quite unsubstantiated theory is given as a fact in Ian Jack's normally careful *English Literature 1815–1832* (1964), p. 105, a note may be warranted. The beautiful and sophisticated Mrs. Jones, who was acquainted with some of Keats's friends, had an elderly Irish "protector," a Donat O'Callaghan, whose summer base was Hastings; Keats had met her there in May or June, 1817, and had seen her (at a theater party) a year later. On October 24, 1818, he described to his brother and sister-in-law an accidental meeting with Mrs. Jones on a London street and his accompanying her to her home. In the letter he said he had "no libidinous thought about her," that she and Georgiana were the only young women he would be content to know for their mind and friendship alone (I, 402–403). There is no need of going into Robert Gittings' arguments for an affair and its reflections in

that he hoped he would never marry: "The roaring of the wind is my wife and the Stars through the window pane are my Children"[3] (October 24: I, 403). Domestic happiness is only one part of his "mighty abstract Idea . . . of Beauty," and he must have a thousand particles, for he lives in a thousand worlds. In his sublime solitude, "shapes of epic greatness are stationed around" him; according to his state of mind, he is "with Achilles shouting in the Trenches or with Theocritus in the Vales of Sicily," or with Troilus waiting like a lost soul for Cressida. Besides, he has a low opinion of the generality of women, to whom he would rather give a sugarplum than his time. If Tom were well and he knew that George and his wife were passing pleasant days, he would be enviably happy. Otherwise, "The only thing that can ever affect me personally for more than one short passing day, is any doubt about my powers for poetry—I seldom have any, and I look with hope to the nighing time when I shall have none." Finally, his greatest elevations of soul leave him "every time more humbled."

In a letter of October 21, concerning the *Quarterly* review of *Endymion*, Woodhouse reverted to a conversation in which Keats had held that there was now nothing original to be written in poetry, that its riches and beauties were exhausted, and that he would write no more but simply try to increase his knowledge for his private gratification (I, 380). Wood-

---

Keats's poetry (*John Keats: The Living Year*, 1954; *The Mask of John Keats*, 1956), since they were demolished by Middleton Murry (*Keats*, 1955) and Aileen Ward (*Keats-Shelley Journal*, X, 1961). The one shred of possible "evidence" is the lyric "Hush, hush! tread softly," and that—even if it related to Mrs. Jones and a lover—proves nothing; it might have been the product of the first flirtation and of Keats's dramatic fancy. Early in 1819 he gave Fanny Brawne his copy of Hunt's *Literary Pocket Book*, and in it she transcribed this lyric; Keats would hardly have given her the song if it represented, even by anticipation, a kind of betrayal of his love for her. In the autumn of 1818 Mrs. Jones sent some presents of game for Tom and sent some more after his death. We do not know how often, or how seldom, Keats may have seen her after their third meeting. Some time during the weeks before January 18–19 (when he left for Chichester) she suggested the superstition about St. Agnes' Eve as a subject for a poem.

[3] A variation on "Society became my glittering bride,/And airy hopes my children" (*Excursion*, iii.735–736)?

house argued earnestly against both Keats's premise and his conclusion: the senses, the passions, and reflection and the moral sense combine in an inexhaustible process of creation; and however low at times the public mind and taste may sink, there are always some spirits who respond to original and genuine poetry. In his reply of October 27 (I, 386–388) Keats stressed two points. First, enlarging on what he had just written to George and Georgiana, he gave his most elaborate exposition of negative capability (though he did not here use that phrase). He emphasized, as we noticed in Chapter 3, the true poet's lack of any fixed identity, his non-moral, unbiased empathy and creativity; he "has as much delight in conceiving an Iago as an Imogen," since his dealings with both evil and good "end in speculation." This lack of identity means, too, that a poet's always shifting ideas—including those Keats had uttered to Woodhouse—must not be taken as a settled creed. We may think that in this, more than in earlier accounts, Keats was led into overstating his doctrine. However wholesome an antidote it was to "the wordsworthian or egotistical sublime," and however much it contributed to the objective method of *Endymion* and *Hyperion,* it was an inadequate basis for the conception of both poems, since the creative imagination cannot work with the moral blindness of photography.

Keats's second point was a more direct disowning of the talk that had disturbed Woodhouse, it was indeed a tacit recognition that creative power is not enough; and it was in part a reaffirming of what he had written to John Taylor on April 27, about his need for study and knowledge. It is not quite clear, however, whether he hopes to rise from merely sensuous to philosophic poetry, or whether he is setting the service—presumably intellectual service—of mankind not only above but against poetry. He is "ambitious of doing the world some good: if I should be spared that may be the work of maturer years." But then poetry, though treated as a kind of prelude to higher things, gets the upper hand:

in the interval I will assay to reach to as high a summit in Poetry
as the nerve bestowed upon me will suffer. The faint conceptions
I have of Poems to come brings the blood frequently into my
forehead—All I hope is that I may not lose all interest in human
affairs. . . .

Keats declares that he feels indifferent to applause even from
the finest spirits; he would write "from the mere yearning
and fondness" he has for the beautiful, even if the night's
labors were burnt every morning. "But," he adds, "even now
I am perhaps not speaking from myself; but from some char-
acter in whose soul I now live." The always admiring and
intelligent Woodhouse paraphrased and endorsed Keats's
principle of negative capability in a letter to Taylor (I, 388–
390).

Whatever his indifference to attacks or applause, Keats was
naturally touched and embarrassed by an odd incident of
early November. Someone using the name "P. Fenbank" sent
him from Teignmouth—where George and he had stayed
successively with Tom—a note for £25 and a poor but lauda-
tory sonnet. The address pointed at once to the Jeffrey sisters,
with whom the three brothers had become well acquainted,
but Keats apparently did not regard them as the donors; the
tributes may have come from Woodhouse or someone Wood-
house had worked on. In the latter half of December, in his
journal-letter to his brother and sister-in-law, Keats still had
the matter in his mind (II, 9, 16–17).

On December 1 Tom died, just after his nineteenth birth-
day. To George and Georgiana, who had already been in-
formed by the faithful Haslam, Keats wrote on December 16:

The last days of poor Tom were of the most distressing nature;
but his last moments were not so painful, and his very last was
without a pang—I will not enter into any parsonic comments on
death—yet the common observations of the commonest people on
death are as true as their proverbs. I have scarce a doubt of im-
mortality of some nature of [for or] other—neither had Tom.
(II, 4)

This last declaration, and a fuller one a few lines further on,
were perhaps the result of grief rather than a steady convic-

tion—although Keats was to take immortality for granted in his account of "Soul-making" on April 21. His friends, he says, have been exceedingly kind, every one of them. After the relative confinement of his long attendance on Tom, Keats now went about a good deal. He saw more of his fifteen-year-old sister. On Charles Brown's invitation, he moved in December from the lodging in Well Walk into Brown's half of Wentworth Place, a double house which he and Dilke had built on John Street, Hampstead. (It is now the Keats House.) A note to Woodhouse on December 18 was in the vein of practical resolution. Woodhouse had conveyed a wish expressed by the Misses Jane and Anna Maria Porter—both authors of historical romance, the former of the once famous *Scottish Chiefs*—to meet the author of *Endymion*. Keats replied that he was flattered but could not afford the time for new acquaintances: "I have a new leaf to turn over—I must work—I must read—I must write" (I, 412).

But this resolution was during the rest of Keats's active life to be both strengthened and shaken by a new star that had swum into his ken. Brown's half of Wentworth Place had been rented for the summer of 1818 by a widow, Mrs. Samuel Brawne; during the autumn and winter she lived elsewhere in Hampstead, and in April, 1819, she rented the Dilke half of the house, where she remained until her death in 1829. The eldest of her three children, Frances (Fanny), had been born on August 9, 1800. The date of Keats's first meeting with her has been much disputed because the scraps of evidence are few and uncertain or belong to a later time. Scholarly opinions have fixed variously on August, September, November, or early December. Without going into the arguments, we may take the middle or the latter half of November as the safest surmise. Much later Keats told Fanny that "the very first week I knew you I wrote myself your vassal" (July 25, 1819: II, 132). But he was very reticent, even with his brother and sister-in-law, about his real feeling for Fanny. His first mention of her, on December 16, in the first section of a journal-letter to George and Georgiana, was short, detached, and critical: she is "beautiful and elegant, graceful, silly, fashionable, and strange"; they have little tiffs now and then, "and she behaves a little better, or I mus[t] have sheered off" (II, 8). Two days later he gave a fuller and no more auspicious account, though we may see significance in its thrusting itself so soon and abruptly into the letter and in its precise observations. (Keats was mistaken about her age; she had become eighteen in August.) The description began with a more than objective item: "She is about my height." It ended thus:

> she is not seventeen—but she is ignorant—monstrous in her be-haviour flying out in all directions, calling people such names—that I was forced lately to make use of the term *Minx*—this is I think no[t] from any innate vice but from a penchant she has for acting stylishly. I am however tired of such style and shall decline any more of it. (II, 13)

We cannot tell whether vassalage to Fanny Brawne was one of the distracting pressures under which Keats worked on *Hyperion*. We have noted already those very trying circumstances, especially Keats's feeling the desperate need of imaginative escape from Tom's bedside (although an uninformed reader of *Hyperion* might well assume that, except for the intrinsic problems of any major work, it had grown out of untroubled serenity). He had begun the poem in the latter half of September. Apart from the references of that month, quoted above, his only other remarks on its composition begin on December 18 (II, 12) and have to do with the difficulty of going on. He could say on December 31 that the poem "is scarce began" (II, 18), but we do not know what that means in relation to his total scheme. The first two books may have been finished by the time of Tom's death (December 1); and the incomplete third book, a new departure in matter and style, may have been added in the winter or early spring. Whatever Keats may have done during those later months (when he was writing very different things), by April 20, 1819, he gave up the effort to complete the poem.

The subject had been long in his mind. *Endymion* contained a number of allusions and an explicit promise (iv.774) of a poem on Apollo. On September 28, 1817, Keats had written to Haydon of "a new Romance which I have in my eye for next summer"; and on January 23, 1818, he had given Haydon—as a possible illustrator—a general notion of it. Whereas *Endymion* had "many bits of the deep and sentimental cast,"

the nature of *Hyperion* will lead me to treat it in a more naked and grecian Manner—and the march of passion and endeavour will be undeviating—and one great contrast between them will be—that the Hero of the written tale being mortal is led on, like Buonaparte, by circumstance; whereas the Apollo in Hyperion being a fore-seeing God will shape his actions like one. (I, 207)

This description hardly fits the fragment we have; but Keats made no further comments on his plan or changes of plan. The war between the gods and Titans came to his mind during the northern tour, and some sculpturesque scenes, recorded in the letters, got into the poem. In his exposition of negative capability to Woodhouse on October 27, when he was at work, he referred to his possible "cogitating on the Characters of saturn and Ops" while he was talking of something else (I, 387). But such items do not take us very far into his narrative and symbolic intention.

To the "meaning" of *Hyperion*—or indeed to the meaning of any of his long poems—Keats's letters give no direct clue, however much they tell us about his views of poetry in general, its present state in England, and his own ambitions. While he disclaimed any settled or serious conviction in the talk that had disturbed Woodhouse, about the exhaustion of poetry in modern times, such gnawing doubts must have been recurrent (along with periods of high confidence in his own powers and the future). W. J. Bate has notably defined Keats's acute and sensitive awareness of the difficulties facing a modern poet, both within the domain of his craft and in relation to the world at large. Whereas earlier poets, all the way back to antiquity, had a more or less assured standing and function, in Keats's age the feeling of alienation, though not unknown in the past, was becoming a more general reality and one based on much deeper facts than, say, the Renaissance scholar-poet's contempt for the unlettered populace. The conspicuous march of science and technology, the kind of civilization being inaugurated by the Industrial Revolution, was removing the poet—now the poet of personal vision rather than of "mimesis" or manners—further from an audience increasingly committed to another set of values. The literary at least were becoming familiar with the idea or the fear that poetry, a primitive art bound up with the unspoiled senses and imagination of the natural man, was doomed to decay and extinction. In his preface to the second edition of *Lyrical Ballads* (1800), Wordsworth could look forward to the poet's embracing science as soon as it was absorbed into general human experience (that is, one might say, when it ceased to be scientific), but other men could be less hopeful. Bacon, Newton, and Locke were Blake's evil trinity. The inevitable erosion of poetry by scientific reason was touched by Hazlitt in his first lecture on the English poets; the pattern of decay was the text of Peacock's partly ironical *Four Ages of Poetry* (which evoked Shelley's *Defence of Poetry*); and it appeared in the young Macaulay's first contribution to the *Edinburgh Review,* his essay on Milton. Four years later the young Tennyson, in his Cambridge prize poem, *Timbuctoo* (1829), saw the magic city of myth shrinking, under the blight of "keen Discovery," into the ugly huts of barbarism.

If the status and function of poetry in general were beginning to look dubious, if the modern world seemed to have small room for the imagination, the heaviest doubts might well center on the epic, which the Renaissance had made the grandest of poetic genres. The composing of a heroic poem had been problematical in Milton's age, even at moments to Milton himself, and such eighteenth-century efforts as Glover's *Leonidas* and Wilkie's *Epigoniad* might confirm the worst fears. The many long narrative poems produced within Keats's lifetime did little toward resuscitating genuine epic.

D

The Story of Rimini we have met. Such earlier and later works as Landor's *Gebir* and the more or less popular tales of Scott, Byron, Moore, and Southey ("An epic from Bob Southey every spring," in the phrase of *Don Juan,* iii.97) were only more elaborate varieties of romance. Blake's prophetic books were little known and anyhow would have been of little use to Keats. Wordsworth had taken the bold step of making Milton's re-creation of the traditional epic a kind of precedent for a modern "epic" on the growth of his own mind; but the *Prelude* of course remained in or on his desk and the *Excursion*—which the young Keats so much admired—was largely discursive rumination. Yet Keats saw Wordsworth as the poet of the human heart, and in *Endymion, Hyperion,* and *Lamia* he might be said to have tried, consciously or unconsciously, to objectify his own version of the Wordsworthian theme of poetry and the poet, of aesthetic, emotional, and ethical experience and growth. As for the mode of objectification, like more learned poets of romantic Hellenism, Continental and English—notably Shelley, whose *Prometheus Unbound* was written at the same time as *Hyperion*—Keats turned instinctively to Greek myth as a vehicle for his highest visions.

Because of his own censure of the Miltonism of *Hyperion,* and because of many modern critics' preoccupation with the recast *Fall of Hyperion,* the earlier poem does not always receive its due as an astonishingly original and powerful achievement. When we think of the preceding year and a half, of the waywardness and lushness that almost buried the serious theme of *Endymion,* or of the thin pathos and prettiness of much of *Isabella,* when we remember too that Keats only reached twenty-three on October 31, we see an almost incredible advance in strength and massiveness of conception, structure, and texture. There were of course other factors than Milton—the general process of Keats's maturing, the Elgin Marbles (and some acquaintance with Egyptian works), and the visual and imaginative effects of northern scenery. The three small volumes of Cary's somewhat Miltonic translation of Dante had been the only books in his knapsack, but we do not know how much he read in them and influence would be hard to demonstrate. The miracle of *Hyperion* was mainly the result of the feasting on Milton that Keats had enjoyed in the spring of 1818. Eighteenth-century Miltonists had commonly thought they were being Miltonic when they wrote unrhymed pentameters in Latinate diction, but Keats had the genius to convert Miltonic nourishment into his own substance and through that creative assimilation he changed from a minor into a major poet. When we are given so impressive a poem, we can hardly afford, whatever its faults and whatever Keats's own verdict, to discount it as an unusual piece of ventriloquism.

The core of the epic material, the gods' overthrow of the Titans, was familiar to Keats long before he settled on the subject, though more materials would accrue afterward. Among handbooks, Lempriere's *Classical Dictionary* seems to have been much less useful than *The Pantheon* (1806) by "Edward Baldwin" (William Godwin, the philosopher).[4] Keats would have got hints or more from some classical and Elizabethan or later poetry, such as Spenser, Chapman's translations of Homer and Hesiod's *Works and Days,* and Sandys' translation of and commentary on Ovid's *Metamorphoses* (Keats cited pages in the 1640 edition). Most of these sources had contributed to *Endymion.* Keats probably read such other things as Hesiod's *Theogony* in Cooke's or another version. Incidental echoes, direct or adapted, come chiefly from Shakespeare (who supplied, for instance, the catalog of omens that dismay Hyperion) and Milton (the minor poems as well as *Paradise Lost*). Keats's range of apparent reminiscence takes in such unexpected items as *Gebir* and Beckford's *Vathek.* All these major or minor materials he used without labored indications of his having got them up for the occasion.

What appears to be the central theme of *Hyperion* was a

---

[4] Cited frequently in the notes on *Hyperion* (and in some on *Endymion*) in my edition of Keats (1959).

deeper reading of what had been the central theme of *Endymion* and had indeed been conceived as far back as *Sleep and Poetry,* though now it had behind it the weight of Keats's fuller experience and thought. But, since he did not manage to state that central theme until just before he abandoned the poem, we may look at things—with very inadequate brevity —as they come. And we need not indulge in vain guesses about the intended length or the total design (of which Woodhouse left a summary, as he understood it was to be shaped).

The first book, opening after the war between the old Titans and the new gods, is mainly a series of statuesque tableaux with a minimum of action, unless varied descriptions and expressions of grief and despair come under that head. The picture of the deposed and helpless Saturn is amplified by the words of Thea, Hyperion's spouse, and by Saturn's impotent efforts to reassert his power; at length she leads him to join the other dispossessed Titans. Meanwhile the one undefeated Titan, Hyperion the sun-god, enveloped by ill omens, rages defiantly in his palace. He is addressed by his celestial father, Coelus (Uranus), who laments the hitherto serene Titans' weakly violent display of human passions and counsels his brightest son to act with decision and to seek Saturn and his company on earth.

The council in book two, with all its general debt to the debate of Milton's fallen angels, is quite different in manner as well as substance. If Keats does not approach his model in dramatic staging and characterization, or in rhetorical force and density, he achieves some dramatic tensions and collisions. The Titans speak, here as elsewhere, with what even the hostile Byron was to praise as Aeschylean sublimity; and the speeches contribute more or less to the development of the theme. Since in some ancient sources (and in the *Excursion,* iii.756–758) Saturn was identified with the golden age, Keats had authority for presenting the Titans as beneficent rulers, not the outlaws of the more familiar myth, so that in his poem—for a reason different from that of Milton's

devils—they cannot understand the meaning of their over-
throw. The spectrum of their reactions might be described in
the words Keats had used about his "Pleasure Thermometer"
in *Endymion*, a "first Step towards the chief Attempt in the
Drama—the playing of different Natures with Joy and Sor-
row." While Coelus could deplore the Titans' lapsing into
the passions of mortal men, he has apparently, like Saturn,
Hyperion, Enceladus, and others, no better plan than the
regaining of sovereignty by force. The debate moves on
higher levels. The wise Oceanus, appealed to by the be-
wildered Saturn, starts likewise from the fact of the Titans'
sinking their divinity in violent passions, but his philosophic
insight enables him to see and explain that the gods' victory
is in accord with the eternal law "That first in beauty should
be first in might." Just as the magnanimous Titans had ex-
celled their predecessors, so in turn they must be excelled by
"A power more strong in beauty." Oceanus recognizes the
rightness of his being superseded by the beautiful Neptune,
and his fellow Titans must also acquiesce in the evolutionary
process. This speech—which recalls Keats's letter of May 3,
1818, on the mansion of life, on Milton and Wordsworth and
the "mighty providence" that "subdues the mightiest Minds
to the service of the time being"—is an utterance character-
istic of the revolutionary and romantic era (witness bits of the
Excursion) put in characteristically Keatsian terms. Yet, book
three seems to prove, the insight of Oceanus is to be taken as
limited; his conception of ideal beauty does not apparently
go beyond the simple, common meaning. And while Oceanus
can, parenthetically, urge upon his hearers a main doctrine
of the *Excursion*—

> for to bear all naked truths,
> And to envisage circumstance, all calm,
> That is the top of sovereignty—

his wisdom is more stoically passive than positive; it rests
upon mere acceptance of nature's law.

Clymene, like the rest, feels the loss of joy and a new

weight of woe, but she has heard the music of Apollo and her
reaction brings her nearer than Oceanus to final truth. For
the new music awakens, not simple joy or simple grief, but
"joy and grief at once"; "A living death was in each gush of
sounds." The significance of the mixture is to become clearer
in later poems, notably in the *Fall;* here, perhaps, it does not
register adequately as a step further toward the concluding
experience of Apollo. As Clymene's "baby-words" are de-
nounced by the simpleminded, wrathful Enceladus, the un-
conquered Hyperion arrives, to heighten both hope and
despair among the fallen Titans.

Whatever length Keats had in mind, he had now got to the
end of book two without much epic action and without de-
fining his main theme, though he had differentiated between
the self-centered Titans who have a "strong identity" (i.114),
who are only "Men of Power" (I, 184), and the two who have
partial but larger and more disinterested intuitions. In book
three, written probably after an interval, Keats seems to have
resolved that he must express that main theme. The style and
tone of this book, as he turns to "antheming a lonely grief,"
avowedly change from epic stateliness to a lush and lyrical
vein, akin to that of *Endymion,* which is for Keats, even now,
"the true voice of feeling." Apollo encounters the majestic
Mnemosyne (mother of the Muses), and learns that she has
been the inspirer of his music, which the whole universe has
heard—like Clymene—"in pain and pleasure." Yet he is
strangely sad, not, like the Titans, because of loss of outward
power, but "Like one who once had wings" (or like the dis-
illusioned Endymion); he feels "curs'd and thwarted," and he
does not know why. The beauty and the thunders of the
world are all about him, while he listens "In fearless yet in
aching ignorance." Apollo is still in the "Chamber of
Maiden-Thought," although he is ready to leave it. And now
he reads "A wondrous lesson" in Mnemosyne's silent face:

> Knowledge enormous makes a God of me.
> Names, deeds, gray legends, dire events, rebellions,
> Majesties, sovran voices, agonies,

Creations and destroyings, all at once
Pour into the wide hollows of my brain,
And deify me, as if some blithe wine
Or bright elixir peerless I had drunk,
And so become immortal.

The last lines tell how "wild commotions shook him,"
"Most like the struggle at the gate of death," or rather a
fierce pang that enables him to "Die into life." Thus Apollo
becomes a god, a true poet, through comprehension of his-
tory and change and human suffering. He has attained a
tragic vision, a vision of the real, complex beauty, far beyond
the simple beneficence of Titanic power (which had turned
to blind frustration in defeat), beyond the limited insights of
Oceanus and Clymene. Whereas Endymion had chosen re-
ality as against abstract idealism (and had found that the one
led to the other), Apollo's poetic experience is more ma-
turely realized, even if Keats has to describe rather than dram-
atize the illumination. (He told Woodhouse that Apollo's
speech "seemed to come by chance or magic—to be as it
were something given to him": K.C., I, 129.) Apollo's accept-
ance of historical process, with all its conflicts and agonies, is,
we may note, the achievement of widened and deepened hu-
man consciousness; it is not the metaphysical reconciliation
of opposites seen by Wordsworth in his apocalyptic passage
on crossing the Alps (Prelude, vi.624–640). The deification of
Apollo, at this stage, perhaps left Hyperion an inevitable
fragment, since there would seem to have been nothing more
to say. Yet Keats must have had a good deal more in view;
for one thing, Hyperion has not yet done much toward ful-
filling his titular role, and, as W. J. Bate says, he is the only
character capable of tragic development.

While we recognize the value, for our understanding of
Keats, of this statement of his mature poetic faith, it may be
admitted that his epic story and epic figures do not go far
enough toward expressive embodiment of it. What does move
us strongly and almost continuously is the local beauty and
power of word, line, image, and rhythm, which are not

merely Miltonic and indeed are often quite un-Miltonic. Keats's negative capability or empathy, in spite of his human- ized creed, for the most part works best on inanimate objects and scenes. And he fully exploits what he called Milton's "stationing" of figures in relation to solid objects. (It is sig- nificant that the random notes he made on *Paradise Lost* have to do less with the theme or characters than with the vividness of particular sensations and images—such as our sense of Satan's being suffocated inside the serpent.) Thus nothing in *Hyperion* is more memorable than the opening description of utter stillness, in which the paralyzed Saturn is hardly more than one of the properties and not immeasur- ably more potent than the light seed or the dead leaf (though at some later moments Saturn has a touch of King Lear). The picture of the dreaming oaks (i.72f.) takes such possession of us that we forget what the simile is intended to illustrate— the manner of Thea's speaking to Saturn. Thinking of these and a multitude of other things (the last word is not casual), we might recall, in a perverted sense, Keats's saying of a year earlier: "the excellence of every Art is its intensity, capable of making all disagreeables evaporate, from their being in close relationship with Beauty & Truth." While the griefs of the Titans do not evaporate, they still seem almost a back- drop for incidental images, rather than the other way about.

It would be idle to go through *Hyperion* and point out what no reader can fail to see and feel, the compelling sen- sory and imaginative actuality of image after image; but, as reminders of Keats's conscious working toward such intensity, we may notice some of his revisions, familiar though these illuminating items are to all students. Some revisions—as in that opening description of stillness—are too complicated to rehearse, but a few small and simple ones will suggest Keats's aims. In the description of Saturn the richly imaginative and emotional "realmless eyes" (i.19) came only after the dis- carding of the rather commonplace "ancient" and the merely pictorial "white-browed." While here the final half-abstract epithet was finely right, in other places the abstract and vague gave place to the concrete and specific: "eased Ixion's toil" (i.30) to "stay'd Ixion's wheel"; "Labouring in pain" (ii.27) to the visual "Heaving in pain." The common "evening star" (i.3) became visually and rhythmically arresting when turned into "eve's one star." Adjectives may be changed into verbal adjectives (i.214: "fiery robes" into "flaming robes"); or participles into verbs (i.139: "not hearing" into "heard not"). Flat and colorless verbs are replaced by more distinctly expressive ones: "On he went" (i.217) by "On he flared"; "Opened his curved lids" (i.351) by "Lifted his curved lids," which carries a sense of effort; "When the prow turns" (ii.355) by the more energetic "When the prow sweeps." "And still they were the same bright, patient stars" (i.353) perfectly suggests the agitated Hyperion's view of the unchanged constancy of the cosmic order; but it was arrived at only through such verbally and rhythmically defective phrases as "And still they all were the same patient stars."

Keats was a highly literary poet, not in the sense that he possessed wide learning but that he instinctively echoed and adapted phrases, images, and ideas from what he had read, especially of course poetry. That is evident from his first to his last writings; but while at all stages he may merely—and perhaps unconsciously—take over useful phrases, in general the process becomes more and more one of individual and suggestive resetting or re-creation. A random example might be the opening lines of *Hyperion:*

> Deep in the shady sadness of a vale
> Far sunken from the healthy breath of morn,
> Far from the fiery noon, and eve's one star,
> Sat gray-hair'd Saturn, quiet as a stone,
> Still as the silence round about his lair;
> Forest on forest hung above his head
> Like cloud on cloud. . . .

This sentence is roughly parallel in its periodic structure to the first five and a half lines of Milton's second book (quoted a couple of pages below), but Saturn in defeat has no Satanic vitality and splendor; we may think instead of Wordsworth's gray-haired leech-gatherer, who appears so lifeless that an elaborate simile compares him to a stone. What may be called a structural as well as a descriptive element is the succession, "morn," "noon," "eve's," which, as M. R. Ridley noted, follows that of Mulciber's fall (*Paradise Lost*, i.742–743): "from morn/To noon he fell, from noon to dewy eve. . . ." Both the words and the pattern of Keats's first line take us back to "Deep in the winding bosom of a lawn," in a poem he knew, *The Castle of Indolence* (ii.6), though Thomson could hardly have conceived "shady sadness." Keats expressed, apropos of Milton, a special relish for the word "vale" (a word very frequent in Wordsworth), and here he may be recalling especially the "shady vale" of *Paradise Regained*, i.304, and two passages he commented on in *Paradise Lost*, i.318–321 and ii.546–561. In Wordsworth's *Michael* (138–139) the word "vale" is associated with "The Evening Star," the name locally given to Michael's house because he and his wife worked so late by their one lamp; Keats's original phrase, we remember, was "evening star." The words "breath of morn" occur in Eve's pastoral speech (*Paradise Lost*, iv.641), but Keats's whole line brings in a contrast like that between city smells and rural purity in *Paradise Lost*, ix.445f., and that at the beginning of *Samson Agonistes*, where Samson, released from his "Unwholesome" prison, feels "The breath of heav'n fresh-blowing." Keats's second-last line may start from the northern scenes that later inspired the picture in the *Ode to Psyche*—

> Far, far around shall those dark-cluster'd trees
>   Fledge the wild-ridged mountains steep by steep—

but the line may include a memory of Satan's first sight of Eden (iv.137f.):

> and overhead up grew
> Insuperable highth of loftiest shade,
> Cedar, and pine, and fir, and branching palm,
> A sylvan scene, and as the ranks ascend
> Shade above shade, a woody theater
> Of stateliest view. . . .

Remembering Keats's youthful translation of the *Aeneid,* we may think too of what Milton had in mind, Aeneas' Libyan harbor with its dark, overhanging grove (*Aeneid,* i.165). And Keats's "Like cloud on cloud" might combine recollections of Atlas, his pine-wreathed head enveloped in clouds (*Aeneid,* iv.246f.), and Wordsworth's leech-gatherer, "Motionless as a cloud." These various "sources" range from the almost certain to the merely possible; but, whatever items may have been in Keats's conscious or unconscious mind, the result is entirely original. Our immediate awareness is not of allusive enrichment, as in Milton or Eliot, but only of the maximal sensuous and emotional rendering of the idea.

The Miltonic devices of style in *Hyperion* have long been familiar in the concrete analyses in De Selincourt's edition of Keats and W. J. Bate's *Stylistic Development,* and they need not and cannot be cataloged here; but it may be repeated that they are rather the outward evidence of a new discipline than a detraction from the greatness of Keats's achievement. A word may be said, however, on a no less complex question, the new strength and control and expressive power the rhythms of *Hyperion* display. If we think once more of the prevailing lack of such qualities in *Endymion* and *Isabella,* or of eighteenth-century Miltonists, we may wonder afresh at a majestic orchestration which permits few lapses. Whatever Keats owed to Milton in metrics as in style, the result is decidedly his own. Perhaps the most obvious features of Milton's epic verse are variety of movement, speed, and the extended interlinking of lines. The verse of *Hyperion* has much less variety, and its most obvious feature is the heavily weighted, slow-moving, single line. The opening of Milton's second book has already been cited as a structural parallel to Keats's first sentence, and the Miltonic lines might be quoted for metrical and rhythmical comparison:

> High on a throne of royal state, which far
> Outshone the wealth of Ormus and of Ind,
> Or where the gorgeous East with richest hand

Show'rs on her kings barbaric pearl and gold,
Satan exalted sat, by merit raised
To that bad eminence . . .

We do not need to go into metrical statistics, which yield slightly different results for different readers, and conventional terminology is misleading anyhow in regard to Milton's syllabic verse, but some approximate conclusions both support and qualify the initial impression of the ear. According to that impression, Milton's lines, at least the first two, are somewhat slower in tempo than usual, but Keats's are slower still. The chief reasons are his higher proportion of end-stopped lines and of spondaic feet; and these reasons are valid for *Hyperion* as a whole. What may run counter to our first impression is the more or less equal number of monosyllabic words, pyrrhic feet (two unstressed syllables), and long vowels; however, the succession of long vowels in Milton's first two lines is unusual, and throughout *Hyperion* Keats goes beyond the Miltonic norm.

Although *Hyperion* can no doubt be called in some sense a failure, it is a greater poem than any other English poet ever wrote at the age of twenty-two and twenty-three; and it remains, by any standard, one of the few great pieces of epic writing in the language.

Apart from the major poems of this winter of 1818–1819, the chief biographical event was one of which Keats's letters gave no hint at all. In a letter of December 13, 1821, Fanny Brawne told Fanny Keats that the Christmas day of 1818— when Keats had dinner at Mrs. Brawne's—was the happiest day she had, up till then, ever spent; and the only reason could be that she and Keats had come to some degree of understanding. While this understanding was certainly not a formal engagement (that was not reached until the autumn of 1819), it meant some kind of new life for both, in relation to each other and to their world at large—although on February 14 Keats could still say, as he had said in his first reports of Fanny, that they have every now and then a chat and

a tiff (II, 59). Obviously such references—and this was the
last, except mere mention on April 16 (II, 89)—leave us as
ignorant as Keats's relatives and friends were of what his real
feelings, and hers, had become; and of what they were to be
we get no direct knowledge until he began to write to her
when they were separated in the summer of 1819.

In the course of the last forty years or so, Fanny has
emerged from clouds of prejudice which, during the preced-
ing century, had established her as a shallow, selfish flirt,
quite unworthy of a great poet's ardent devotion. Keats
clearly did not find her so, even if, at eighteen, she was in
some respects immature, as in her great concern with dress
(and that was fitting enough in a young cousin of Beau Brum-
mell). Certainly she was not of the bluestocking type that
Keats abhorred, although she knew French well and had pos-
sibly begun to study German; she enjoyed mainly light read-
ing and doubtless had something of the sharp wit for which
she was noted in later life. Certainly too she had abundant
vitality. But, in spite of her later letters to Fanny Keats—
which, when published in 1937, did much to redress the in-
justice done her—we do not know enough to explain what
became a consuming passion; we can only accept it, knowing
something about Keats and his scale of values. Nor can we
assess the physical beauty that was so constantly and intensely
in his thoughts. If Fanny was naturally social, even flirtatious,
she loved Keats for himself, and he was not at all the kind of
man who would normally have attracted a girl of her back-
ground and supposed shallowness.

Some lesser items belong to Keats's artistic biography,
though the first one does not. A few days before Christmas,
Haydon—who for some time had been unable to work be-
cause of his eyes—made known his need of money, and he
became increasingly urgent, even hysterical, when Keats—
who was not the most affluent of his friends—was finding it
difficult to get hold of a large amount.

On December 31, writing to George and Georgiana, Keats
spoke of his growth in aesthetic appreciation. (Two weeks

earlier he had recorded his disgust with Hunt's often mere-
tricious taste.) As always, he "never can feel certain of any
truth but from a clear perception of its Beauty" (II, 19), and
he finds himself "very young minded even in that perceptive
power," but he is maturing. He now sees nothing in the
verse of Mrs. Tighe and Beattie, which had once delighted
him; and he can now begin to read Raphael's cartoons, which
a year before he had not understood at all. He has lately been
excited by reproductions of the frescoes of the Campo Santo
at Pisa, which are full of romance and tender feeling, with
magnificent draperies, yet "Grotesque to a curious pitch,"
and are impressive because they leave so much to the imag-
ination. These were the engravings that, a generation later,
were to excite the Pre-Raphaelite painters.

In the same letter, on January 2, Keats copied three recent
poems, *Fancy*, "Bards of Passion," and the song, "I had a
dove." *Fancy* was a light, spontaneous, and rapid survey of
the mainly external pleasures nature affords to the flitting
senses. It has some affinity with Keats's earliest catalogs of
"wonders" and "luxuries," but there are differences. Now he
writes in a spirit and meter and with a crisp economy that
recall *L'Allegro* and still more his own earlier "outlaw"
verses on Robin Hood and the Mermaid Tavern. And now
there runs through the poem a serious note that is to be
sounded more deeply in the odes: the sensuous phenomena
of nature, tied to natural processes, may perish or cloy as the
ideal creations of the roving, unfettered mind do not. "Bards
of Passion," another slight and shorter piece, "on the double
immortality of Poets," is a kind of variation on the same
theme, the relation and the contrast between transient actu-
ality and ideal permanence.

Late in December Keats was to have joined Charles Brown
in a visit at the home of Dilke's parents in Chichester, but,
because of his continued sore throat, he did not leave Hamp-
stead until January 18 or 19. He was away about two weeks.
Nine or ten of the days were spent at nearby Bedhampton,
with Dilke's sister and brother-in-law. On January 25 they

all attended the dedication of an ornate chapel at Stansted; details from the chapel Robert Gittings has seen in Keats's next two poems. The first of these, *The Eve of St. Agnes,* he had finished, or almost finished, by February 1 or 2, when he returned to Hampstead.

The superstition connected with St. Agnes' Eve (January 20), which Mrs. Jones had suggested as a subject, invited all the emotional warmth now awakened in the relatively happy lover of Fanny Brawne. The result was a gorgeous tapestry of 378 lines, Keats's first and much his most elaborate exploitation of the "medievalism" that was one element of romantic inspiration. *The Eve of St. Agnes* is by far the most beautiful short narrative of its age, or perhaps of any age of English poetry, and it is of course at the opposite pole from the grandeurs of *Hyperion* (which Keats had been unable to go on with but had not yet given up). In one central respect, however, the two poems are akin. In spite of the personal emotion that Keats was now qualified to pour into a tale of young love, this narrative, like *Hyperion,* lives rather in its richness of setting and detail than as a poem of human experience and feeling. Although the *Eve* is much finer in craftsmanship than *Isabella,* it is a question if Madeline is more of a living creature than her predecessor. Romeo and Juliet would of course be active presences in Keats's mind as he wrote, yet the response his title evokes in us is not so much sympathetic involvement with his hero and heroine as the abstract idea of young love seen against a background of picturesque contrasts, of family hatred, feeble age and youth, religious and quasi-religious piety and erotic passion, winter cold and storm and interior luxury, music, and color. And the poet's sympathy does not preclude touches—more gentle than those in Marlowe's *Hero and Leander*—of skepticism about the validity of romantic dreams.

Keats's empathy and negative capability are still manifest largely in his consummate power of rendering local—and in a sense peripheral—sensation. No part of the poem captures our senses and imagination more completely than the de-

scription of bitter cold in the opening stanzas—the owl, the
trembling hare, the silent flock, the Beadsman with his numb
fingers and frosted breath, the sculptured dead in icy hoods
and mails; these are more vividly conceived and communi-
cated than the feelings of Madeline and Porphyro. And this
is true of all the animate and inanimate figures and proper-
ties throughout the poem, from old Angela to the casement
in which, as a climactic glory, "A shielded scutcheon blush'd
with blood of queens and kings." All these innumerable de-
tails, as in *Hyperion,* approach, or attain, the "material
sublime." If we think of the letters of the preceding year, or
of Apollo's tragic vision, we recognize that Keats wrote the
poem with only a part of his mind; that was no doubt made
inevitable by the choice of such a subject and by the conven-
tions of romantic narrative. He himself implied this in-
adequacy when, in November, 1819, he said he wished "to
diffuse the colouring of St Agnes eve throughout a Poem in
which Character and Sentiment would be the figures to such
drapery" (II, 234). If, in the present of the story, the warmth
of youthful love is set against cold, hate, and aged piety and
palsy, the last stanza thrusts the whole vision into the far-off
past, where the young in their turn must encounter decay
and death (or possibly—like Romeo and Juliet—immediate
death, if Keats thought of them as perishing in the storm).
Here at least romance seems to touch reality.

A few recent critics have discerned a philosophical theme
in the poem, another projection of such ideas of the visionary
imagination as Keats had expressed in "I stood tip-toe" and
Endymion. At the climax of Porphyro's passion, just before
he melts into Madeline's dream, we do have some words that
had special significance in *Endymion*—"Those looks im-
mortal"; "Beyond a mortal man impassion'd far"; "Ethereal"
—but it is hard to see in these and other phrases anything
beyond their direct erotic value. And the fulfillment of Made-
line's dream is a world away from the symbolism Keats at-
tached to the dream of Milton's Adam (I, 185). Indeed, as
Jack Stillinger has remarked, the philosophical interpretation

of the *Eve* implies that "both Madeline and Porphyro have read *Endymion*, Keats's letters, and the explications of the metaphysical critics."[5] Moreover, while Keats was not given to interpretative comments on his poems, we may remember his later reaction to the fears of Taylor the publisher and his adviser, Woodhouse, about the altered lines (eventually not printed) which made the consummation slightly more explicit; Keats said "that he should despise a man who would be such an eunuch in sentiment as to leave a maid, with that Character about her, in such a situation . . ." (*K.C.*, I, 92; *Letters*, II, 163). This remark is not metaphysical. Of course Keats often thought of love and all beautiful things as partaking of "the mighty abstract Idea . . . of Beauty"; but this poem is surely not a Neoplatonic parable.

Like his other serious poems, the *Eve* draws in motifs, images, and phrases from his reading. Apart from his central use of the folklore of St. Agnes' Eve, the plot is in a familiar romantic convention. Along with *Romeo and Juliet*, there are, for instance, *Lochinvar* and the tale of Margaret and Lord Cranstoun in the second canto of *The Lay of the Last Minstrel*. The *Lay* as a whole seems to have furnished atmospheric and numerous particular hints, including the idea of moonlight colored by a red window (218: *Lay*, II.xi.127–128). There are as usual echoes of Shakespeare (notably of Iachimo's description of Imogen in bed) and Milton, and probable or possible reminiscences of such various works as Chaucer's *Troilus*, *The Faerie Queene*, Wieland's *Oberon*, Mrs. Radcliffe's novels, and *Christabel*. Although we associate *Britannia's Pastorals* mainly with Keats's earlier days, his picture of Madeline undressing has long been related to a passage of rather pallid conceits in Browne (I.v.807f.).

In the *Eve of St. Agnes*, as in *Hyperion*, Keats's revisions were numerous, sometimes inspired, and altogether they add up to a good deal, even in the negative way of eliminating, or almost eliminating, weakness. Some of the positive revisions,

5 "The Hoodwinking of Madeline: Scepticism in 'The Eve of St. Agnes,' " *Studies in Philology*, LVIII (1961), 533–555.

as in the stanza on the "casement high and triple-arch'd," are too complex to go into, but a number of simple items will suggest ways in which Keats heightened intensity. Although in texture and tone the *Eve* is so different from *Hyperion*, many of the changes, mostly immediate, are of the same kind: the replacement of vague, abstract words and images by the concrete, pictorial, tactile, and olfactory. In line 4 the commonplace "sheltered fold" becomes "woolly fold." The rooms in the castle at first "Seem'd anxious to receive a thousand guests" (33); this weak and strained personification was changed to "Were glowing. . . ." Old Angela was first seen "Tottering along" (92); she was seen and heard in "Shuffling along." "Unclasps her bosom jewels" (228) was only faintly descriptive; "her warmed jewels" brought a vital sense of flesh and blood. The unhappy excess of flesh in "Loosens her bursting boddice" disappeared in "Loosens her fragrant boddice," an idea much more in keeping with a romantic heroine. Both of these last items remind us of Keats's Miltonic use—begun in *Isabella*—of a verb as the first word in a line. And "warmed jewels" is one of many examples of energy added through the use of past participles as epithets ("frosted breath"; "deep-damask'd"; "iced stream"). In this same stanza a first effort was "Her sweet attire falls light"; this relative flatness gave way to the actively visual and auditory "Her rich attire creeps rustling." The simultaneous appeal to more than one sense is exemplified in "Pale, lattic'd, chill, and silent as a tomb" (113); "silken, hush'd, and chaste" (187). Many of these and many other phrases, original or revised, may not, individually, seem important, but—like so much of Keats's best writing—they remind us of his earlier remark, an echo of Hazlitt on Shakespeare, about "The innumerable compositions and decompositions which take place between the intellect and its thousand materials before it arrives at that trembling delicate and snail-horn perception of Beauty" (April 8, 1818: I, 264–265).

With the more or less negligible exceptions of Keats's first poem, *Imitation of Spenser,* and his last, *The Cap and Bells,* the *Eve of St. Agnes* was his only experiment with the Spenserian stanza, but there is assured mastery in his handling of it. If we think of the grandiose rhetoric of *Childe Harold* or the impetuous rush of *Adonais*, Keats's stanzas give an immediate impression of relative nearness to the slow but fluid movements of Spenser himself (an impression heightened by the partial affinity of romantic, pseudo-medieval narrative and by Keats's loading of every rift with ore). W. J. Bate's technical analysis demonstrates that the slowness of pace here is due to the same causes as in the blank verse of *Hyperion*, the use of end-stopped lines, spondaic feet, and long vowels. Also, Keats goes a little beyond Spenser in observing a stop at the end of each quatrain of the nine-line stanza. Through such technical minutiae, metrical and verbal, which were becoming more and more instinctive, Keats was able in a few days to produce a longish poem of very limited import, to be sure, but of very real magic.

Returning to Hampstead on February 1 or 2, Keats stayed indoors a week and a half in an effort to cure his sore throat. On February 13, after a day in the city, he began *The Eve of Saint Mark,* and in the next three or four days wrote all or most of the 119 lines. What started him, and what his theme was to be, we do not know. The fragment provides only the setting of a stage: a Sunday evening in a cathedral town and a young woman who has all day been absorbed in an old book containing the legend of St. Mark's life and martyrdom; as darkness comes on, she leaves the window to strike a light and pursue her reading. That is all that happens. Near the end is a passage of "Middle English," purportedly taken from the legend in the book; it has a degree of correctness that testifies to Keats's study of Chaucer.

The poem is a tantalizing fragment in what was for him a new mode, and one he never tried again. Whereas the *Eve of St. Agnes* was the natural and opulent flowering of Keats's Spenserian manner, this poem of two or three weeks later was, as everyone knows, destined to delight Rossetti and Morris as an anticipation of their own ideals of purity of line and tone. We may remember Keats's delight in the pre-Raphaelite frescoes of the Campo Santo, in which he had seen a combination of romance, tenderness, grotesqueness and a simplicity that left much to the imagination.

According to his comment, of seven months later, the poem was

quite in the spirit of Town quietude. I th[i]nk it will give you the sensation of walking about an old county Town in a coolish evening. I know not yet whether I shall ever finish it. (II, 201)

After copying it, he added: "I hope you will like this for all its Carelessness"—though the artistry seems careful as well as novel. Keats's main comment covers only lines 1–23, 40–47, and 57–68, which describe the countryside around the town and the streets, trees, and birds of the cathedral square. Part of the first paragraph packs into single lines and phrases contrasts that bring a discordant complexity of view into what might have been a simple, unified attitude:

> Upon a Sabbath-day it fell;
> Twice holy was the Sabbath-bell,
> That call'd the folk to evening prayer;
> The city streets were clean and fair
> From wholesome drench of April rains;
> And, on the western window panes,
> The chilly sunset faintly told
> Of unmatured green vallies cold,
> Of the green thorny bloomless hedge,
> Of rivers new with spring-tide sedge,
> Of primroses by shelter'd rills,
> And daisies on the aguish hills.

These four-beat lines recall *Fancy* and "Bards of Passion," but the seven-syllable trochaics of those poems have given place to octosyllabic iambics, and the shift involves a shift from speed and vivacity to the relatively slow and sedate. Keats's meter and manner may have been indebted to Chatterton's *The Unknown Knight* (the name Bertha no doubt came from Chatterton's *Ælla*) and to two poems that had contributed to the *Eve of St. Agnes, Christabel* and especially the *Lay of the Last Minstrel.* One couplet from this last (III.xxiv.305–306) might have had a place in Keats's poem:

> So passed the day—the evening fell,
> 'T was near the time of curfew bell.

The fragment as a whole, like the *Eve of St. Agnes,* turns on implicit or explicit contrasts between life and death, past and present, outdoor and indoor scenes, the externals of ordinary life and human dreams and aspirations; but these differ greatly in substance as in manner. In *Saint Mark,* medievalism is confined to Bertha's book and its associations, while the actual setting is a modern cathedral town that reflects Keats's recent acquaintance with Chichester. Bertha is the pole of two special contrasts. Her fervently religious reading and imagining are set against the quietude of the town and the placid Sabbath piety of its people; and her "homely room," her humble self, and her black dress, against the exotic decorations of her book and screen and the eerie play of light and shadow about her. While Keats's title seems to point directly to the superstition concerning St. Mark's Eve (April 24),[6] the poem, so far as it goes, does not give any supporting hints. It has been argued (by Walter Houghton) that—like a heroine of George Eliot—Bertha was dreaming of the glories of martyrdom and sainthood (although that is not the kind of theme we should expect Keats to choose). At least there seem to be serious implications or possibilities; perhaps Keats did not quite know where he was going either when he began or when he stopped.

6 According to D. G. Rossetti's widely accepted surmise, the poem was to be based on the old belief that if on St. Mark's Eve one stood near a church porch at twilight, one would see going in the apparitions of people of the parish who during the next year would be gravely ill, and who, if the figures did not come out again, would die. In our century there turned up two copies of sixteen more lines of "Middle English" which told of the superstition and would seem to have been intended for use in the poem, though they may have been an afterthought. At any rate Keats did not incorporate the lines in the text he copied in his letter of September 20, 1819.

The article by Walter Houghton cited in the next sentence of the text is "The Meaning of Keats's *Eve of St. Mark*," *ELH: A Journal of English Literary History,* 13 (1946), 64–78.

The sonnet "Bright star" was dated 1819 by Charles Brown, but there is no substantial clue to a more precise date; the early months of the year may seem more probable than the last months.[7] Keats made great improvements in the version he wrote in a volume of Shakespeare about October 1, 1820, when he and Severn were on shipboard off the Dorset coast, on their way to Italy. The first six lines have a cosmic sublimity of vision and phrase that we hardly expect outside of *Hyperion;* Keats may have started from Shakespeare's allusions to the North Star in Sonnet cxvi and *Julius Caesar* (III.i.60). But the lines are pure and original Keats (I quote the later version):

> Bright star! would I were steadfast as thou art—
>   Not in lone splendour hung aloft the night
> And watching, with eternal lids apart,
>   Like nature's patient, sleepless Eremite,
> The moving waters at their priestlike task
>   Of pure ablution round earth's human shores. . . .

The stars (to borrow from David Perkins' comment) had always been for Keats like figures of myth, objects or beings who, if they could move and even "pant with bliss," were still above the mortal world of flux; here the North Star is as fixed, remote, and passionless as a supreme deity, an un-

---

[7] It seems likely that the sonnet was written when Keats and Fanny were not under the same roof. Arguments for July rest partly on several supposed echoes of Keats's letters, partly on his supposed state of mind when he was in Shanklin. But—even if all of these were real echoes—Keats's echoes of himself may occur after a short or a long interval and are not valid evidence for a date. Moreover, the sonnet expresses a contentedly wishful rapture, not the painful conflicts that run through his letters of the summer to Fanny. And—though this is a dubious point—would the image of snow be used as Keats uses it by a poet writing in July in the southernmost part of England? As between the early and the last part of 1819, the former may appear more probable. Keats had been Fanny's vassal from the first; at Christmas, 1818, they reached some sort of understanding; and soon afterward he celebrated young love in the *Eve of St. Agnes.* During the autumn they became engaged, but at that time Keats's mounting troubles might not have allowed an utterance of such happy serenity. The sonnet "The day is gone" is likewise serene, but that sonnet records daytime intimacy and was presumably the product of reunion after the summer's separation, whereas in "Bright star" there is a sense of distance. Also, the other poems written to Fanny in late 1819 or early 1820 are in a vein of raw feeling and nowhere near the poetic quality of "Bright star."

moved mover. The last six lines of the sonnet, however natural for an ardent lover and however characteristic in their association of love and death, recall Keats's earlier swooning lovers and are a poetic descent from the grandly impersonal opening. The semi-religious aura of the octave is almost if not quite lost in the transition to the lover's dream. The sonnet has its place in Keats's view of things—the wish, admittedly vain, that the world of process, of human experience, might be stable and permanent. If we were to let ourselves think of the progressive erosion of his earlier visions of the ideal, of earthly happiness and love transposed to an "immortal" plane, we might say that the contrast between the two kinds of stability described in the sonnet would permit or invite disillusioned irony; but of course there is no hint of irony in Keats's earnest longing—as there was to be no overt irony in the odes that turn on a similar contradiction. However, there is no self-deception.

6

The Great Year: II (March–May, 1819)

SINCE EARLY WINTER, apparently, Keats had found himself unable to continue *Hyperion,* though he had written two very distinctive if not quite major poems, the *Eve of St. Agnes* and the unfinished *Eve of Saint Mark.* The latter he broke off on February 17. The next two months were—apart perhaps from the fragmentary conclusion of *Hyperion*—the longest unproductive period Keats had between the end of his medical studies and his last illness. We know that *La Belle Dame sans Merci* and the five odes were to come in April and May, but Keats lived from day to day without knowing that, and his letters from January into April are studded with reports of a barren inertia he cannot escape from: "I see by little and little more of what is to be done, and how it is to be done, should I ever be able to do it" (II, 32). Two months later, on March 8, he takes stock of himself, quite unjustly: "I am three and twenty with little knowlege and middling intellect. It is true that in the height of enthusiasm I have been cheated into some fine passages, but that is nothing" (II, 43). Keats might have been somewhat braced if he had understood more clearly that spells of fallowness and fertility are common enough in the life of the artist. But possibly his lassitude already indicated incipient disease.

There is no evidence that his relations with Fanny Brawne were at this time disturbing. In the middle of February, as we observed before, he could speak, in the same terms he had

used at first, of their having "every now and then a chat and
a tiff," but we do not know what his or her real feelings were.
There were certainly other anxieties and vexations. Keats
had been told by Richard Abbey that the money due him
from Tom's estate would not be available until Fanny Keats
reached the age of twenty-one, that is, five and a half years in
the future; it has appeared to some recent investigators that
Abbey had been drawing on the Keats funds for his own
purposes. Moreover, Abbey had removed Fanny from school
and made difficulties about Keats's writing to her. (Keats, by
the way, sent her a book to help her prepare for confirmation,
and, as "Your affectionate Parson," added quite knowledge-
able instruction in a letter.) The letters reveal various other
causes of harassment: Haydon's pressure for money; lack of
news from George; Keats's persistent sore throat; the advance
sale of four thousand copies of the fourth canto of *Childe
Harold;* the power wielded by the reviews; the failure of
Endymion; Keats's occasional thought of going to Edinburgh
to study to be a physician; his old friend Bailey's jilting of
Mariane Reynolds for another (Keats's severe view, that of
the Reynolds family and James Rice, was, it may be said, less
than fair to Bailey). This last topic, oddly enough, leads to
one of Keats's most suggestive and most familiar sayings: "A
Man's life of any worth is a continual allegory. . . . Lord
Byron cuts a figure—but he is not figurative—Shakspeare
led a life of Allegory; his works are the comments on it" (II,
67).

On March 12 and 13 Keats joyfully quoted at great length
from Hazlitt's powerful denunciation of William Gifford,
the editor of the *Quarterly.* On the nineteenth—after men-
tioning a black eye received at cricket—he described his
present exquisite state of languor, or laziness, in the partly
pictorial terms he was to use in the *Ode on Indolence.* But
then news of the expected death of Haslam's father—along
with the recent transcriptions from Hazlitt, thoughts of
Hazlitt's and his own concern with disinterestedness, and
even the Bailey affair—sets him off on some of his most seri-

ous ethical reflections, though he knows he is young and only
"straining at particles of light in the midst of a great dark-
ness"; "Circumstances are like Clouds continually gathering
and bursting—While we are laughing the seed of some
trouble is put into the wide arable land of events" (II, 79).
Most men pursue their aims with the animal eagerness of a
hawk or a stoat; yet there is a purifying fire in human nature
(he recalls Wordsworth's "we have all of us one human
heart"), although only two men, Socrates and Jesus, have
been completely disinterested. He had earlier quoted Hazlitt
in regard to the imaginative excitement and pleasure derived
from reading of the ravages of a beast of prey, and he now
adds the example of a quarrel in the street; we enjoy both
because of the sense of power abstracted from the sense of
good. From that he moves to the energies, bad along with
good, represented in poetry: "and if so it is not so fine a thing
as philosophy—For the same reason that an eagle is not so
fine a thing as a truth." This is a decided qualification of
Keats's former exalting of non-moral negative capability, and
it indicates a more mature wisdom in his conception of
poetry.

Then he copies a sonnet, "Why did I laugh to-night?",
which he had not intended to send George and Georgiana
because, apparently, it would sound weak-spirited; but he ap-
peals to the preceding part of his letter as proof that he has
it in him to bear the buffets of the world. Yet the rather
rhetorical sonnet is not an isolated utterance. The opening
and repeated question links itself with Keats's remark, quoted
in the last paragraph, about our laughing while seeds of
trouble are sown in the wide arable land of events; the
first ten lines, on the mysterious mixture in man of ignorance
and capacity for both suffering and high imagining, recall the
sonnet written on the top of Ben Nevis and the aching ig-
norance of Apollo in *Hyperion;* and the final choice of death
as an intensity beyond "Verse, Fame, and Beauty" both
echoes "When I have fears" and anticipates the *Ode to a
Nightingale.*

The journal-letter extending from February 14 to May 3—
an unusual stretch of time, because Keats was hoping daily
to hear from George—covered the period that began with
the *Eve of Saint Mark* and, after two months of uneasy lassi-
tude and depression, ended with *La Belle Dame sans Merci*
and the *Ode to Psyche*. As late as April 15, however, Keats
could think of moving to Westminster (as the Dilkes had just
done) and presumably trying journalism. In April or early
May the Brawnes moved into the Dilkes' half of Wentworth
Place, so that, until the end of June, Keats and Fanny were
under the same roof. He managed to find £30 for the im-
portunate Haydon, although he had been informed by Abbey
that his resources were much smaller than he had thought,
and although—as he told Haydon on April 13—he had lent
to various persons nearly £200, of which he was not likely
to see much again or soon. Keats was more keenly afflicted by
coming upon some of the correspondence between Tom and
"Amena Bellefila," a supposed woman supposedly in love
with him—a crude hoax that had been perpetrated in 1816
by C. J. Wells, a former schoolfellow (who in 1824 published
a notable play, *Joseph and His Brethren*). One vivid and
diverting item is Keats's account of a chance meeting and
walk with Coleridge (April 11) and of the sage's monologue,
a steady stream of heterogeneous associations, from nightin-
gales and dreams to volition and mermaids (II, 88–89). On
April 16, the day he reported this dreamlike encounter,
Keats copied the sonnet "As Hermes once," a confessedly
quite inadequate description of an intoxicating dream he had
had, after many days of low spirits, a dream based on Dante's
episode of Paolo and Francesca.

There had been a gap of nearly a month (March 20–April
14) in this journal-letter, and Keats nowhere mentions *Hy-
perion*, but perhaps during early April he composed the frag-
mentary third book, so different in style from the first two
books. Having at last set forth his main theme, Apollo's ar-
rival at tragic understanding, he gave up the effort to round
out the poem and let Woodhouse have the manuscript (along

with the manuscripts of the *Eve of St. Agnes* and *Eve of Saint Mark*). On April 21 Keats copied in his journal-letter two very different things, a brief review for the *Examiner* of Reynolds' *Peter Bell*, a wicked anticipatory parody of the early poem Wordsworth was about to publish, and *La Belle Dame sans Merci*, which he had partly written that day and apparently finished in the letter.

On this ballad of sinister magic Keats gives no comment except a jocular explanation of the precision of "kisses four." He may at this time have been torn by the opposed feelings he avowed to Fanny Brawne in the following July—the painful sense of lost freedom along with intense love—but we have no evidence; Keats's imagination could develop a timeless theme without, or with only a hint from, personal experience. The same thing may be said in regard to "sources"; we remember too Keats's own episode of Glaucus and Circe in the third book of *Endymion* and the Dantesque conclusion of "As Hermes once." This sonnet had described a dream he wished he could have every night; its obverse side appears in *La Belle Dame*. It is chiefly with medieval ballad and romance that we associate the idea of a fairy woman's loving and leaving a mortal man, but the main material of Keats's poem seems to be a conflation—whether unconscious or half-conscious—of two contrasting episodes in the *Faerie Queene*, the witch Duessa's seduction of the Red Cross Knight (I.ii.14, 30, and 45) and Arthur's inspiring dream or vision of the "Faerie Queene" herself (I.ix.13–15).[1] All these

[1] Some details may come from other passages, II.vi.14 and 18, and perhaps III.vii.17 and xi.29 and 46. While Keats may have had many things in mind, his poem is much closer to Spenser than to various other suggested sources, such as Coleridge's *Love* and Allan Cunningham's ballad, *The Mermaid of Galloway*. The plot of Thomas Love Peacock's long narrative, *Rhododaphne* (1818)—the seduction of a young man by a witchlike beauty—was possibly to leave its mark on *Lamia*, and some lines in the first canto (in which the opening question is twice repeated) suggest Keats's first stanzas:

> What ails thee, stranger? Leaves are sear,
> And flowers are dead, and fields are drear. . . .
> . . . .
> And streams are bright, and sweet birds sing.

passages were more or less marked in Keats's copy of Spenser.

La Belle Dame is far removed from prototypes by its *femme fatale* and romantic subjectivity, by its blended simplicity and sophistication of style and rhythm, and by the suggestive power of its narrative particulars. In his picture of anguish after ecstasy Keats approximated the experience of the Red Cross Knight more fully than that of Arthur, but of course his ballad is "pure poetry" with none of Spenser's moral and religious meaning. Yet there is a suggestion, beyond the merely erotic, of human loneliness, of the wasting futility of supramortal aspiration, of the whole mystery of life. And though the knight is not presented as a poet, he is akin to Endymion in his disillusioned return to actuality after a glimpse of the ideal. But while Endymion was granted a saving revelation, the knight remains desolate; the truth he awakes to is not the fulfillment of Adam's dream. His partial affinity with the Lycius of *Lamia* belongs to the future.

The second version of the poem—printed in Hunt's *Indicator* on May 10, 1820—is one notable exception to the rule that Keats's revisions were always improvements; it is not clear whether the changes were early or late or a mixture. In any case they tend to sacrifice the arresting to the conventional. In the first line the change from "knight-at-arms" to "wretched wight" gives up chivalric associations for a vague and redundant stereotype; and the lady's demonic power shrinks with the replacing of "And there she lulled me asleep" by "And there we slumber'd on the moss."

In the evening of April 21, the day he wrote *La Belle Dame*, Keats, going on with his journal-letter, remarked on the odd effect of reading at the same time Robertson's *History of America* and Voltaire's *Le Siècle de Louis XIV*. From that point—since for him every point of thought is the center of an intellectual world—he launched on an elaborate parable of life as "The vale of Soul-making," a kind of sequel

---

Keats's "And no birds sing" has commonly been linked with William Browne's "Let no bird sing" (*Britannia's Pastorals*, II.i.244). However that may be, the poignant effect of Keats's short, slow last lines is his own.

to the "mansion of life" of May 3, 1818. This statement, no less familiar than important, of Keats's growing ethical concern amounts to a tacit repudiation of his earlier and cherished doctrine of negative capability. For although he is discussing men in general, he does not exclude poets as a privileged species; and whereas the chief point of his former creed was the poet's necessary lack of any positive identity, his theme now is the necessity of harsh experience, of pains and troubles, for the achieving of identity, of character, of "a soul." Keats had approached this question a month before, when he wrote of circumstances gathering and bursting upon the heads of unsuspecting mortals. Indeed, as far back as that letter to Bailey of November 22, 1817, so much quoted for its aesthetic credo, he had spoken of a man's misfortunes calling upon "the resourses of his spirit" (I, 186; cf. I, 141). Now he sees identity attained through the medium of the heart, "And how is the heart to become this Medium but in a world of Circumstances?" (II, 104). All this may be seen as a practical expansion of the tragic knowledge that flooded in upon Apollo at the end of *Hyperion*. The importance of this ethical creed is not in novelty—it has none—but in its being a product of Keats's own experience and thought; it marks a stage in his development. And, in a lesser way, it proves that he has come out of his prolonged and depressing inertia.

We might not expect this discourse to go along with the poems Keats proceeded to copy, the sonnets on Fame (two) and Sleep, the *Ode to Psyche,* and the sonnet on the sonnet ("If by dull rhymes our English must be chain'd"), although not merely the *Ode* but the sonnets—notably *To Sleep*— have their degrees of value. In the second sonnet on Fame Keats can, in the spirit of some letters, put aside the craving for fame as "a fierce miscreed" in contrast with the natural growth that brings true salvation. But these sonnets have a special technical interest. On January 2, after copying *Fancy* and "Bards of Passion"—which he called "specimens of a sort of rondeau"—Keats said he thought he would cultivate this genre "because you have one idea amplified with greater ease and more delight and freedom than in the sonnet" (II, 26). On May 3, before he copied the fourth of the new sonnets, he remarked that he had been "endeavouring to discover a better sonnet stanza than we have": the "legitimate" (Petrarchan) pattern does not suit English well on account of its pouncing rhymes, and the English form is too elegiac (the term referred to the alternative rhymes of the three quatrains) and its final couplet is rarely pleasing. But Keats was almost done with sonnets; by this time he had written over sixty. These late experiments contributed to the various complex stanzas he used with such power in the odes. He had of course begun to experiment with irregular stanzaic patterns two years earlier, in the "Hymn to Pan" in *Endymion* and in the ode to Maia of May 1, 1818; and no doubt Spenser's *Epithalamion* and *Lycidas* had been in his mind all the way along.

The continuity of technical effort is apparent in the *Ode to Psyche,* which Keats copied on April 30, after the first three sonnets: although the rhyme schemes of the stanzas vary, they are all closer to the sonnet pattern than the more compact stanzas of the later odes. Keats said, by way of prelude, that this was the first and only poem with which he had taken even moderate pains, that for the most part he had dashed off his lines in a hurry (a remark that seems hardly true of *Hyperion* or even *Endymion*): "This I have done leisurely—I think it reads the more richly for it and will I hope encourage me to write other thing[s] in even a more peacable and healthy spirit" (II, 106).

Keats's five great odes, from *Psyche* to *Autumn,* have long been such peaks in the poetical landscape that they are likely to constitute our first instinctive associations with the word "ode." The more or less Pindaric tradition, beginning with Ben Jonson, established by Cowley, and carried on by Dryden, Gray, and Collins, was predominantly in "the Big Bow-wow strain" of public declamation; and this was continued even by Coleridge ("To turgid ode and tumid stanza dear," as Byron said). Of that tradition Keats's juvenile *Ode to*

Apollo was a small echo. But there had been examples, such
as Collins' *Ode to Evening,* of the private, quiet, reflective
ode; the great examples nearer Keats were of course Cole-
ridge's *Dejection* and Wordsworth's *Intimations of Immor-
tality.* Yet to think of these is to realize at once how far Keats
re-created (and shortened) the reflective ode. He had already,
in the first and fourth books of *Endymion,* written two elab-
orate odes which, though both cataloged more or less ex-
ternal details, inclined respectively toward the two kinds: the
"Hymn to Pan" glorified the romantic imagination, and the
Bacchic processional, while ostensibly the main body of an
"Ode to Sorrow," remained a tapestry. The serenely beauti-
ful fragment of an ode to Maia had promised to be in the
reflective line. But one of the distinctive elements of the
later odes is their dramatic structure.

Before copying the *Ode to Psyche,* Keats provided, chiefly
from Lempriere, the bit of information that had given him
his cue: that Psyche was not a goddess of primitive Greek
myth but was "embodied" by the post-Augustan Platonist,
Apuleius, so that she "was never worshipped or sacrificed to
with any of the ancient fervour—and perhaps never thought
of in the old religion—I am more orthodox that [*for* than]
to let a hethen Goddess be so neglected."

In spite of—or perhaps because of—the special pains Keats
took over this poem, his first steps were uncertain. A brief
and not very felicitous invocation leads, with somewhat
forced abruptness, into a vision of Cupid and Psyche couched
in a timeless embrace in the kind of green recess Keats was
so fond of. There is no such outdoor meeting in Apuleius or
in Mrs. Tighe's romance, and the picture, apparently draw-
ing scenic details from the Elizabethan translation of Apu-
leius, is a Keatsian and "pagan" metamorphosis of Milton's
Adam and Eve in their paradisal bower (cf. "two fair crea-
tures," "side by side," and "roof," and *Paradise Lost,* iv.741,
772, 790). Keats asks at the start—as he was to ask after the
actual hearing of the nightingale's song—if his vision was a
dream; its imaginative validity the ode must establish. (We

may remember again his early assertion that "The Imagina-
tion may be compared to Adam's dream—he awoke and
found it truth.") Whatever his symbolic purpose, Keats is of
course far more intent than Milton on immediate sensation,
and two lines are a prime example of Keatsian synesthesia,
since they appeal to four of the five senses:

> 'Mid hush'd, cool-rooted flowers, fragrant-eyed,
> Blue, silver-white, and budded Tyrian . . .

We have noticed that Keats's empathy often works more po-
tently with things than with persons, and here the flowers
are more real than the immortal lovers.

From this close-up, wholly sensuous picture Keats rises
toward his abstract theme:

> O latest born and loveliest vision far
> Of all Olympus' faded hierarchy!

He goes on to tell in "historical" terms of Psyche's lack of a
temple, altar, virgin-choir, incense, priesthood, all the happy
pieties of a time

> When holy were the haunted forest boughs,
> Holy the air, the water, and the fire.

The chief sources of the details are very different—John
Potter's *Archaeologia Graeca* (a book Keats owned and was to
use for *Lamia*) and the exultant account in Milton's *Nativity*
of the dispersal of the pagan gods from their shrines. But
now nostalgia gives place to positive affirmation, "So let me
be thy choir," and to repetition, with a new meaning, of the
ritualistic observances the poet can supply. The adjuration,
indeed the whole poem, is as typical of the quietly contem-
plative side of Keats as the somewhat later prayer to the West
Wind, "Make me thy lyre, even as the forest is," was typical
of the revolutionary Shelley. We may think too of *Kubla
Khan*, in which an objective description of an imagined
scene becomes a metaphor for poetic creation.

In the final stanza the role of the poet in building a temple
of the mind is set forth in a tissue of metaphors from nature,

E

partly transmuted from the pictorial details of the opening vision:

> Yes, I will be thy priest, and build a fane
>   In some untrodden region of my mind,
> Where branched thoughts, new grown with pleasant pain,
>   Instead of pines shall murmur in the wind:
> Far, far around shall those dark-cluster'd trees
>   Fledge the wild-ridged mountains steep by steep. . . .[2]

The last two of the quoted lines—a reminiscence of Keats's northern tour (I, 306; cf. *Endymion*, i.86) and perhaps also of Milton and Mrs. Radcliffe—are at once strongly pictorial and suggestive of the wilder and more dangerous reaches of the poetic imagination. Yet that suggestion is only local and momentary; this one bold and massive image is quickly smothered as Keats relapses into the cozy world of Flora and old Pan, a private world of "soft delight." The ode ends with a return to the myth and the union of Love and Art in "shadowy thought"; but the whole conclusion falls short of its symbolic purpose. Psyche is assuredly no Lamia, yet the poet, so far as his words go, is uncomfortably close to the dreamer Lycius.

To postpone for a bit the question of expressive adequacy, the style in itself is uneven; along with manifest and uniquely Keatsian beauties of phrase and rhythm there are flaws in detail and diction that take us back to the earlier Keats: "soft-conched ear"; "fainting with surprise"; "At tender eye-dawn of aurorean love." While these phrases remained, some others were improved—though "delicious moan" (30) seems, even for pagan religion, an ultra-aesthetic replacement of "melodious moan." In one of the lines quoted above, the too botanical "freckle(d) pink" gave way to the

---

[2] The adoption of the priestly and architectural role may have been aided by remembrance of Spenser's worshipfully amorous lines (*Amoretti*, xxii):

> Her temple fayre is built within my mind,
>   in which her glorious ymage placed is,
> on which my thoughts doo day and night attend,
>   lyke sacred priests that never thinke amisse.

Cf. also *Psyche*, line 5, and *Amoretti*, lxxvii.1.

cool, clear, satisfying "silver-white." "O bloomiest" (36), an unfortunate throwback, became "O brightest." Some of the chief poetic echoes have been mentioned already. Some—"happy, happy dove," "virgin-choir," the "fane-pain" rhyme, "untrodden"—perhaps came from Mrs. Tighe's *Psyche*, which Keats had long and avowedly outgrown but which his theme might have brought back to his subconscious mind. The second line of the ode is, in its context, an unhappily audible echo of *Lycidas*—and Mrs. Tighe. The description of Vesper as "amorous glow-worm of the sky" and the turning of Psyche's lamp into a torch may have been both suggested by Coleridge's *Nightingale* (68–69): "while many a glow-worm in the shade/Lights up her love-torch."

Incidental blemishes are only a partial indication of a pervasive quality that makes this one of Keats's weaker odes. To take such a view of *Psyche* is to go against some notable critics—and it is not to deny that the ode would make the fortune of a lesser poet—but it may be thought that the almost wholly luscious imagery, especially in the final stanza, results in a debilitated rendering of a serious theme. The idea of the poet-priest, however richly developed, does not reach a plane of inclusive complexity or set up anything of the central tension that is the strength of the greater odes. There is not, as in *Kubla Khan*, a reconciliation of the Apollonian and Dionysian, nor indeed is there any recognition of the actual world. The phrase "pleasant pain" may touch on Keats's perennial concern with mixed and unmixed joy and sorrow, but here it is an ineffectual cliché. Keats proclaims an imaginative exploration of "untrodden" ways, of "stars without a name," of the new subjective poetry, yet Psyche and her temple are not products of the poet's realistic imagination; she does not become an adequate symbol of "vision," but remains a creation of sensuous and erotic fancy in a "rosy sanctuary." While forward-looking in technique and presumably in theme, the ode is really a sophisticated continuation of, or reversion to, the simple blend of nature, myth, and poetry of the youthful Keats. The theme is akin to that of the "Hymn to Pan," but the "Hymn," with all its faults, was bolder and tougher; what should in the *Ode to Psyche* be a climactic vision of the imagination's creative power does not rise above lush reverie.[3] As a metaphorical statement of Keats's mature conception of poetry it comes nowhere near the comprehensive wisdom and strength of the letters, least of all the section on "The vale of Soul-making" written within a few days of the ode. Even *Endymion* had partly explored "the Chamber of Maiden-Thought"; *Hyperion* and *La Belle Dame* had in large and small ways framed a tragic outlook; but the *Ode to Psyche* seems to come from "the infant or thoughtless Chamber." Perhaps Keats's concern here with formal problems made him unaware of how much he had left unsaid or attenuated by a texture and tone of merely or mainly sensuous luxury. He may well have intended to set forth the strong and comprehensive idealism, transcendental or naturalistic, that some critics find, but it is very hard to discern that in the poem he actually wrote.

No such disappointment can arise in regard to the two supreme odes that followed. *Psyche* was clearly the first of the series; on April 30 Keats said it was the last thing he had written. The *Ode to a Nightingale* was dated "May" by Brown and Woodhouse, and presumably came early in the month. In a few lines added to his journal-letter on May 3, Keats said nothing of any more poems but, reporting the "delightful forwardness" of spring, included a remark which, somewhat altered, was to find a place in the *Ode:* "the violets are not withered, before the peeping of the first rose." It is generally agreed, though we lack evidence about dates and sequence, that the other odes, the *Grecian Urn, Melancholy,* and *Indolence,* were written during the same month. Such concentrated productivity never ceases to be astonishing. While the odes were not composed as parts of any coherent

---

[3] We might compare Shelley's prettified rendering of poetic creativity in his major vision of a new world, *Prometheus Unbound* (I.737f.):

> On a poet's lips I slept,
> Dreaming like a love-adept. . . .

program, they are naturally linked together as variations on some central ideas and questionings which had long been active in Keats's mind and had been more or less touched in earlier poems, notably *Endymion*.

The account of the genesis of the *Nightingale* given later by Brown is one of the most familiar of literary anecdotes, but it must be quoted (*K.C.*, II, 65):

In the spring of 1819 a nightingale had built her nest near my house. Keats felt a tranquil and continual joy in her song; and one morning he took his chair from the breakfast-table to the grass-plot under a plum-tree, where he sat for two or three hours. When he came into the house, I perceived he had some scraps of paper in his hand, and these he was quietly thrusting behind the books. On inquiry, I found those scraps, four or five in number, contained his poetic feeling on the song of our nightingale.

The autograph manuscript that survives was probably a second draft and we do not know how much revision it embodied. Also, according to Brown, Keats had listened to the bird before this particular morning. Whether the poem had been taking shape in his mind over several days or was composed in several hours, it has none of the faltering, padding, and other defects that attended the leisurely and studied writing of the *Ode to Psyche*. Keats was able to achieve such miraculous felicity because his ideas and feelings were ripe for utterance, because sureness of design and expression had become a habit which now rarely failed him, and because he had—as he had not in *Psyche*—a concrete object and symbol to start from.

Psyche was a completely happy poem, a picture of harmonious, single-souled creativity uncrossed by any shadow. The first stanza of the *Nightingale* sets up a conflict which, progressively enriched and deepened, governs the structural and emotional pattern. This initial conflict is of limited scope: the poet's heartache, his drowsy, deathlike numbness, comes from the acute intensity of his happiness in the song of the bird. Along with this internal antithesis, there is the antithesis between the simple joy of the nightingale, singing

of summer in full-throated ease, and the mingled joy and
pain of the human listener—joy and pain that are as yet
purely sensuous and aesthetic. And, as yet, the listener as well
as the singer lives only and fully in the moment; as Keats had
said in his *Epistle to Reynolds,*

> It is a flaw
> In happiness to see beyond our bourn—
> It forces us in Summer skies to mourn:
> It spoils the singing of the Nightingale.

But the scope of conflict is now enlarged. The poet's crav-
ing to share fully in the bird's happiness suggests recourse to
wine; yet this means of heightened enjoyment turns into a
means of escape,

> That I might drink, and leave the world unseen,
> And with thee fade away into the forest dim.

The escapist impulse, though, leads only into a grim picture
of the world the poet would escape from, the world of suffer-
ing and age and death which the bird has never known. The
third stanza, no product of drowsy numbness or sensuous
rapture, sums up all that *Psyche* had left out, what Keats a
year before had identified with the "Chamber of Maiden-
Thought"—"sharpening one's vision into the heart and na-
ture of Man—of convincing ones nerves that the World is
full of Misery and Heartbreak, Pain, Sickness and oppression"
(I, 281). The poetic picture is more ample, and no more
generalized, than the happy pastoralism of stanza 2; it firmly
establishes the criterion of reality that conditions the whole
poem.

Escape from that world, however, cannot be achieved
through wine, through the senses; only the poetic imagination
(as described in the less serious *Fancy*) seems to have the
power. The line "Though the dull brain perplexes and re-
tards" suggests the numbness of the opening and the realistic
mind of earth ("Where but to think is to be full of sorrow"),
and perhaps Keats's old antithesis between sensation and
thought. The poem had begun in an hour of sunlight; now,

when the poet's imagination has carried him to join the bird in the forest, it is midnight, in a secluded fairy world of sense that is almost cut off from moon and starlight. Escape has been accomplished, after a fashion, and in stanza 5 the poet enjoys for the moment the rich—if still half-drugged—stability of "embalmed darkness," feeling (in the words of *Endymion*) "a sort of oneness" with untroubled nature. Yet this serenely happy passiveness admits, almost unwittingly, the fact of process, of transiency, of death along with life:

> Fast fading violets cover'd up in leaves;
> And mid-May's eldest child,
> The coming musk-rose, full of dewy wine. . . .

The sixth stanza recalls and enlarges an idea expressed in earlier poems and just hinted at in the opening lines of this one —of death as the supreme ecstasy, the ultimate escape. But such a luxurious death wish is seen at once as illusory, even in the utterance—"half in love," "seems it rich." The poet's sense of actuality—which has maintained an open or tacit countermovement that prevents any lapse into mere unconscious escapism—tells him that such a desire is self-defeating:

> Still wouldst thou sing, and I have ears in vain—
> To thy high requiem become a sod.

The brute fact of death, real death, opens all the stops for what now becomes the dominant theme, the contrast between the mortality of man and the immortality of art:

> Thou wast not born for death, immortal Bird!
> No hungry generations tread thee down. . . .

We need not be exercised over the logical flaw in Keats's forgetting the mortal singer when he makes its song a symbol of enduring art; there is a deeper logic in the contrast between art and human life. The most wonderful thing about this stanza—so beautiful in every detail of phrase and rhythm —is that the climactic affirmation is also a tissue of implicit irony. For the conscious rejoicing in the immortal life and power of art turns—as it were unconsciously and inevitably, and hence with stronger and more subtle impact than overt irony would bring—into recognition of the perpetuity of pain and sorrow through all generations of mankind. The clown, along with the emperor, suggests that there were hungry generations in the past and that high and low were alike subject to human ills. Ruth perhaps was comforted, but she was still a grieving exile, sick for home. The last and fullest item adds to history the world of romantic imagination, and —like the quoted lines about the flowers—combines positive and negative more distinctly: the song charms open magic casements in fairylands, but they open on perilous seas and the fairylands are forlorn.

The word "forlorn," the funeral bell that tolls the poet back to himself and life in this world, finally shatters the whole illusion that his imagination had built up. His experience has been a fuller and truer version of Endymion's: he has been brought back, after a glimpse of ideal beauty, to a sense of real, inescapable things. And here there is no simple "Platonic" resolution; there can be only acceptance.

In this dialectical pattern the slow rise to a climax includes elevations and depressions and contradictions before the final subsiding, and yet the whole describes a perfect curve in which no essential note is lacking or slighted or overstressed and no non-essential note is touched. Moreover, passages of "softness" are not, as in *Psyche*, uncriticized idealism but, however beautiful and seductive, become the half-unreal material for realistic skepticism. There may be one or two dubious phrases, such as "blushful Hippocrene," but they are mere specks, if that. Of the known revisions, the chief items were at the end of the sixth stanza, where "the wide casements" became "magic" and "ruthless" or "keelless" became "perilous"—both great gains. These two lines may owe more to some of Mrs. Radcliffe's casements and violent waves than to Claude's peaceful painting *The Enchanted Castle* (which Keats had described in his *Epistle to Reynolds*); the phrase

"perilous seas," if it came from Coleridge's *Fears in Solitude*
(87), acquired a new aura.

Keats's probable or possible literary echoes (including rem-
iniscences of his own letters and poems) are perhaps even
more numerous here than usual, and, as usual in his mature
writing, they pass through his own sensibility into his own
idiom; they are part of his imaginative process of conception
and composition. The first two lines of the ode may be wholly
original, or they may fuse memories of Horace's draining of
a Lethean bowl (*Epodes*, xiv.1–4)—Keats owned a copy of
Horace; of Adam's dream in *Paradise Lost* (viii.288–291),
which includes the "dissolve" of Keats's line 21; of Marlowe's
"as if cold hemlock I had drunk" (*Ovid's Elegies*, III.vi.13);
and of Mrs. Tighe's "drowsy dullness . . . Benumbs each
torpid sense" (vi.16). The picture of "Dance, and Provençal
song, and sunburnt mirth" seems to combine various scenes
in Mrs. Radcliffe with the "sunburn'd sicklemen . . . be
merry" of *The Tempest* (IV.i.134–135). The "purple-stained
mouth" goes back to Horace (*Odes*, III.iii.12). Line 23, "The
weariness, the fever, and the fret," blends Wordsworth's "the
fretful stir/Unprofitable, and the fever of the world" (*Tin-
tern Abbey*, 52–53) with Macbeth's words on King Duncan,
"After life's fitful fever he sleeps well" (*Macbeth*, III.ii.22).
Line 26, "Where youth grows pale, and spectre-thin, and
dies" (happily revised from "Where youth grows pale and
thin and old and dies"), brings up the wasting away of Tom
Keats and Wordsworth's "While man grows old, and dwin-
dles, and decays" (*Excursion*, iv.760); and the next two lines
of the *Excursion* can be heard behind Keats's "No hungry
generations tread thee down." "Darkling I listen" recalls the
allusion to the nightingale in Milton's invocation to Light
(*Paradise Lost*, iii.38–40). The not entirely biblical picture
of Ruth amid the alien corn—one of those Keatsian and
kinetic epithets that distill and dramatize a wealth of meaning
—may draw in the "forlorn" heroine of Wordsworth's *Ruth*
and surely *The Solitary Reaper;* while the reaper's "plaintive
numbers" remain alive and beautiful in Wordsworth's heart,

E*

the nightingale's joyous song becomes, for the disenchanted listener, a "plaintive anthem." The last two lines of the ode may echo a variety of things, from *The Merry Wives of Windsor* (III.v.141) to Hazlitt's comment on Spenser as "the poet of our waking dreams . . . lulling the senses into a deep oblivion of the jarring noises of the world, from which we have no wish to be ever recalled." Whatever of these and other items flowed into Keats's memory, they were as much a part of himself as any other kind of experience; and, whether or not we recognize them (or peruse footnotes and commentators), such associations enrich the emotional resonance of words and phrases.

Keats had little time, after *Psyche,* for further experimentation with stanzaic patterns, but somehow he arrived quickly at the shorter and firmer stanzas of the *Nightingale* and later odes. The perfection of this new formal vehicle (which had its minor variations) must be allowed to speak for itself. But a word may be said on another topic which also would invite many pages and embraces an infinity of variations. The functional felicity of sound in Keats's mature poetry was not merely the random result of instinct. He early developed a theory about the combination and permutation of open and close vowels which—though Bailey's attempted explanation (*K.C.*, II, 277–278) does not take us very far—can be understood from its disciplined results, results that go beyond the obvious uses of alliteration, assonance, and contrast. Any of Keats's best writing, from *Hyperion* onward, would serve for illustration, and one fine specimen would be the seventh stanza of this ode, which a reader may study for himself. Such interweaving of sounds Keats may have learned especially from Spenser and Milton.

In the *Ode on a Grecian Urn,* as in the *Nightingale,* the poet starts from a solid object and symbol, in this case an inanimate, anonymous artifact which in itself can be called immortal, since it has survived and presumably will survive through many centuries. But that fact of silent immortality, while it remains the major premise of the whole poem, gives

way to the immediate question of mortal or immortal ex-
perience (again we remember *Endymion*). The young people
．e depicted on the urn in a moment of sensuous ecstasy, men
pursuing women amid the music of pipes and timbrels; and
there is the repeated question: are they "deities or mortals,"
"men or gods"? But the question shifts to the central contrast
between the unending happiness arrested in art and the
brevity of happiness in mortal life. This contrast is developed
in the second and third stanzas, though the tone becomes sub-
dued. To the crowded scene of amorous pursuit is now added
the piper beneath the trees, and in both stanzas the happiness
of the piper and the leafy trees is unclouded; the marble
piper will, unwearied, pipe songs for ever new, and the
marble trees will never shed their leaves. But the erotic theme
brings in frustration and negation. The poet thinks first of
the perpetual unfulfillment of love, although his overt em-
phasis is on consoling affirmation: the lover can never catch
and kiss, yet—as if the pair were alive—"For ever wilt thou
love, and she be fair!" The third stanza repeats the pattern of
affirmation in regard to trees, piper, and lover, love being as
before the climactic theme, and there is fuller stress on the
ideal state of eager expectation; such pictured love has all the
joys and none of the pangs that go with actual human passion
and satiety.

These three stanzas have had a coherent development, at
once describing and interpreting the scenes on the urn in
terms of the contrast between its timeless world and the hu-
man world of time and change; and the material has been
entirely that of the senses, springtime and youth and music
and especially love. Except for the line and a half on the
frustrated lover, there has been no hint of anything but per-
fection in the life presented on the urn and complete—
though envious—contentment in the mortal beholder. We
might recall the somewhat gushing Severn's report of Keats's
talk about "the Greek spirit,—the Religion of the Beautiful,
the Religion of Joy, as he used to call it"; and Severn quoted

him as saying: "It's an immortal youth, . . . just as there is no
Now or *Then* for the Holy Ghost."[4]

The fourth stanza, the most beautiful in the poem and one
of Keats's supreme achievements, is a total digression from
the line pursued so far. The new scene, a sacrificial proces-
sion, turns away from the sensuous and erotic to the happy
communal pieties treated in the opening pages of *Endymion*
and touched in the *Ode to Psyche*. But here, in contrast with
the handling of the erotic theme, the positive is quietly sub-
merged in the negative; it is not the pictured procession that
dominates the poet's mind, but his unpictured thought of the
emptiness and silence of the deserted town. The eternity of
joy and beauty becomes an eternity of joyless desolation. The
half-unconscious ambivalence, or failure of illusion, is like
that in the seventh stanza of the *Nightingale*.

The *Grecian Urn* is obviously different in structure from
the *Nightingale*. In the longer poem every step in the poet's
psychological experience is recorded in consecutive detail.
In the *Grecian Urn* the poet's attitude is soon made clear
and amplified—with some intrusive negations—in succeeding
stanzas; and these are relatively separate pictures presented
with contemplative detachment and in circular rather than
progressive sequence. The poet himself is central throughout
the *Nightingale;* in the *Grecian Urn* he does not exist except
as the eye and voice of man in general.

Criticism has concentrated on various things in the final
stanza, especially the last two lines. The first four and a half
lines reassert the poet's conscious theme, the preservation of
beauty and love in enduring marble. The phrase "tease us
out of thought" (which had occurred in the tormented *Epistle
to Reynolds,* line 77) seems to say that the urn raises the be-
holder above this world—"Where but to think is to be full
of sorrow"—into the world of art that is exempt from vicissi-
tude and decay. The next few lines are a more explicit affir-
mation: the urn will continue to soothe and exalt distressed

4 William Sharp, *Life and Letters of Joseph Severn* (London: Sampson Low,
Marston, 1892), p. 29.

humanity through ages to come. Yet between these positive
statements of the poet's ostensible theme comes the exclama-
tion "Cold Pastoral!" If, as Keats's habits of feeling and
phrase would lead us to expect, he had said "Cool Pastoral,"
the idea of refreshment would fit perfectly the affirmations
that precede and follow (and would be a kind of reply to "A
burning forehead, and a parching tongue"). But, taken along
with the earlier negations that had obtruded themselves upon
the poet's affirmative intention, "Cold Pastoral" sounds al-
most like a Freudian slip, a revelation of his imperfect con-
tentment with the eternal but unfelt happiness of the figures
on the urn; these "marble men and maidens" are cold, and
human experience, with all its deficiencies, is warm and
panting.

The last two lines have, in our time, attracted more, and
more adverse, criticism than any other passage in Keats's ma-
ture poetry, and a good deal of it may be thought wide of the
mark. There have been three points at issue: the identity of
the speaker; the meaning and value of the assertion that
"Beauty is truth, truth beauty"; and the question of artistic
propriety, of Keats's lapsing into the didacticism he abhorred.
The first point involves bibliographical data as well as logic
and may be put into a note;[5] the only possible conclusion,

[5] In the transcripts of the ode made by Brown, Woodhouse, Dilke, and
George Keats (Brown's at least probably from Keats's copy), and in the text
(probably supplied by Keats) that was printed in *Annals of the Fine Arts*
(IV, no. 15, published early in 1820), there were no quotation marks. In
Keats's volume of 1820 the lines read:

"Beauty is truth, truth beauty,"—that is all
Ye know on earth, and all ye need to know.

This form either makes the first five words the utterance of the urn and the
rest the poet's comment, or it merely emphasizes the aphoristic part of two
lines spoken by the urn. When the volume was in the press, Keats was ill and
may not have scrutinized all proofs with minute care; but even if he did do
so, the context rules out the first alternative. Earlier in the stanza Keats has
been speaking of mankind, including himself, in terms of "us" and "ours";
he could not now address mankind as "ye," nor could he, a poet on earth,
speak of men "on earth." In my own edition (1959) I put the last two lines
in quotation marks.

one may think, is that all of the last two lines are the speech
of the urn to mankind.

As for the second point, whatever Keats the man might
have said, it is a question if in the poem he thought of the
urn's oracular wisdom as limited by its own character. And,
whatever subtleties his mind could entertain, there seems to
be no novel complication here. While he is not, any more
than in parallel assertions in his letters, using the strict
language of aesthetic philosophy, he appears to be simply
reaffirming a main article of his creed, that beauty is the
criterion and proof of truth, of reality, and that reality—
which includes "all our Passions"—is the creative matrix of
beauty: "What the imagination seizes as Beauty must be
truth—whether it existed before or not" (I, 184). So austere
a moralist as Matthew Arnold found no difficulty, though his
comment took in only the first half of the idea: "For to see
things in their beauty is to see things in their truth, and Keats
knew it." The poet does not say in so many words whether
he means beauty in the obvious and conventional sense of
Oceanus' speech or as embracing Apollo's tragic vision; but
the fuller and deeper conception seems to be indicated by the
second half of the dictum, by the picture of the desolate
town, and by the acceptance of "woe" as the human lot.

Finally, there is the complaint that an abstract generality
is illegitimately imposed upon an otherwise dramatic poem.
The complaint is nullified if we take the two lines as the
words of the urn; while they voice the sentiment of the poet,
they are in fact the only dramatic utterance in the whole ode,
since all that precedes is the poet's direct description and in-
terpretative comment. A far more important point is the total
effect. Those two lines are a logical summary of the central
argument, a celebration of the immortal beauty of art in
contrast with fleeting human lives and loves. The lines are
not, however, in accord with the half-unconscious counter-
movement or undertone which gives this ode, though less
openly than in the *Nightingale,* much of its strength—the
feeling we are left with that the poet has not quite convinced

himself, that his human instincts (like Endymion's) cleave to flesh-and-blood experience, with all its pains, rather than to the cold, remote perfection of the marble urn. Keats does not, as in the *Nightingale,* acknowledge his rapture to be a momentary illusion, but he betrays something of the same skepticism. Thus, with its divided emotions, the half-denial of its main intention, the ode as a whole is more complex than the *Ode to Psyche*—or than *Sailing to Byzantium,* in which Yeats, for all his attachment to flesh and blood and his fierce awareness of man's inward divisions, turns away with more unified confidence from the Many to the aesthetic One.

Almost from the beginning Keats's imagination had been stimulated by painting and sculpture as well as literature, and the *Grecian Urn* is a cardinal example of combination and transmutation. We need not speculate about what old vases or modern imitations or engravings he had seen (he made a tracing of one vase, the Sosibios), but some literary items may be recorded, whether as "sources" or as illustrative parallels. No one seems to have suggested a source for the first four lines, which are pure Keats; he is, among other things, the poet of stillness. The picture of revelry that follows may fuse recollections of Poussin's paintings of Bacchanals and "triumphs" with some lines from Collins' *The Passions* (the word "brede" in Keats's last stanza is surely from Collins' *Ode to Evening*):

> They saw in Tempe's vale her native maids,
> Amid the festal sounding shades,
> To some unwearied minstrel dancing. . . .

The "unwearied minstrel" may have been telescoped with William Browne's "lovely shepherd's boy" who

> Sits piping on a hill, as if his joy
> Would still endure. (II.ii.33–35)

The fourth stanza may gather in items from various works that Keats knew: a sentence in Lempriere ("Hyacinthia") about a city left "almost desolate, and without inhabitants" during the last days of a festival; Sandys' lowing heifer at the

altar (*Ovid,* ed. 1640, p. 47); Claude's *Sacrifice to Apollo,*
which Keats had briefly described in his *Epistle to Reynolds;*
Raphael's cartoon, *The Sacrifice at Lystra,* which showed a
temple outside the city (Acts xiv.13), the assembled crowd,
the priest, and the garlanded victim;[6] and the sacrificial pro-
cession, with a victim perhaps more mature and robust than
a heifer, in the Elgin Marbles. In general, although the poem
is written in Keats's most finely characteristic idiom, it has,
in harmony with its subject and some of its sources, a plastic,
sculptural quality which distinguishes it from his other odes;
yet it would not be easy to put a finger on the words that
create that pervasive impression. We may not agree with
Arnold—though he was a better judge of what is Greek than
most of us—that the picture of the little town is "as Greek as
a thing from Homer or Theocritus . . . composed with the
eye on the object, a radiancy and light clearness being
added"; but at least we agree on Keats's possessing the rare
gift of "natural magic."

We have observed that *Psyche* embodies single-hearted
affirmation, that the joy celebrated in the *Nightingale* is ad-
mittedly fleeting, and that the enduring beauty of the Grecian
urn yields less than complete happiness. The latter two are
the finest of the odes of this spring in craftsmanship, and
in them the poet's realistic awareness of life hinders his os-
tensible escape into the ideal world of art and beauty and
thus creates tensions that are none the less potent for being
partly unstated. In the short *Ode on Melancholy* the theme
of transiency and permanence and the poet's conflicting atti-
tudes are open and central, all the more so because the poem
is wholly given to exhortation and definition and has no stage
setting or controlling symbol. But there is some unconscious
revelation also.

The ode's three stanzas constitute a beginning, a middle,
and an end, though its subject and brevity obviously forbid

6 The picture was exhibited at the British Gallery during this spring and
Haydon published an essay on it (*Examiner,* May 2 and 9; *Annals of the
Fine Arts,* IV, no. 13). See J. R. MacGillvray, *T.L.S.,* July 9, 1938, p. 465.

either the vertical curve of the *Nightingale* or the friezelike
circle of the *Grecian Urn*. The original first stanza was a
catalog of images of horror which, though explicitly distin-
guished from genuine melancholy, made a tissue of gothic
invention that Keats, whatever his reason, wisely deleted. The
second stanza, which became the first, is a parallel catalog of
more traditional symbols of melancholy and death—Lethe,
various herbs, the beetle, death-moth, and owl—which the
truly melancholy mind is likewise urged to shun. Keats was
no doubt recalling the banishment of pathological melan-
choly in the prelude of *L'Allegro,* but his sense of proportion
failed him when he let a recital of negatives occupy a third
of the poem; the probable cause was the poet's fascinated
gusto that makes the images of death almost nullify his dis-
missal of them. The reason for the dismissal does not become
clear until the second stanza, which is needed also to explain
the last two lines of stanza 1:

> For shade to shade will come too drowsily,
> And drown the wakeful anguish of the soul.

The traditional macabre symbols belong to simple melan-
choly, whereas a more profound melancholy, "the wakeful
anguish of the soul," arises from acute consciousness of the
impermanence of beauty; the first kind, drowsily sought or
indulged, would smother the second. (Keats's mood and the
drugged rhythm resemble the opening lines of the *Nightin-
gale,* though the direction and emphasis differ.)

In stanza 2 Keats turns from the homeopathic prescription
he has rejected to allopathic treatment—not that he is seeking
a cure. When a sudden fit of melancholy comes, like a weep-
ing cloud that "hides the green hill in an April shroud" (an
image of both fertility and death), it may be consciously
nourished and enriched by the contemplation of beautiful
things:

> Then glut thy sorrow on a morning rose,
> Or on the rainbow of the salt sand-wave,
> Or on the wealth of globed peonies;

>Or if thy mistress some rich anger shows,
>   Emprison her soft hand, and let her rave,
>   And feed deep, deep upon her peerless eyes.

The first three items are more logical examples of transitory beauty than the last, which suffers also from "let her rave," a lapse that recalls the very youthful Keats. While we know the extraordinary intensity of Keats's responses to beauty in nature and woman, his images here are at once strained and inadequate. The monosyllabic "glut" has "unpoetical" force, but that force is half-squandered on "a morning rose" (not that one would disparage roses). Both the rose and the rainbow lack the poignant simplicity of Wordsworth's images of sensuous loss:

>The rainbow comes and goes,
>And lovely is the rose. . . .

In the last stanza the theme is generalized. Melancholy

>   dwells with Beauty—Beauty that must die;
>And Joy, whose hand is ever at his lips
>Bidding adieu; and aching Pleasure nigh,
>   Turning to poison while the bee-mouth sips:
>Ay, in the very temple of Delight
>   Veil'd Melancholy has her sovran shrine,
>   Though seen of none save him whose strenuous tongue
>Can burst Joy's grape against his palate fine;
>   His soul shall taste the sadness of her might,
>   And be among her cloudy trophies hung.

The idea had long been in Keats's mind. Endymion's goddess had exclaimed (ii.823–824):

>Endymion: woe! woe! is grief contain'd
>In the very deeps of pleasure . . . ?

(The word "deeps" was originally "shrine.") We remember Keats's concern with a significant difference between simple, unmixed joy and pain and the mixture—though the basis of such concern varies in breadth and depth. In this ode the keenest pangs of loss are reserved for those whose sensitivity is most acute, whose "palate" is most "fine." The last stanza seems to owe part of its power—even if it hardly widens the limits of the experience—to recollections of Hazlitt and Shakespeare. In his first lecture on *The English Poets* Hazlitt had said: "The poetical impression of any object is that uneasy, exquisite sense of beauty or power that . . . strives . . . to enshrine itself, as it were, in the highest forms of fancy, and to relieve the aching sense of pleasure by expressing it in the boldest manner. . . ." (Both Hazlitt and Keats would be thinking of Othello's "the sense aches at thee.") And Shakespeare's Troilus, the self-conscious amorist, in his feverish expectation of Cressida, asks himself, in a speech Keats underlined throughout:

> What will it be
> When that the wat'ry palates taste indeed
> Love's thrice-repured nectar? Death, I fear me;
> Sounding destruction; or some joy too fine,
> Too subtile-potent, tun'd too sharp in sweetness
> For the capacity of my ruder powers.

There is also Shakespeare's Sonnet xxxi:

> Thou art the grave where buried love doth live,
> Hung with the trophies of my lovers gone.

But Keats's ode supplies no adequate ground or object for "the wakeful anguish of the soul"; here "Sorrow" is less "Wisdom" than luxury. His examples are not major occasions of human suffering. The solemn exaltation of language and rhythm in the last stanza only half-conceals the fact that, however much Keats's thoughts embraced, his words set forth a purely and thinly sensuous aestheticism. *Melancholy* is the obverse of the confident serenity of *Psyche,* but, like *Psyche,* this poem—in spite of "strenuous tongue" and other indications of vitality—would support the old notion of Keats as an epicure of voluptuous sensation. We cannot ask, to be sure, that every short poem should say or imply everything, yet we can hardly fail to recognize in these two odes a relative poverty of theme, however intense the emotions they grow from. These poems certainly express an essential and distinctive element of Keats's temperament and genius, without which he could not have written his greater things; but they do not express the Keats who had undergone and who understood the more common and more real misery and heartbreaks of humanity, who could bear the buffets of the world, who could see life as a passage through the vale of soul-making, and who could jump down Etna for any great public good. *Melancholy* is the only poem of Keats's that might be said, not altogether unjustly, to approach the "decadent." For a reminder of the normal Keats, we might recall a bit from a letter of about the same time, a rejection of perfectibility and a realistic accept- ance of the human condition (April 21, 1819: II, 101):

The point at which Man may arrive is as far as the paralel state in inanimate nature and no further—For instance suppose a rose to have sensation, it blooms on a beautiful morning it enjoys it- self—but there comes a cold wind, a hot sun—it can not escape it, it cannot destroy its annoyances—they are as native to the world as itself: no more can man be happy in spite, the world[l]y elements will prey upon his nature.

After producing these four odes within a few weeks, Keats was entitled to compose an *Ode on Indolence*. It was also fitting that this relaxed poem should be pitched in a much lower key than its predecessors (of which it has verbal echoes); but it seems odd that he could say in June that he had en- joyed writing it more than anything he had done this year (II, 116). For the vision of Love, Ambition, and "my demon Poesy" passing before him "like figures on a marble urn," Keats went back to a daytime reverie of March 19 (II, 79), when, after sleeping late, he felt a careless and delightful languor of both mind and body (which honesty would com- pel him to call laziness). The account of this sensation had come between the report of a black eye caused by a cricket ball and the reflections—cited early in this chapter—on circumstances bursting upon one, the common predatory in- stincts of man and beast, and the rarity of true disinterested- ness.

While this ode ranks far below the others, it grew out of a

mood Keats often experienced, a mood which varied importantly between sterile and unhappy torpor (such as had preceded the writing of the odes) and the passive, sensuous receptivity that—as the thrush said—yielded positive nourishment. Here we are reminded of various earlier utterances. A phrase that echoes the epistolary account—"Pain had no sting, and pleasure's wreath no flower"—takes us back to Endymion's Cave of Quietude; Love, Ambition, and Poesy recall the sonnets "When I have fears" and "Why did I laugh to-night?" In the not altogether coherent last stanzas, a craving to follow the three figures, now recognized, conflicts with the pleasure of honied indolence; but surrender ends with a dismissal of the "three Ghosts" that includes what seems here a halfhearted assertion,

> I yet have visions for the night,
> And for the day faint visions there is store.

We have come two-thirds of the way through Keats's great year, and, when we think of the chief poems already written and of those to come, we have a renewed sense of his growth in artistic power and insight. To use some earlier remarks of my own,

The verbal and rhythmical richness of the odes does not—like Keats's northern lakes and mountains—make one forget youth and age, life and death, permanence and transience, joy and suffering, which are at the center of the poems; the sensuous images, individually so potent—Ruth "amid the alien corn"—are elements in a view of life. The dealings of such a poet as Wallace Stevens with the senses and imagination and the nature of reality are doubtless far more subtle and complex than Keats's, yet they may be thought far more remotely and even inhumanly intellectual. Most of Keats's major poems have to do with the nature and experience of the poet, and might therefore seem foreordained to be precious; but Keats is in a way the natural man raised to the *n*th degree, and his meditations are so central that he speaks, with "the true voice of feeling," for no small part of humanity.[7]

[7] *John Keats: Selected Poems and Letters* (Boston: Houghton Mifflin Company, 1959), p. xvii.

7

The Great Year: III
(June–September, 1819)

THE MONTH OF MAY had not been a period of un-
disturbed creativity. On May 12, after months of waiting,
Keats received news from George, news that he—putting up a
cheerful front—could call "tolerably good too all consid-
ered." But the George Keatses were expecting a baby soon;
they had been disappointed about a settlement in Illinois and
moved on to Louisville; and George was in need of money—
an object that Keats, because of Richard Abbey's hostility,
was ill qualified to promote. His own problems at this time
are summed up in his letters of May 31 and June 9 to the
brothers' Teignmouth friend, Sarah Jeffrey. He has "the
choice as it were of two Poisons," going for a few years as
ship's doctor on an East Indiaman or "leading a fevrous life
alone with Poetry"; he would prefer the latter, and might live
cheaply in Devon (Brown was as usual renting his house for
the summer). Keats is still haunted by the necessity of achiev-
ing "some grand Poem" (the odes being apparently minor
items); but he must cope with circumstances and in some way
or other earn money for George and himself.

I have been always till now almost as careless of the world as a
fly—my troubles were all of the Imagination—My Brother
George always stood between me and any dealings with the
world—Now I find I must buffet it—I must take my stand upon
some vantage ground and begin to fight—I must choose between

despair & Energy—I choose the latter—though the world has taken on a quakerish look with me, which I once thought was impossible—

> 'Nothing can bring back the hour
> Of splendour in the grass and glory in the flower'

I once thought this a Melancholist's dream—(II, 113).

On June 9, although he had given up the idea of the Indiaman, Keats defends it on the ground that his mental energies would be strengthened by life among strangers on a ship. Going on to England's neglect of its great writers, contrasted with the bountiful patronage of Italy, he speaks of Boiardo as

a noble Poet of Romance; not a miserable and mighty Poet of the human Heart. The middle age of Shakspeare was all clouded[?] over; his days were not more happy than Hamlet's who is perhaps more like Shakspeare himself in his common every day Life than any other of his Characters. . . . I dare say my discipline is to come, and plenty of it too. I have been very idle lately, very averse to writing; both from the overpowering idea of our dead poets and from abatement of my love of fame. I hope I am a little more of a Philosopher than I was, consequently a little less of a versifying Pet-lamb. (II, 115–116)

(This last phrase echoes the *Ode on Indolence*—"A pet-lamb in a sentimental farce"—which he then mentions as what he has most enjoyed doing in 1819.)

On June 8 Keats had accepted the proposal of his sickly but lively friend, James Rice, that they stay for a time on the Isle of Wight. He was resolved, as he wrote a month later to his sister, "to try the fortune of my Pen once more." But now Keats received a shock from Richard Abbey, who reported that Keats's aunt, Mrs. Midgley Jennings, was filing a claim against the grandmother's estate; and, Abbey wrongly said, all money would be tied up until the suit was settled and he, Abbey, would have to pay the legal expenses (in fact the suit was never brought and in any case would not have touched the Keatses' share). Keats at once asked Haydon and others for the repayment of loans, but he received nothing and had to borrow himself from Brown and later from Taylor. On June 27 he and Rice went down to Portsmouth. As an outside passenger exposed to heavy rain, Keats caught a cold which hung on for weeks. They settled in Shanklin, on the Isle of Wight, which Keats had visited before.

On June 29 he wrote to Fanny Brawne a letter he was glad had not been posted, since it was too much like Rousseau's *Nouvelle Héloïse*. His second, "more reasonable" letter (July 1) was that of a passionate but not completely happy lover:

I have never known any unalloy'd Happiness for many days together: the death or sickness of some one has always spoilt my hours—and now when none such troubles oppress me, it is you must confess very hard that another sort of pain should haunt me. Ask yourself my love whether you are not very cruel to have so entrammelled me, so destroyed my freedom. (II, 123)

The words are, to be sure, a tribute to her, but they are ominous too. Moreover, while Keats could center his happiness in her, he cannot hope to engross her heart entirely—yet he would hate a successful rival. He is almost astonished, he tells her on July 8, that though absent she has such "luxurious power" over his senses. His love of beauty is so intense that he is miserable without her. He had never believed in such love, and had feared it would burn him up. Why—even if she does protest—should he not speak of her beauty, since without that he could never have loved her? The very first week he knew her, he says on July 25, he wrote himself her vassal (literally, though he had burned the letter because, the next time he saw her, he thought she showed some dislike):

You absorb me in spite of myself—you alone: for I look not forward with any pleasure to what is call'd being settled in the world; I tremble at domestic cares—yet for you I would meet them, though if it would leave you the happier I would rather die than do so. I have two luxuries to brood over in my walks, your Loveliness and the hour of my death. O that I could have possession of them both in the same minute. . . . I will imagine you Venus tonight and pray, pray, pray to your star like a Hethen. (II, 133)

During this summer of 1819, Keats was the partly happy, partly tormented victim of two intense emotional drives that were in conflict with each other—the almost desperate resolve that he must write and achieve success by writing, and the distracting force of his passion for Fanny. There were too the secondary but not minor anxieties about money for his and George's needs and about his own health. By the end of July, Rice left Shanklin and was replaced by Brown. Keats worked hard, first on *Lamia*—at the same time collaborating with Brown on a tragedy, *Otho the Great*—and then on *The Fall of Hyperion.* "Thank God for my diligence!" he wrote to Fanny on August 5–6; "were it not for that I should be miserable." He was now "in a train of writing" and feared to disturb it: "let it have its course bad or good—in it I shall try my own strength and the public pulse." On August 12 Keats and Brown moved to Winchester, in order—though the hope proved vain—to be near a library. On the sixteenth he wrote to Fanny what at the end he called a "flint-worded Letter"; it was mainly an account of his efforts, for the sake of his work, to steel his heart against thoughts of her. He has no idle leisure to brood over her, and perhaps luckily, since he could not have endured the throng of jealousies that used to haunt him before he "had plunged so deeply into imaginary interests." Now he is "in complete cue—in the fever"; his mind "is heap'd to the full; stuff'd like a cricket ball," and he must drive ahead without interruption for a couple of months longer.

A week later Keats, who for three months had been living on loans from Brown, made an embarrassed appeal to John Taylor (the money sent to him, as from the firm, was supplied by the faithful Woodhouse). He feels every confidence, he told Taylor, that if he chooses he may be a popular writer, yet

that I will never be; but for all that I will get a livelihood—I equally dislike the favour of the public with the love of a woman —they are both a cloying treacle to the wings of independence. (II, 144)

This is a flint-worded utterance for a passionate lover, although, as we saw, Keats could express these, with other feelings, to Fanny herself. The next day, August 24, he wrote in a partly similar strain to Reynolds. He has, he thinks, the power to become a popular writer, and also the "strength to refuse the poisonous suffrage of a public." His own being, his own soul, is a world more real and important than the shadowy crowd—apart from the friends he could not do without. If he were as strong as an ox, he could pass his life "very nearly alone though it should last eighty years." But his body will not support mental activity at its height; "I am obliged continually to check myself and strive to be nothing." However, "this state of excitement . . . is the only state for the best sort of Poetry—that is all I care for, all I live for" (II, 147).

Keats had written the first act of *Otho the Great,* from Brown's synopsis, by July 11, before Brown arrived in Shanklin; the play was finished by August 23. For the most part collaboration had proceeded in a way that might have seemed altogether fatal—Keats, without knowing what lay ahead, writing scene by scene as Brown unfolded the plot, though Keats largely took over the handling of the fifth act. Considering both the method and the speed of composition and the general character of tragedy at the time, we may say that *Otho* is much better than we might have expected: most of the characters, except the hot-blooded Ludolph, are silhouettes and stereotypes, and the complications of the plot are unclear; but the play does gather shape, momentum, and rhetorical energy. Critics have seen affinities between Ludolph and Auranthe and Lycius and Lamia and the knight and lady of *La Belle Dame sans Merci.* Keats's motives were of course partly practical: he hoped to win fair success, bolster his reputation (so badly damaged by the reviews), and make some much-needed money. But, while he cracked jokes about the play and had no illusions about its merits, he evidently looked upon it as something better than hackwork. We remember how long he had cherished dramatic aspirations and had thought of Shakespeare as the supreme model, however unapproachable. Even if *Otho*—which naturally has its Shake-spearian echoes—was inferior to Beaumont and Fletcher and Massinger, Keats's sights remained high. One of his ambi-tions, he wrote to Bailey on August 14, was "to make as great a revolution in modern dramatic writing as Kean has done in acting." He saw Kean as the only tragic actor in London or Europe and it was with him in mind that he fashioned Lu-dolph. However, a few days after the drama was completed, this hope was extinguished by the news that Kean had ar-ranged an American tour for the autumn and winter.

While working on the first act of *Otho* Keats had gone on with *Lamia,* his chief new enterprise, and by July 11 he had finished the first part, "about 400 lines." That day he wrote to Reynolds that he had great hopes of success, because he was making use of his judgment more deliberately than he had done hitherto. He has had many days and nights of thinking and has gained a soberly realistic view of worldly success and failure:

I have of late been moulting: not for fresh feathers & wings: they are gone, and in their stead I hope to have a pair of patient sublunary legs.

By September 5 Keats was done with *Lamia* (except for re-vision) and was revising the *Eve of St. Agnes* and studying Italian, by way of Ariosto. On September 18 he wrote to George of his hopes for *Lamia:*

I am certain there is that sort of fire in it which must take hold of people in some way—give them either pleasant or unpleasant sensation. What they want is a sensation of some sort. (II, 189)

A few days later, in a letter to Woodhouse, Keats pronounced *Isabella* too unsophisticated for the public, the *Eve of St. Agnes* also, but he saw "no objection of this kind" to *Lamia.*

Every reader of *Lamia* feels at once the sophisticated brilliance of the writing, and feels too an unexpected hard-ness of surface that can accommodate bits of semi-Byronic mockery. Both as a story and as a poetic texture the poem may have less attraction than the "naïve" beauty of the *Eve of St. Agnes;* if that poem was Keats's *Romeo and Juliet,* *Lamia* might be called his *Troilus and Cressida.* Notwithstanding the beauty and mature power of particular lines and passages, we are drawn to *Lamia* chiefly by the question of its "meaning." Keats gave no hint of that, although his letters and other poems provide the essential clues; however, his changing attitudes toward love, beauty, truth, and poetry have in the past given grounds for various one-sided interpretations. But first we may look at the story.

In *Lamia* Keats made 708 lines out of something more than one bare circumstance. He would have some general awareness of the archetype of ancient myth and folklore, the serpent-woman who is both seductive and destructive (and to whom the Geraldine of *Christabel* is related).[1] The short tale in the *Anatomy of Melancholy* was already slanted, since it appeared in the section headed "Heroical love causing melancholy. His Pedigree, Power, and Extent." Keats's opening episode, which occupies nearly a fifth of the poem, was his chief addition to the plot. The amorous Hermes has come to earth in quest of a lovely nymph who, because she was grievously beset by raw suitors, had been granted invisibility and happy freedom through the compassion of the serpent-woman, Lamia. Lamia agrees to show the nymph to Hermes if he will change her herself from her serpent form into the woman she once was, so that she may gratify her own passion for a young man of Corinth, Lycius. The bargain is carried out, the artless nymph responds to the ardent Hermes, and

1 In elaborating Burton's anecdote (III.ii.1.1), Keats may have got suggestions from many sources; they are fully described and assessed by Bernice Slote, *Keats and the Dramatic Principle* (Lincoln, Nebr.: University of Nebraska Press, 1958), pp. 164f. Peacock's *Rhododaphne,* in cantos vi–vii, has a palace erected by magic, with a sumptuous banquet room, and the enchantress who seduces the hero is destroyed by Uranian Love. W. W. Beyer has invoked, in Wieland's *Oberon,* the enchantress who tries to win Huon. Keats also knew the story of *Undine* (II, 173). The opening episode of *Lamia,* that of Hermes and the nymph, was apparently adapted, with echoes of Sandys, from Ovid's tale of Mercury, Herse, and Aglauros (*Metamorphoses,* ii.708–832); the same tale may have contributed to the final blighting of Lamia. There are, as usual, incidental echoes of other poets, especially of Milton, and Miltonic idioms are conspicuous.

Into the green-recessed woods they flew;
Nor grew they pale, as mortal lovers do.

This self-contained incident is a mythic example of "the faery power/Of unreflecting love" (to quote "When I have fears"); the simple passion of two immortals—even if it be only an immortal dream—is a prelude and contrast to the fatal passion of the mortal Lycius and the half-human, half-demonic Lamia.

As a serpent (with a woman's mouth, teeth, voice, and eyes), Lamia from the start is not a very sympathetic figure, and she is still less so when she undergoes a convulsive metamorphosis into a beautiful woman. She then transports herself to a place where she may encounter Lycius. He, his mind lost in Platonic shades, approaches and, the moment he is addressed by Lamia and sees her beauty, he becomes her adoring slave. At first she holds back, with coy cruelty: since these hills and vales are "Empty of immortality and bliss," what purer air can Lycius provide to soothe her "essence" and please all her senses? But then she bewitches him again with a kiss and song and avows herself a real woman, a dweller in Corinth, and as deeply in love as he is. The pair make their way into the city. When in the street they pass a bald, sharp-eyed philosopher, Lycius shrinks into his mantle and Lamia shudders. Lycius identifies him as

> Apollonius sage, my trusty guide
> And good instructor; but to-night he seems
> The ghost of folly haunting my sweet dreams.

They take up their abode in Lamia's home, a palace mysterious and magical, unknown to the townspeople.

Part II begins with lines both flippant and ominous. Then, as the lovers recline, half-asleep, the thrill of trumpets reminds Lycius of the noisy world

> For the first time, since first he harbour'd in
> That purple-lined palace of sweet sin.

The anxious Lamia, knowing "That but a moment's thought is passion's passing bell," accuses him of deserting her. But

Lycius affirms his ever-deepening devotion; he would claim
her in marriage before all Corinth. At that proposal Lamia
is profoundly upset; it would be, in Woodhouse's synopsis,
"a forfeiture of her immortality." But Lycius, grown cruel in
his turn, insists, even though he has thought, and still thinks,
that she is an immortal. Lamia submits; she is alone in the
world, yet she will welcome his many guests, all except
Apollonius. However, the sage comes, uninvited, to the wed-
ding feast.

As music and wine free "every soul from human tram-
mels," wreaths are distributed among the guests, and the poet
pauses to name appropriate garlands for the three main fig-
ures: for Lamia, willow (from Desdemona's song?) and the
kind of fern called adder's tongue; for Lycius, leaves from the
Bacchic thyrsus, to bring forgetfulness; for Apollonius, spear-
grass and spiteful thistle. This last award is prolonged into a
generalized attack on "cold philosophy," which "will clip an
Angel's wings," "Unweave a rainbow," anatomize the mys-
teries of the world of sense and imagination. The apparent
purport of the whole story would appear to require at least
a tinge of irony in these lines, but they may seem, in their
angry directness, a momentary revelation of one of Keats's
contradictory attitudes.[2] Yet, of the three persons, Apollonius
alone has a hold, however limited in its reasoned negations,
upon reality, and he alone survives.

As the banquet proceeds, Apollonius fixes his steady gaze
upon the bride and Lycius feels her growing cold and hot;
she loses her color and voice and almost her consciousness.
Lycius fiercely denounces the sage, who replies that he, the

2 While the clipping of wings is a proverbial phrase (and occurs in Burton
a few pages before his tale of Lamia), it is a mark of Keats's sincerity here
that he is echoing that first lecture of Hazlitt's on *The English Poets* which
he had echoed before. Hazlitt had said that "the progress of knowledge and
refinement has a tendency to circumscribe the limits of the imagination, and
to clip the wings of poetry" (*Works*, ed. Howe, V, 9). We remember, too,
Haydon's "immortal dinner" of December 28, 1817, when Keats and Lamb
agreed that Newton had destroyed all the poetry of the rainbow by reducing
it to its prismatic colors, and all the guests—in a highly convivial state—
drank Newton's health and confusion to mathematics.

young man's old mentor, will not see him "made a serpent's prey." At the repeated "Serpent" Lamia vanishes with a frightful scream and Lycius, his "arms . . . empty of delight," dies. This conclusion differs significantly from Burton's summary statement that "she, plate, house, and all that was in it, vanished in an instant. . . ."

Interpretations of *Lamia* have turned on the questions whether the theme is love, or love and poetry, as against philosophic reason, and whether Keats is making a clear-cut decision for one or other or is reflecting a divided attachment to all three. Such varying views indicate difficulty; and the difficulty that belongs properly to Keats's conscious intention, whatever that was, seems at moments to be aggravated by his ambivalent feelings, by elaboration of the plot and background, and perhaps most of all by his dramatic method. But recent criticism has made the poem more coherent by fully recognizing its complexity.

The personal emotions and attitudes that would have some bearing on *Lamia* were a mixture of new and old. Keats's letters of this summer to Fanny Brawne show how acutely he was torn between his love for her and his love of freedom and poetry; and that conflict was sharpened by his knowledge that he could not hope to marry unless he made money, and that he could write only when apart from her. In February(?), 1820, after his fatal illness had begun, he thus recalled the summer:

My sweet creature when I look back upon the pains and torments I have suffer'd for you from the day I left you to go to the Isle of Wight; the ecstasies in which I have pass'd some days and the miseries in their turn, I wonder the more at the Beauty which has kept up the spell so fervently. (II, 263)

Then there was Keats's long-continued awareness of the different and sometimes opposed kinds of truth open to the poetic senses and imagination and to the philosophic reason; and, on the whole, the mature Keats inclined more to the latter. There were the opposed claims of poetic contemplation and humanitarian action. Finally, as we have often observed, nearly all of Keats's poems, early or late, center or touch on the conflict between idealistic aspiration and realistic disenchantment, between the desire for imaginative transcendence and rational acceptance of things as they are. It would be strange if such a major work as *Lamia* were not involved with this complex of emotions and convictions—and they were to find more direct expression in the poem that immediately followed *Lamia*, the *Fall of Hyperion*.

On the story level, Lamia is a kind of *belle dame sans merci* who lives only for possessive love. She is not positively evil, but she is unreal, an agent of corruption, a sort of semi-Spenserian Acrasia. On a more abstract level, the poem is a disillusioned reworking of the themes of *Endymion* and *Hyperion*, to name only two stages in Keats's developing view of the poet's nature and experience. The serpent whom Hermes overhears longing for passionate love is not the Indian maid, the warm human creature, overheard by Endymion; still less is she a Cynthia or Mnemosyne. Lamia is not ideal at all, except as a symbolic object of sensuous dreams. She herself, while a serpent, could send her spirit abroad to dream among mortals (i.202–215), but she is not deceived like the simple Lycius. After her restoration to womanly form she is described as having more than mortal knowledge (though her magical powers are limited):

> Not one hour old, yet of sciential brain
> To unperplex bliss from its neighbour pain.

And when she waylaid Lycius,

> every word she spake entic'd him on
> To unperplex'd delight and pleasure known.

Such promises—which are to have only temporary fulfillment —recall Keats's continual concern with the mixture or the separation of these opposites: here Lamia's ability to separate them marks her as non-human, as specious illusion. In the

end both she and Lycius vanish, like—and unlike—the happy
Hermes and the nymph at the beginning.

Since most of Keats's chief poems are concerned with the
nature of poetry and the poet, we may assume that Lycius
represents not merely a lover but a poet, although a projec-
tion of only one part, and not the strongest part, of Keats him-
self. Like Endymion, Lycius is captured by what he takes to
be an ideal and immortal love; luxuriating in his bower of
bliss, he does not heed either the trumpets of action or the
wisdom of philosophy. He is a mortal dreamer who gladly
retreats from reality into a world of fantasy. In demanding
marriage he is not, as the poet's later ironical comment puts
it, profaning secret joys (ii.146f.), but is trying to make a
dream substantial and lasting. Unlike Endymion, he does not
grow into devotion to the real; unlike Apollo, he does not
attain comprehension of the world of suffering. Rather, Ly-
cius is—somewhat like Tennyson's innocent Lady of Shalott
—a cloistered artist who lives on illusions and is killed by the
shock of reality—that is, in *Lamia*, by philosophic truth. Yet
Apollonius is a coldhearted realist who can only see through
everything—a very imperfect symbol of what Keats meant by
philosophy. Thus none of the three chief figures represents
an ideal; they are all more or less fatally flawed parts of an
ideal.

If something like this was Keats's conception, it was no less
valid than complex. Yet, in spite of the apparent firmness of
control, we do not feel the theme as we do in many other
poems of Keats's, even poems well below his best. Instead of
being moved, we apply ourselves with cool detachment to sift
the evidence and work out a coherent pattern; and the pat-
tern, however convincing, does not quite dispose of equivocal
elements that seem to reveal unresolved tensions.

Although the serious theme links itself with Keats's deepest
personal and poetic problems, *Lamia*, as a piece of craftsman-
ship, gives the impression of coming from the top of his
mind; perhaps his compulsive effort to make some popular
appeal—for all his scorn of the public—had its effect. Cer-

F

tainly the poem has "a sort of fire" and does give "a sensa-
tion," but it does not show the best kind of Keatsian warmth
and intensity; it is in fact far more artificial than *Hyperion*.
And the narrative crispness and lacquered style are not a
compensation for the relative want of the human feeling
manifest even in *Endymion* and *Isabella*. In suggestive rich-
ness of imagery—as distinguished from merely vivid descrip-
tion—there are only a few parallels to the phrase used of
Hermes, "the star of Lethe," which Lamb finely praised. The
picture of the streets of Corinth (i.350–361) a good critic,
M. R. Ridley, has called "a miniature masterpiece," and no
doubt it is; but does the almost wholly visual and objective
passage create the life and atmosphere of the simpler lines at
the beginning of the *Eve of Saint Mark? Lamia* also contains
lapses in diction and tone which are odd at this late stage and
take us back to Keats's early uncertainties of taste. While the
storytelling is far more disciplined and brisk than it was in
early poems, Keats's decorative instincts can still sometimes
get out of hand. The coloring of the snake and its convulsions
(i.47f., 146f.) should be arresting, since this is no ordinary
reptile; but the brilliancy is overdone, even as oblique
mockery. And, though the account of the hall and banquet is
much more than competent, the furnishings and manners
give the effect of having been got up—as indeed they largely
were, from a book Keats owned, John Potter's *Archaeologia
Graeca, or the Antiquities of Greece*.

Keats evidently took pains with his heroic couplets. Evi-
dently also, in metrics as in storytelling and tone, he learned
much from Dryden's *Fables*, perhaps too from Sandys' terse
translation of Ovid. Instead of the erratic or deliberate loose-
ness of *Endymion*, couplets here are neatly, even smartly, but-
toned up; the first line often runs over into the second, but
a couplet tends to be a unit rather than to run on into an-
other. The old feminine rhymes, with their air of jauntiness,
have disappeared. As in Dryden, sequences of couplets are
diversified in pace and emphasis by Alexandrines and occa-

sional triplets. Half-lines are often balanced in the Augustan way:

> With no more awe than what her beauty gave,
> That, while it smote, still guaranteed to save.

But, in general, Keats has grown to be his own master; in minutiae as well as in the main principles of versification *Lamia* is both imitative and independent.

Letters of July 25 and August 14, to Fanny Brawne and Bailey, seem to say that, while working on *Lamia* and *Otho*, Keats was also writing *The Fall of Hyperion*. We may well wonder how—even if he had had nothing else on his mind— he could thus carry on three works in every way so different. He had in the spring given up the effort to finish the epic in its original form and now set about recasting it as "A Dream." Such a subtitle reminds us of his old instinct for the visionary approach and implies a subjective reworking of the objective epic. The *Fall* has, along with the odes, been of special interest to modern critics; that interest has focused much more on the entirely new induction, the first three hundred lines, than on the portion of the narrative that was recast, although this has its significance too.

In the first paragraph Keats develops the idea that all men, including religious fanatics and savages, have their visions and are potential poets, even if only the few have the gift of utterance. The not uncommon idea had been set forth by Wordsworth in the *Excursion* (i.77f.), and Keats, in one of his early anti-Wordsworthian moments, had made a similar remark: "Many a man can travel to the very bourne of Heaven, and yet want confidence to put down his halfseeing" (February 3, 1818: I, 224). But there is something of the solemnity of a last testament in the lines in the *Fall,* especially in "When this warm scribe my hand is in the grave." We may think, *mutatis mutandis*, of Keats's comment on Milton: ". . . but there was working in him as it were that same sort of thing as operates in the great world to the end of a Prophecy's being accomplish'd: therefore he devoted himself rather to the Ardours than the pleasures of Song. . . .'"

The induction as a whole is Keats's final effort, an effort both cool and feverish, to discover his own poetic identity. The latter part of the parable is clear enough, and self-inquisition grows more tortured as it grows more explicit. But in the first half the symbolic meaning of the successive stages cannot be interpreted with confidence. Every reader recalls the phases of poetic growth outlined in *Sleep and Poetry* and *Endymion,* in the letters on the mansion of life and the vale of soul-making, and feels that Keats must here be following a similar pattern. Yet, if we stay within the poem, the first phases of the vision might apply as well to the spiritual evolution of the race as to that of the poet. And throughout there is a sense of the mystery, only in part apprehended, of human existence.

The vision opens on a scene that blends a Keatsian arbor with the Miltonic Eden, a paradise of nature and the senses with trees, fountains, flowers, and abundant fruits. Our first and perhaps correct instinct is to see here another version of the realm of Flora and old Pan, of the infant or thoughtless chamber of life or the initially "pleasant wonders" of the second chamber. The poet eats deliciously and drinks sweet juice, pledging all the mortals of the world and all the illustrious dead: "That full draught is parent of my theme." The "elixir"—a word associated with Apollo's rebirth in *Hyperion*—proves overpowering and brings on a cloudy swoon, the Keatsian state of vision. When he awakens, the garden and arbor are gone, and he finds himself in a lofty sanctuary, an "eternal domed monument" which makes gray cathedrals seem only decrepit relics; and around him are strange vessels, large white draperies,

> Robes, golden tongs, censer, and chafing dish,
> Girdles, and chains, and holy jewelries.

Such a scene does not readily relate itself to the parable of a poet's growth; to take the sanctuary as the temple of Knowl-

edge is to leave much unexplained. Later (221f.) the temple
is identified with the reign of Saturn, and that, in *Hyperion,*
was a golden age of simpleminded, beneficent power, which
must give way to mature understanding and acceptance of
reality. The structure that has replaced idyllic pastoral na-
ture, the properties assembled from Old Testament and
ecclesiastical tradition (and perhaps Potter's *Archaeologia
Graeca*), and the phrase "in that place the moth could not
corrupt"—all these in themselves suggest the historical re-
ligions of mankind, of which only the buildings and trappings
survive to inspire awe. We may remember the awe with
which Endymion, under the sea, beheld the relics of bygone
civilizations, among them

> mouldering scrolls,
> Writ in the tongue of heaven, by those souls
> Who first were on the earth.

Such an idea would link itself with the opening lines of the
Fall, the references to fanatics' dreams of a sectarian paradise
and savages' guesses at heaven. And it is perhaps strengthened
by what follows: the poet looks at a range

> Of columns north and south, ending in mist
> Of nothing; then to Eastward, where black gates
> Were shut against the sunrise evermore.

The whole picture seems less suggestive of knowledge than
of ignorance, "the pious frauds of Religion" (II, 80), though
here contemplated with imaginative sympathy; the garden
and the temple might stand for phases in the development of
man—and in particular the poet—from innocent illusion
through superstitious delusion toward experience and self-
dependence.

The poet looks to the west and sees a huge image, at its
feet an altar with many steps. His turning from the east to
his proper goal in the west may imply a turning from the
dead past to the future; it recalls too the prelude to the
fourth book of *Endymion,* on the movement of poetry from
the East to the West. Approaching the shrine, which sends

forth blissfully intoxicating incense, the poet is told by a
voice that, unless he can quickly climb "these immortal
steps," he will die and wither into nothingness. We assume
that, as in *Endymion*, "immortal" is related to imaginative
intuition. A palsied chill mounts through his body and only
after deathlike effort can he touch the lowest stair; at the
touch new life pours in at his toes and he ascends, as the
angels flew up Jacob's ladder. The whole experience seems to
parallel the struggles of Apollo, in *Hyperion*, as he dies into
life and becomes a poet of tragic vision.

The narrator now asks the veiled prophetess of the shrine
why he has thus been saved from death.[3] The dialogue that
follows is a debate between Keats and himself, especially
between his present and his earlier poetic self, and symbolism
is abandoned for anguished directness. Moneta replies that
none can usurp this height

> But those to whom the miseries of the world
> Are misery, and will not let them rest.
> All else who find a haven in the world,
> Where they may thoughtless sleep away their days,
> If by a chance into this fane they come,
> Rot on the pavement where thou rotted'st half.

Yet, he answers, are there not thousands of people

> Who love their fellows even to the death;
> Who feel the giant agony of the world;
> And more, like slaves to poor humanity,
> Labour for mortal good?

Why then is he here alone? Such people, says Moneta, are no
visionaries, no weak dreamers; they are simple, selfless lovers
and servants of mankind who have no thought of coming to

[3] Apollo's mentor in *Hyperion*, Mnemosyne (Memory, mother of the Muses),
is in the *Fall* given the equivalent Latin name of Moneta (which Keats got
from a book he owned, *Auctores Mythographi Latini*), perhaps because of her
more active role and the Latin root-meaning, "warn," "advise." Moneta's
function is akin to that of Dante's Virgil and Beatrice (who in *Purgatorio*,
c.31, opens her veils like Moneta), and to that of Milton's Michael, who takes
Adam to the top of a hill to show him a vision of human history. The trial of
the steps may have been suggested by the references in cantos 9, 11–13, 17,
21, 25, and 27 of the *Purgatorio*.

this place, whereas the poet is here because he is less than
they (but presumably can learn a saving lesson):

> What benefit canst thou do, or all thy tribe,
> To the great world? Thou art a dreaming thing;
> A fever of thyself—think of the Earth;
> What bliss even in hope is there for thee?
> What haven? every creature hath its home;
> Every sole man hath days of joy and pain,
> Whether his labours be sublime or low—
> The pain alone; the joy alone; distinct:
> Only the dreamer venoms all his days,
> Bearing more woe than all his sins deserve. . . .

The last five lines are Keats's last and most explicit utter-
ance on that theme we have met so often. But the idea, or its
application, seems opposed to that in the lines in *Lamia:* now
joy and pain are said to be separate in the mass of natural,
normal people, whereas it is the mixture that afflicts the poet,
who in imagination undergoes all kinds of experience at once
—for (if one may quote Oscar Wilde),

> he who lives more lives than one
> More deaths than one must die.

This is the penalty of the active imagination, not merely of
the dreamer; Shakespeare was "a miserable and mighty Poet
of the human Heart." We recall—not to mention many lines
of verse—Keats's saying that "the Man who thinks much of
his fellows can never be in Spirits" (I, 175); and his remark,
apropos of his sister-in-law's disinterested happiness, that
women must owe such happiness to lack of imagination (I,
293).

In a more general way the exchanges in the poem remind
us of the humanitarian sympathies that run through the
letters and of Keats's comparative ranking of goodness and
genius, of active beneficence and contemplative detachment,
of philosophy and poetry. Early in 1818 he had spoken of
Bailey's "probity & disinterestedness" as "the tip top of any
spiritual honours, that can be paid to any thing in this
world" (I, 205); he himself "would jump down Ætna for any

great Public good" (I, 267), and saw "no worthy pursuit but
the idea of doing some good for the world" (I, 271). On
March 19, 1819, writing to George, he had spoken of Socrates
and Jesus as the only completely disinterested figures in his-
tory, and of the fine if perhaps erroneous energies manifested
in poetry; "and if so it is not so fine a thing as philosophy—
For the same reason that an eagle is not so fine a thing as a
truth" (II, 81). Two utterances especially relevant to the pas-
sage in the *Fall* belong to the time when Keats was working
on the poem. On August 14 he wrote to Bailey:

I am convinced more and more every day that (excepting the
human friend Philosopher) a fine writer is the most genuine
Being in the World—Shakspeare and the paradise Lost every
day become greater wonders to me—I look upon fine Phrases like
a Lover. (II, 139)

Ten days later he wrote in a similar vein to Reynolds:

I am convinced more and more day by day that fine writing is
next to fine doing the top thing in the world; the Paradise Lost
becomes a greater wonder. (II, 146)

The striking thing here is that these signal exceptions are
made in moments of the most ardent poetic exaltation.

In order "that happiness be somewhat shar'd," the poet,
unworthy yet "In sickness not ignoble," has been admitted to
the garden and the temple, and he is grateful. But he humbly
offers a defense of poetry as not useless (187f.): surely a poet
is a sage, "A humanist, Physician to all men," even if he
himself cannot claim the title; but then what is he, and what
is his "tribe"? Moneta now distinguishes, not as before be-
tween doers and writers, but between true and false poets:

> Art thou not of the dreamer tribe?
> The poet and the dreamer are distinct,
> Diverse, sheer opposite, antipodes.
> The one pours out a balm upon the world,
> The other vexes it.

The agitated poet does not defend himself but amplifies—
and particularizes—the charge with half-hysterical violence:

Apollo! faded, farflown Apollo!
Where is thy misty pestilence to creep
Into the dwellings, thro' the door crannies,
Of all mock lyrists, large self-worshipers,
And careless Hectorers in proud bad verse.
Tho' I breathe death with them it will be life
To see them sprawl before me into graves.

Both Moneta's speech and the poet's answer recall the lines in
Sleep and Poetry (230f.) in which Keats had contrasted the
egotistical strain in the Lake poets with the calm healing
power of true poetry. This passage in the *Fall* (187–210) he
had, according to Woodhouse, marked for cancellation, and
it is clear that he intended at least to rewrite it, since bits of
it, somewhat altered, appear in the passage that follows.
Critical explanations have varied: Keats may have felt the
raw crudity of the lines or he may have modified his senti-
ments. At any rate he had written them, with conviction, and
although he put the worst blame on other poets, he accepted
a good part of it himself as one of "the dreamer tribe." (His
repeated used of "dreamer" may echo the *Excursion*, i.634f.,
iii.333f.) This outburst, even if rejected by the total logic of
the induction, is Keats's last and most painful avowal of
poetic inadequacy, in spite of all that he had accomplished.

Moneta, weeping, now turns toward the epic story. This
temple is all that remains from the war of gods and Titans,
the image is Saturn's, and she herself is "Sole priestess of his
desolation." Recognizing the poet's good will, she will make
the story visible to his mortal eyes. She parts her veils.

> Then saw I a wan face,
> Not pin'd by human sorrows, but bright blanch'd
> By an immortal sickness which kills not;
> It works a constant change, which happy death
> Can put no end to; deathwards progressing
> To no death was that visage; it had pass'd
> The lily and the snow. . . .

In *Hyperion* (iii.107) Apollo had been "in fearless yet in
aching ignorance," and here the poet-narrator

F*

> ached to see what things the hollow brain
> Behind enwombed: what high tragedy
> In the dark secret Chambers of her skull
> Was acting, that could give so dread a stress
> To her cold lips, and fill with such a light
> Her planetary eyes. . . .

This is a kind of ache far beyond that engendered by the nightingale's song; and there is here no aesthetic or erotic association of death with ecstasy. Nor is Moneta's suffering that of the dreamer who venoms all his days because his imagination is self-centered and ineffectually overactive. If this is negative capability, it is not merely non-moral, half-irresponsible creativeness; it works on the highest level, where it is not opposed to but fused with the poet's ethical identity and all-embracing compassion. The relative obscurity of the descriptive language implies something more than the direct revelation given to Apollo. In this last attempt to suggest the "immortal" knowledge of the true poet we seem to have, as D. G. James has said, a Keatsian and naturalistic parallel to Christ taking upon himself the sins of the world.

The epic action is now, through the agency of Moneta, beheld in a prolonged and painful vision by the poet, who has been given the power "To see as a God sees" but who still can declare:

> Without stay or prop
> But my own weak mortality, I bore
> The load of this eternal quietude.

As a concerned observer, who has had a "film" removed from his eyes, the poet is less like Dante than like the Adam of the last two books of *Paradise Lost*. While there is truth in the conventional view that the recasting of *Hyperion* meant a shift from the Miltonic to the Dantesque mode, the *Fall* seems to embody also a new and deeper apprehension of Milton than Keats had shown in his rather callow remarks to Reynolds on May 3, 1818.[4] As extracts from letters have in-

---

[4] Stuart M. Sperry, "Keats, Milton, and *The Fall of Hyperion*," *Publications of the Modern Language Association*, LXXVII (1962), 77–84.

dicated, he was enthusiastically rereading *Paradise Lost* in August, when he was at work on the *Fall*, but Miltonic influence is not a matter of fine phrases or overt imitation; it is rather a non-Christian poet's partial assimilation of, or partial affinity with, Milton's view of the human situation and of human history. There is first Milton's total picture of man's losing his primal innocence and moving, through suffering and knowledge, to the promise of redemption; in particular, as we have noted, there is the angel Michael's unfolding to Adam, through vision and narrative, of the sad history of sinful man. Differences, to be sure, are as great as resemblances, and, so far as Keats carried the *Fall*, there is no release from suffering for the Titans (the world) or Moneta or the poet. Oceanus' law of progress was now far behind him, and if there was to be any catharsis, it does not emerge in what he wrote.

> Oftentimes I pray'd
> Intense, that Death would take me from the vale
> And all its burthens—Gasping with despair
> Of change, hour after hour I curs'd myself. . . .

Critics have asked if, or how far, the experience and insight of Keats's letters got into his poetry, and if the poetry was sometimes more or less behind; in the *Fall* at least there is no gap—unless this vale of despair falls short of the vale of soul-making. Rather, the two seem to merge.

The fragmentary third book of *Hyperion*, in which Keats described the "lonely grief" and the deification of Apollo, was in its semi-lyrical lushness a step backward; in the induction to the *Fall*, on a parallel theme, he took a long step forward and achieved a mature, half-modern, and thoroughly individual idiom. If it lacks much of the verbal and rhythmical beauty of the first two books of *Hyperion* (and the rich luxuriance of the odes), it speaks, even in its uncertain symbolism, in something nearer Keats's natural, unstrained voice; and such mastery looks easier than it is. Language and rhythm together create a style and tone which are elevated and pregnantly suggestive and yet not far above a semi-colloquial plainness. More or less of the same quality is carried over into the recast narrative, but here not every reader may think the gains a full compensation for the losses. For instance, the simile of the dreaming oaks (i.372–377) certainly becomes more economical and functional, but it loses much of its animistic vividness and mystery; and the human weakness of Saturn is emphasized by a querulous speech that he pours out—rather oddly—to Pan (i.412f.). The narrative is not taken far enough for us to say how such radical revision would have affected the whole, but, so far as it goes, it lacks a good deal of the immediacy and force of the original.

When in the spring of 1819 Keats had given up the first *Hyperion*, the chief reason, we may suppose, was the difficulty of making a traditional epic the vehicle for a parable about the nature of poetry and the poet; and when in the third book he grappled with his real theme, the true poet's response to the human situation, he turned away from epic action and the grand style. A further testimony to his un-epical state of mind at that time is in the shorter poems he wrote, from the *Eve of St. Agnes* through the odes. We may also suppose that when in the half-allegorical *Fall* Keats tried to blend the objective with the subjective, the old problem was still there; moreover, since he set forth his theme in the induction, it might appear that the narrative had nowhere to go. On September 21 he let Reynolds and Woodhouse know of his decision to give up the poem. He wrote to Reynolds that he had just composed *To Autumn*, that he always somehow associated Chatterton with that season, and that Chatterton "is the purest writer in the English Language . . . genuine English Idiom in English words," and then he went on (II, 167):

I have given up Hyperion—there were too many Miltonic inversions in it—Miltonic verse cannot be written but in an artful or rather artist's humour. I wish to give myself up to other sensations. English ought to be kept up. It may be interesting to you to pick out some lines from Hyperion and put a mark X to the false beauty proceeding from art, and one || to the true voice of feeling. Upon my soul 'twas imagination I cannot make the distinction—Every now & then there is a Miltonic intonation—But I cannot make the division properly.[5]

On September 24 Keats wrote in the same vein to his brother (II, 212):

The Paradise lost though so fine in itself is a curruption of our Language—it should be kept as it is unique—a curiosity. a beautiful and grand Curiosity. The most remarkable Production of the world—A northern dialect accommodating itself to greek and latin inversions and intonations. The purest english I think—or what ought to be the purest—is Chatterton's. . . . I prefer the native music of it to Milton's cut by feet I have but lately stood on my guard against Milton. Life to him would be death to me. Miltonic verse cannot be written but it [for in] the vein of art— I wish to devote myself to another sensation.

Keats's notion of Chatterton's English was unsophisticated, and his view of Milton's English—like similar views expressed before and after him—was a greatly exaggerated misrepresentation of the facts; these anti-Miltonic sentiments, by the way, are cited more often than the candid avowal in the extract quoted from the letter to Reynolds. At any rate, in making Miltonic inversions his main obstacle, Keats was only clutching at a straw; the real reasons went much deeper than that. But we understand the force and truth of his wishing to give himself up to "other sensations"—represented, we might say, by *To Autumn*.

Keats had been anxious enough about the supposedly impending Chancery suit and financial prospects in general, and now disastrous news came from George: on the advice of the friendly businessman, J. J. Audubon (who became the famous naturalist), George had invested the larger part of his

5 At the moment Reynolds and Woodhouse were together in Bath. While Keats would naturally be speaking of the *Fall*, neither of his friends had a copy of this new work, so that—in the letter quoted—he must have been asking Reynolds to test and mark the first *Hyperion*. In the separate letter to Woodhouse, Keats quoted from the *Fall* three passages that he thought might be of interest. Although he was now abandoning the *Fall*, he tried to work on it later in the autumn.

money in a Mississippi cargo boat that sank, and he was con-
vinced that Audubon had swindled him. Keats at once, on
September 10, went up from Winchester to London to see
Richard Abbey. Abbey, while expressing sympathy, know-
ingly or unknowingly misled Keats in regard to the suit and
the condition of the family funds, and Keats could only re-
port to George that "We are certainly in a very low estate."
He himself had been living on loans and his hopes of profit
from *Otho the Great* had lately been dashed by the report of
Kean's American tour. However, he did what he could to
cheer up George.

On September 13 Keats sent a note to Fanny Brawne ex-
plaining that he loved her too much to go to Hampstead and
see her, that it would not be "paying a visit, but venturing
into a fire." He has been trying to wean himself from her;
though he cannot cease to love her, he "cannot bear the pain
of being happy" (II, 160). Yet, writing to George four days
later, he could say, in regard to Haslam:

Nothing strikes me so forcibly with a sense of the rediculous as
love—A Man in love I do think cuts the sorryest figure in the
world—Even when I know a poor fool to be really in pain about
it, I could burst out laughing in his face.

And the next day he copied for George and Georgiana the
page-long description from Burton's *Anatomy* of a lover's
mistress in all her actual and disgusting ugliness—this of
course need imply nothing except enjoyment of a verbal
cloudburst. From that he turns, after a glance at "Lord
Byron's last flash poem," to a survey of English and European
history and the slow growth of liberalism.

While in London, Keats showed Woodhouse a fair copy of
the *Eve of St. Agnes,* with some changes he had made. These
included, at the very end, a bit of what Woodhouse described
as the Byronic "mingling up of sentiment & sneering"; there
were also the phrases that made plain Porphyro's consumma-
tion of his love, to which, as we saw before, Woodhouse and
later Taylor strongly objected (II, 162–163). As for the Byron-

ism, we have noted touches of flippancy—along with frequent brittleness of tone—in *Lamia;* and Keats's first version of part of the banquet scene, copied in a letter to Taylor of September 5, had some jarring lines. Such items indicate the strain and the degree of disenchantment Keats felt during this summer.[6]

On September 15 he returned to Winchester and, since Brown had gone off visiting, to solitude. Although disposed to write, he feels every day more and more content to read and think: "Books are becoming more interesting and valuable to me—I may say I could not live without them" (II, 220). Among other things he was learning Italian and reading Ariosto at the rate of six or eight stanzas at a time. On September 21, two days after he wrote *To Autumn,* he made some remarks in a journal-letter to George that would apply to that ode, though not, unhappily, to the future, since there was to be no future:

Some think I have lost that poetic ardour and fire 't is said I once had—the fact is perhaps I have: but instead of that I hope I shall substitute a more thoughtful and quiet power. I am more frequently, now, contented to read and think—but now & then, haunted with ambitious thoughts. Qui[e]ter in my pulse, improved in my digestion; exerting myself against vexing speculations—scarcely content to write the best verses for the fever they leave behind. I want to compose without this fever. I hope I one day shall. (II, 209)

On the same day Keats wrote the letters to Reynolds and Woodhouse that were cited in connection with the *Fall of Hyperion;* they come up again because the one gives us the background, the other the first text, of his last great poem. His words are, as usual, quiet and unpretentious:

6 One might add his much quoted comment on Burton: "Here is the old plague spot; the pestilence, the raw scrofula. I mean that there is nothing disgraces me in my own eyes so much as being one of a race of eyes nose and mouth beings in a planet call'd the earth who all from Plato to Wesley have always mingled goatish winnyish lustful love with the abstract adoration of the deity. I don't understand Greek—is the love of God and the Love of women express'd by the same word in Greek? I hope my little mind is wrong—if not I could—Has Plato separated these loves? Ha! I see how they endeavor to divide—but there appears to be a horrid relationship."

How beautiful the season is now—How fine the air. A temper-
ate sharpness about it. Really, without joking, chaste weather
—Dian skies—I never lik'd stubble fields so much as now—Aye
better than the chilly green of the spring. Somehow a stubble
plain looks warm—in the same way that some pictures look warm
—this struck me so much in my sunday's walk that I composed
upon it. (II, 167)

That phrase, "the chilly green of the spring," takes us back
to the *Eve of Saint Mark*:

> The chilly sunset faintly told
> Of unmatured green vallies cold,
> Of the green thorny bloomless hedge,
> Of rivers new with spring-tide sedge,
> Of primroses by shelter'd rills,
> And daisies on the aguish hills.

As David Perkins has especially emphasized, the great bulk
of Keats's poetry—and notable passages in the letters—are
rooted in the inescapable fact and idea of process. The second
stanza of the "Hymn to Pan" had looked forward to summer's
ripening of all growing things, all the "completions" of "the
fresh budding year." In the *Ode to a Nightingale*, "Fast fad-
ing violets" were joined with "The coming musk-rose." In *To
Autumn* this strain in Keats's consciousness receives its last
and most concentrated statement.

It seems to be generally agreed that this poem is flawless in
structure, texture, tone, and rhythm; that it is purely im-
personal, objective description (as the odes of the spring were
not); and—though it has had only a tiny fraction of the
exegesis given to the *Nightingale* and the *Grecian Urn*—some
would say that it is Keats's most mature ode and the most
subtle in what it says and what it suggests. If we think of the
overt conflicts that constitute the themes of the *Nightingale,*
the *Grecian Urn,* and *Melancholy, To Autumn* may at first
seem beautiful but shallow, a poem of untroubled serenity,
of unquestioning surrender to sensuous luxury. If, too, we
think of Keats's recent and immediate anxieties or torments
about money, about Fanny Brawne, and—in the *Fall*—about

his own poetic career and integrity, we might suppose that in some miraculous way he had exorcised these specters and achieved the complete escape his realistic mind had not allowed in the earlier odes. But such a view of *To Autumn*, though it has been held, is quite inadequate.

The first two stanzas build up, or appear to build up, a wholly happy picture of summery warmth and bursting ripeness in everything, of vines and trees and fruits and nuts and bees fulfilling their creative destiny. (Since Keats had read Theocritus, one wonders if the conclusion of the seventh Idyl was linked in his mind with what he saw in and around Winchester.) In the first stanza the sense of fullness and heaviness is given through mainly tactile images; in the second they are mainly visual. Here the personified spirit of autumn becomes a mythic figure, a kind of immortal; although reaping and cider-making are not lifted out of the practical world, they are invested with the dignity and aura of seasonal rites. Yet even in these stanzas there is the overshadowing fact of impermanence. The summer has done its work and is departing; and if autumn comes, winter cannot be far behind. Precise hints are few—the bees "think warm days will never cease," the cider reaches its "last oozings"—but we cannot escape the melancholy implications of exuberant ripeness. What in the first stanzas is largely implicit becomes dominant, if only half-explicit, in the last, where, in keeping with the initial question, the images are chiefly auditory. While the poet sets up the music of autumn against the songs of spring, we have, in a subdued and objective form, the return from vision to actuality, the kind of return recurrent in *Endymion* and most notable in the conclusion of the *Nightingale*. But here the poet is not openly cut off from an abstract ideal or acknowledging an illusion. Whereas in the first stanza fruits as well as bees seemed almost conscious of fulfillment, in the last every item carries an elegiac note. The day is dying and gnats and lambs and crickets and birds all seem to be aware of approaching darkness.

In the sonnet of the spring of 1818, "Four seasons fill the

measure of the year," Keats had, in abstract generalities, directly applied the character and sequence of the seasons to the mind and life of man. It is not the least remarkable thing about *To Autumn* that, although it nowhere mentions man and admits no generalized reflections into its catalog of observed particulars, we instinctively follow what we take to be the poet's feeling and transpose the whole into human terms. In the "Hymn to Pan" Keats had moved from natural phenomena to a climactic glorifying of the romantic imagination's power of transcending life; in the *Ode to Psyche* he had attained contemplative serenity through a soft and rosy view of life and art; in the *Nightingale* and *Grecian Urn* he had tried to "burst our mortal bars" and fallen back in more or less avowed failure (not poetic failure); in *Melancholy,* as in *Psyche,* his vision had been limited or dominated by an intense but thin aestheticism. In *To Autumn* he does not evade or challenge actuality; he achieves, by implication, "the top of sovereignty," the will to neither strive nor cry, the power to see and accept life as it is, a perpetual process of ripening, decay, and death.

8

The Last Chapter
(October, 1819–February 23, 1821)

KEATS'S poetical career was now virtually ended, although he was in this autumn to do some new things and some revision, and although he could at times look hopefully to the future. The hemorrhage that was to open his last year of life did not occur until February 3, 1820, but his health must have been deteriorating long before that. From September 10, 1819, when he learned of George's financial disaster, he was for months anxious about him and doing what he could to raise money. His own prolonged plight we have seen; on November 11 he received from Abbey the first money he had had from him in ten months. The effect of such pressures is illustrated in his altered reactions to Haydon. When in December, 1818, Haydon was in straits, Keats, while trying to assist him, had said it would be a breach of friendship if he sold a drawing; in September, 1819, having been so long in debt himself, he declared that friendship was at an end because Haydon had not sold his drawings (though he wrote a friendly letter to Haydon on October 3). About October 8 Keats and Brown returned from Winchester to London. Keats had already decided to live in Westminster and support himself by journalism, "on the liberal side of the question." For some days in October he did live there, first in lodgings and then—after a weekend at Mrs. Brawne's—with the

Dilkes; but about October 21 he was back with Brown at Wentworth Place.

Meanwhile, there was Fanny Brawne, whom Keats had not seen since he had gone to the Isle of Wight in June. He spent October 10 with her, and the next day he wrote to her from Westminster: he was "living to day in yesterday. . . . I feel myself at your mercy." On the thirteenth he wrote: "My love has made me selfish. I cannot exist without you—I am forgetful of every thing but seeing you again—my Life seems to stop there—I see no further. You have absorb'd me." For three days in the middle of the month, a "three days dream," Keats stayed, as we noted, with the Brawnes in their half of Wentworth Place.

Of the five poems addressed to or concerned with Fanny, probably three or four belong to this autumn and early winter, although dates are a matter of wide conjecture, and one or more of the pieces may have been written in 1820. The relatively quiet and relatively good sonnet, "The day is gone," might have followed the daylong reunion of October 10. The other sonnet, the feverish "I cry your mercy," and the two small odes, "What can I do to drive away" and "Physician Nature," like "I cry your mercy," count rather as painful outcries than as poetry. They are more or less paralleled by many letters of 1819–1820 which express the torments of unfulfilled desire and morbidly possessive jealousy; both emotions were to be aggravated by the inroads of disease. "What can I do to drive away" (assigned to October or thereabouts by Lord Houghton and most modern scholars) has an interest in addition to Fanny. It contains a violent denunciation—kindled no doubt by thoughts of George's recent calamity—of "that most hateful land," the United States; the description was a congeries of recollections from Keats's old favorite, Robertson's *History of America*. The occasion of "Physician Nature" was evidently a winter dance to which Fanny was going without Keats—a fact which might suggest a time after February 3, 1820. Whatever the dates of these poems, and their distressful and distressing substance, they hardly seem to come from the author of the grand octave of "Bright star"; and by this time Keats's feelings had got beyond the comparatively serene intensity of the sestet. Some time between Keats's return from Winchester and the end of the year he and Fanny became engaged, though the event was not made public; and Fanny's mother was not happy about it.

During this autumn Keats's anxiety over George's affairs and the Chancery suit took him frequently to the city. On November 10 he told Severn that he had been "very lax, un-employed, unmeridian'd, and objectless these two months." Two days later he wrote to George that recent attempts at writing had not had much success: "Nothing could have in all its circumstances fallen out worse for me than the last year has done, or could be more damping to my poetical talent" (II, 231). "You had best put me into your Cave of despair," he said to Severn, who had lately done a painting of the Spenserian scene. On November 17 he wrote more hopefully to John Taylor. While he was determined not to publish the poems he had written, he was also determined to publish a fine one before long. Since he feels more at home with men and women than with "wonders," and prefers Chaucer to Ariosto, he wishes to give the coloring of the *Eve of St. Agnes* to more dramatic material. Two or three such poems, done in the next six years, would nerve him up to "the writing of a few fine Plays—my greatest ambition—when I do feel ambitious. I am sorry to say that is very seldom" (II, 234). But he thinks well of the Earl of Leicester as a sub-ject and to that end he has been reading Holinshed's *Chroni-cles*. The four scenes of the tragedy *King Stephen,* which Brown dated as of both August and November, may have been written at either time, or, as Miss Ward suggests, Keats may have done the first three in August and the fourth in No-vember. The fragment is not mere Shakespearian pastiche; it has impressive vigor. In December *Otho the Great* was ac-cepted at Drury Lane, but for the following season; and Keats and Brown, after making some changes, sent the play to Covent Garden, which proved unreceptive (both theaters were having financial and other troubles). In spite of what he had said to Taylor a month earlier, on December 20 Keats told his sister that he was very busy preparing his poems for publication in the spring.

Charles Brown recorded that during the late autumn Keats was engaged with two very different tasks, the revising of the abandoned *Fall of Hyperion* and the composing of the satirical extravaganza, *The Cap and Bells, or, the Jealousies.* This unfinished piece, of almost eight hundred lines in Spenserian stanzas, has a place in the Keatsian canon partly akin to that of *Swellfoot the Tyrant* in the Shelleyan, since both works utilized the notorious marital troubles of the Prince Regent and his wife; but Keats has a far lighter touch and is far more readable. His fantasy, if in some degree an imitation and burlesque of the manner of *Don Juan,* is predominantly in a vein of Keats's own which recalls *A Midsummer Night's Dream* and Drayton's mock-heroic *Nymphidia*. Its satire, genial or caustic, takes in court life and London, and includes such particular targets as Byron's farewell to Lady Byron, Keats's own *Eve of Saint Mark,* and, according to Robert Gittings' evidence, Hazlitt, Hunt, Lamb, Wordsworth, and Southey. If we are surprised, and even pained, by the thought of *The Cap and Bells* as Keats's last large effort in poetry, we may remember the similar strain in the revised (but unprinted) ending of the *Eve of St. Agnes* and its conspicuous presence in *Lamia*. Middleton Murry defended the poem as "authentic Keats, both in diction and feeling," and we may agree with him that Keats "was deliberately keeping himself on the surface of things, for fear of letting the intensity of his inward experience get the upper hand. . . ."[1]

In the manuscript of the *Cap and Bells* Keats wrote eight lines of another kind and quality:

> This living hand, now warm and capable
> Of earnest grasping, would, if it were cold
> And in the icy silence of the tomb,

[1] *Poems of John Keats* (London: Peter Nevill, 1948), p. 17.

So haunt thy days and chill thy dreaming nights
That thou wouldst wish thine own heart dry of blood
So in my veins red life might stream again,
And thou be conscience-calm'd—see here it is—
I hold it towards you.

These lines have in the past been connected with Fanny Brawne, but they are wholly unlike the poems addressed to her; they have the character and tone of dramatic dialogue and were probably a speech for a projected play.

George Keats, in need of repairing his badly damaged fortunes with money from the family funds, had resolved on direct action. He arrived in London about January 8, 1820, and remained until the twenty-eighth. In the intervals of business and George's social engagements, the brothers enjoyed their reunion and George made copies of many of Keats's poems to take back with him. George was able to get from Abbey the sum of £700, partly his share of Tom's estate, partly what John regarded as loans from his own. George later defended his handling of affairs against the resentful accusations of some of John's friends, who may have been less than just; but he seems to have shown less than brotherly concern for the straits John was in. John had doubtless gone along, generously, with all that George did. In her letter of May 23, 1821, to Fanny Keats, Fanny Brawne recorded that Keats himself "never thought so very badly" of George's behavior, although he "used to say, 'George ought not to have done this he should have recollected that I wish to marry myself—but I suppose having a family to provide for makes a man selfish'—They tell me that latterly he thought worse of George, but I own I do not believe it."[2]

Soon after George left, Keats suffered the blow that marked the beginning of his long last illness. He had ended the northern tour of 1818 with a sore throat that continued for some time to be troublesome, though it was evidently not tubercular. The tour itself showed that Keats was a pretty

2 Letters of Fanny Brawne to Fanny Keats 1820–1824, ed. Fred Edgcumbe (London: Oxford University Press, 1937), p. 34.

robust person, but it left him weakened; and then came three months of close attendance upon the dying Tom. To this the best modern medical opinion ascribes the beginning of Keats's disease; it probably reached an active stage in the fall of 1819. At times during that year, most lately on December 22, he had spoken of being unwell (and mental troubles were always in the background or foreground). On the very cold night of February 3, 1820, Keats (who had not worn his greatcoat because of a thaw) returned from the city to Hampstead on the outside of a coach, and apparently, in the darkness, had a severe hemorrhage. Getting home in what seemed to Brown a strangely excited state, he went to bed; a cough brought another drop of blood. Keats at once recognized it as arterial blood and his "death-warrant" (K.C., II, 73). The physician Brown summoned proceeded to bleed him. In regard to that and all the other wrong things done, for Tom and now and later for John, we must remember that nothing was known of tubercle bacilli or of the need for ample food and fresh air.

Perhaps on February 4 Keats sent a brief note to Fanny Brawne, next door, saying that he "must remain confined to this room for some time," and asking her to come and see him frequently. From now on, about every other day, he wrote more or less short letters to Fanny, reporting his condition, assuring her of "the Love which has so long been my pleasure and torment," and asking for assurances of hers. On the night of his hemorrhage, when, nearly suffocated, he felt that he might not survive, he had thought of nothing but her. Although he remains weak and nervous from illness, medicine, and a vegetable diet that would starve a mouse (this last phrase in a letter to Fanny Keats), his condition seems to be improving, very slowly, and he can at times look forward "to Health and the Spring and a regular routine of our old Walks." But he is not allowed to read poetry, much less to try to write: "I wish I had even a little hope." Apparently he offered to release Fanny from their engagement, but she refused. "Then," he said, "all we have to do is to be patient."

One letter to Fanny, quoted in earlier pages, recalls "the pains and torments, . . . the ecstasies . . . and the miseries" Keats had undergone since he had left her in June to go to the Isle of Wight, and his growing wonder at "the Beauty which has kept up the spell so fervently" (II, 263). Now that he has wakeful nights as well as long days, other thoughts intrude upon him:

"If I should die," said I to myself, "I have left no immortal work behind me—nothing to make my friends proud of my memory— but I have lov'd the principle of beauty in all things, and if I had had time I would have made myself remember'd."

Such thoughts came very feebly while he was in health and every pulse beat for her; now his reflections are divided between her and "That last infirmity of noble mind." He loves her more and more as an ever new being, not merely for her beauty but as one who loves him.

To James Rice, who had had so many years of illness, Keats wrote on February 14 with melancholy candor (II, 260):

I may say that for 6 Months before I was taken ill I had not passed a tranquil day—Either that gloom overspred me or I was suffering under some passionate feeling, or if I turn'd to versify that acerbated the poison of either sensation. The Beauties of Nature had lost their power over me. How astonishingly (here I must premise that illness as far as I can judge in so short a time has relieved my Mind of a load of deceptive thoughts and images and makes me perceive things in a truer light)—How astonishingly does the chance of leaving the world impress a sense of its natural beauties on us. Like poor Falstaff, though I do not babble, I think of green fields. I muse with the greatest affection on every flower I have known from my infancy—their shapes and coulours are as new to me as if I had just created them with a superhuman fancy—It is because they are connected with the most thoughtless and happiest moments of our Lives—I have seen foreign flowers in hothouses of the most beautiful nature, but I do not care a straw for them. The simple flowers of our sp[r]ing are what I want to see again.

In spite of occasional cheerful remarks, the earlier letters seem in the main to imply no strong hopes of recovery. On

March 8 Brown informed Taylor that two days before Keats had been seized with "violent palpitations at the heart" and would not be able for a long time to prepare his poems for the press. Yet on the tenth Brown repeated the doctor's assurance—incredible as it now appears—that "there is no pulmonary affection, no organic defect whatever,—the disease is on his *mind,* and there I hope he will soon be cured" (II, 275). Two or three days later Keats was, Brown said, "greatly altered for the better" and was revising *Lamia.* Keats himself wrote to Fanny with more positive hope for the summer and a future. On March 20, however, he told Fanny Keats of several recent attacks of palpitation; but his only trouble was debility, and his present diet would restore his strength. One day when he felt "much better," he wrote to Fanny Brawne that "there is a great difference between going off in warm blood like Romeo, and making one's exit like a frog in a frost" (II, 281). We are surprised to learn that on March 14 and 25 Keats was able to go to town, on the second occasion for a private exhibition of Haydon's painting *Christ's Entry into Jerusalem* (which he had begun before he met Keats). The *Morning Post* noted the presence, among others, of Lamb, Keats, and Bryan Waller Procter (who had lately sent Keats his poems); and the triumphant Haydon noted "Keats and Hazlitt . . . in a corner, really rejoicing."

During April Keats's accounts of himself grew better, although, with his medical knowledge, he could hardly find full reassurance in his doctor's verdict that there was nothing the matter with him "except nervous irritability and a general weakness of the whole system" due to the anxieties and poetic excitements of recent years. He was advised, and for a short time intended, to sail with Brown on a smack to Scotland; but he gave up the notion, though he accompanied Brown on the smack as far as Gravesend. Brown had as usual rented his house for the summer, so that Keats had to find another domicile. On May 4 he moved to Wesleyan Place, Kentish Town, a couple of miles away. There he had seven weeks of solitary brooding, relieved or agitated by calls from Fanny Brawne. Near the end of April he had sent to his publishers the manuscript of his *Lamia* volume, and toward the middle of June he was reading proof. About June 18 he was able to visit an exhibition of mainly seventeenth-century portraits at the British Institution, and he could report to Brown that he continued "to improve slowly, but, I think, surely." On June 22, however, there were further hemorrhages, and the next day Keats was moved to the nearby house of Leigh Hunt in Mortimer Terrace, where he would not be alone and without care.

Removal from Wentworth Place, along with illness and hopelessness, seemed to raise to a fever Keats's passion for Fanny Brawne and his possessive jealousy. Whatever her thoughts and feelings about her lover, much of her life went on as before and included some parties. She may, he says, think him selfish and cruel in wanting her to be unhappy, to be wholly wrapped up in him as he is in her, yet he can "see *life*" in nothing but the certainty and completeness of her love. "I long to believe in immortality I shall never be able to bid you an entire farewell." In June and July, indeed months earlier, there was talk of Keats's going to Italy, but he was sure that he could never recover if he were to be separated from her so long. Her "habit of flirting with Brown" had been unendurable; although he has owed so much to Brown, he "will never see or speak to him again until we are both old men, if we are to be" (II, 303); the rest of this letter is such an exposure of naked torment that one cannot bring oneself to quote it. With all our profound sympathy for Keats's sufferings in body and mind, we cannot in fairness accept at their face value the charges that, in his morbid state, he threw out against either Brown or Fanny. We may blame Brown for going off for the summer in his accustomed way and leaving Keats to fend for himself, although we should remember, as Keats did, that for a long time he had been living chiefly on loans from Brown (who had to borrow money for Keats's summer expenses), and that Keats was now said to be improving. Also, before and after the bitter declaration cited above, he could write to Brown in friendly, even very affectionate, terms. In any matter that touched Fanny, Keats could not now be his normal fair-minded self; neither he nor she can be blamed for his overwrought fancies and demands. What seems to have been his last letter to her (August?: II, 311–312) was another avowal of consuming love and despair. If he had the strength, he would write a poem showing "some one in Love as I am, with a person living in such Liberty as you do":

I am sickened at the brute world which you are smiling with. . . . I wish you could infuse a little confidence in human nature into my heart. I cannot muster any—the world is too brutal for me— I am glad there is such a thing as the grave—I am sure I shall never have any rest till I get there At any rate I will indulge myself by never seeing any more Dilke or Brown or any of their Friends. I wish I was either in your a[r]ms full of faith or that a Thunder bolt would strike me.

God bless you—J.K—

About June 21 Keats had written to Brown (II, 298):

My book is coming out with very low hopes, though not spirits on my part. This shall be my last trial; not succeeding, I shall try what I can do in the Apothecary line.

At the beginning of July, 1820, appeared one of the richest volumes in the history of English poetry. Along with the poems named in the title, *Lamia, Isabella, The Eve of St. Agnes, and Other Poems,* there were five odes (the *Nightingale,* the *Grecian Urn, Psyche, To Autumn, Melancholy*), the first *Hyperion, Fancy,* the "Ode" beginning "Bards of Passion and of Mirth," and the two light "outlaw" poems, *Lines on the Mermaid Tavern* and *Robin Hood.* The most notable omissions were the fragmentary "Ode to Maia," *The Eve of Saint Mark, La Belle Dame sans Merci,* and the *Fall of Hyperion;* and no sonnets were included. A prefatory note from the publishers said that they alone were responsible for the inclusion of the unfinished *Hyperion,* since

it was printed at their particular request, and contrary to the
wish of the author. The poem was intended to have been of equal
length with *Endymion*, but the reception given to that work dis-
couraged the author from proceeding.

This well-meant apology (written by Taylor or Woodhouse)
angered Keats, who in one copy scratched it out and wrote
above it "This is none of my doing—I was ill at the time";
and below, "This is a lie."

While there were half a dozen jabs in the Lockhart-Croker
vein, for the most part the new volume evoked a new kind of
respect and, along with some censure of strained originality,
affected diction, and the like, there was high praise, backed
up by abundant quotation, and some reviewers recalled the
unfair attacks on *Endymion*. Charles Lamb's prompt review
—which Hunt reprinted in the *Examiner* of July 30—was
very laudatory but, from our standpoint, ill-balanced. He
quoted four stanzas from the *Eve of St. Agnes* as examples of
Keats's extraordinary powers of description, and gave the rest
of his space to *Isabella*, "The finest thing in the volume," and
Lamia; he did not mention the odes or *Hyperion*. The
Monthly Review (July) was wiser than Lamb in pronouncing
Isabella "the worst part of the volume" and *Hyperion* the
best, despite its un-Greek character; "the power of both
heart and hand which it displays is very great." *To Autumn*
was quoted in full as a perhaps unequaled picture of "the
reality of nature." Keats's poems show "the ore of true poetic
genius," mingled with much dross in the way of mannered
boldness, obscurity, and indecorum. In the *Indicator* (August
2 and 9) Leigh Hunt summarized the narrative poems, with
comments, quoted the whole of the *Ode to a Nightingale* and
much from *Hyperion* and other pieces, and wound up with a
general eulogy of Keats's now perfected versification, re-
strained imagination, and "calm power," his uniting of en-
ergy, voluptuousness, and "a high feeling of humanity"—
qualities which have replaced his early impatient exuberance.
"Mr. Keats undoubtedly takes his seat with the oldest and
best of our living poets."

August also brought a more influential judgment on both *Endymion* and the new volume from Francis Jeffrey in his own journal, the *Edinburgh Review;* he may have been stirred to action by letters from Reynolds. A year earlier Keats had declared to George that the *Edinburgh* did not know how to deal with *Endymion* and was afraid to touch it (II, 200). In his belated account of that poem, which occupied most of his article, Jeffrey was fair according to his lights. While reprehending Keats's mythological material and formless extravagance, he found *Endymion* "at least as full of genius as of absurdity." In a brief glance at the 1820 volume he spoke chiefly of *Isabella;* the subject of *Hyperion,* like that of *Endymion,* was too remote from human interest. Jeffrey concluded by saying that "Mr Keats has unquestionably a very beautiful imagination, and a great familiarity with the finest diction of English poetry," but that he must not misdirect and misuse his gifts. The *Quarterly* ignored the book. *Blackwood's* (September), though continuing its gibes at the Cockney school, admitted Keats's "talents" and "much merit in some of the stanzas" in his new volume. The *British Critic* (September) reaffirmed its "especial contempt" for "Mr. Examiner Hunt," made some apology for its harsh treatment of *Endymion,* and censured "the morality of the principal poems" in the new book, but recognized its author as "really a person of no ordinary genius," who, if he will follow Spenser and Milton instead of Hunt, may attain "a very high and enviable place in the public esteem." The distinguished *London Magazine* (September) denounced the unprincipled abuse Keats had received and, while mildly noting some faults, gave full and high praise, quoting at length from the *Nightingale,* the *Eve of St. Agnes,* and *Hyperion;* this last is "one of the most extraordinary creations of any modern imagination." In the widened and altered response to his poems Keats may not now have found much savor. On August 14 he wrote to Brown that his book had had good success among literary people and, he believed, a moderate sale. Some days or perhaps weeks later he reported that the sale was very slow, although the book "has been very highly rated." One reason for its lack of popularity (an odd reason, we may think) he has heard from various quarters, that women take offense because in his poems "they never see themselves dominant."

On July 12 Mrs. Gisborne, Shelley's friend, recorded in her journal: "We drank tea at Mr Hunt's; I was much pained by the sight of poor Keats, under sentence of death from Dr. Lamb. He never spoke and looks emaciated." At the same time Severn wrote to Haslam that Keats's shocking appearance reminded him of Tom and that Keats himself was pre-possessed with the conviction that he could not recover. The state of his mind may be judged from his reaction to an incident in which the Hunts—who had been doing their best to look after and entertain him—were quite blameless: a letter, apparently from Fanny Brawne, was given to him, opened, two days after it had come to the house, because of the spiteful behavior of a servant who was being discharged. Keats wept for several hours, Mrs. Hunt told Mrs. Gisborne, and returned at once (August 12) to Hampstead. For the next month he lived with the Brawnes.

On this same August 12 Keats received from Shelley—who had heard from John Gisborne—a cordial invitation to spend the winter with him and his family in Pisa. Keats's reply (August 16) seemed to say that he would if he did not die first; but he contemplated the Italian journey "as a soldier marches up to a battery." Shelley's letter had included some ill-timed counsel, apropos of *Endymion,* on the writing of poetry, and Keats, somewhat nettled, went on, with more critical wisdom than graciousness, to chide Shelley for being too much of a crusader: "you might curb your magnanimity and be more of an artist, and 'load every rift' of your subject with ore." After apologizing, as the author of *Endymion,* for offering advice, he adds more, on Shelley's excessively rapid production of *Prometheus Unbound.* Remembering perhaps his own rather rapid writing, he says that his new volume "would never have been publish'd but from a hope of gain";

Keats had not forgotten, and in fact recalls here, that Shelley had advised him against publishing his *Poems* in 1817. In this as in some other matters, during his last year Keats was not in full possession of his normal warmth of charity; besides, Shelley had always set him on edge. The letter ended "In the hope of soon seeing you" (II, 322–323). Although Keats is sometimes said to have declined Shelley's invitation (and certainly he did not act upon it), both his opening and closing words read like an acceptance, if a vague one. They evidently seemed such to Shelley, who in October wrote to Mrs. Hunt to ask where Keats was and say that he was anxiously expecting him in Italy; he promised that every possible attention would be given to preserving the "most valuable life" of a rival who would far surpass Shelley himself. A similar proposal came a few days later from a less illustrious person and a stranger, the Scottish John Aitken, a bank clerk and minor literary figure, whose admiration for Keats had inspired a protest to Lockhart against his abusive review, and who now, having read in the *Indicator* of Keats's illness, warmly urged him to visit him and his sister in Dunbar.

During August Keats made preparations for the voyage to Italy. He sent John Taylor a sort of memorandum for a will: since he had no assets except hopes of royalties, he wanted these applied first on his debts to Brown and Taylor. He asked Abbey for a loan for expenses but was refused. (We may remember that he and George did not know of the considerable funds left by John Jennings and held by the Court of Chancery, from which they might have drawn upon application at any time after they became twenty-one.) On September 16 there was a formal assignment to Taylor of Keats's several copyrights; Taylor's generous arrangements in regard to the past, present, and future wiped out debts and yielded £180 in cash and credit. Obviously Keats could not travel to Italy by himself, and he hoped that Brown might go with him; but Brown did not learn of the plan for some time and, though he returned home, he just missed Keats. Other friends, however much concerned about him, for various

reasons were unable to go—all except Joseph Severn, who,
against his father's strong opposition, agreed and got ready in
the few days left. Along with his admiration and affection for
Keats, Severn could, as an ambitious painter, have the hope
of profiting from a sojourn in Italy; but, even so, it was an act
of loyal friendship, and, as things turned out, attendance
upon Keats grew more and more exacting and left him
little time for art.

On September 17 Keats and Severn boarded the *Maria
Crowther,* a small freighter, which was lying off the Tower.
Taylor, Haslam, and Woodhouse accompanied them as far as
Gravesend. The ship had one cabin with six beds, for the
captain and the four passengers; the other two were women,
one of them a young consumptive. A woman friend of one of
those on board, who was evidently devoid of imagination and
tact, looked at Keats and Severn and asked which was the
dying man. It came out later that the ship in which Brown
was returning home had been anchored close to the *Maria
Crowther* at Gravesend. They sailed from Gravesend the
night of the eighteenth. In the English Channel storms
caused delays and extreme discomfort to the passengers. Con-
trary winds caused further delays. At Portsmouth on Septem-
ber 28 Keats and Severn landed and visited Mr. and Mrs.
Snook at Bedhampton, where Keats had written most of the
Eve of St. Agnes; Brown was then, they learned, in nearby
Chichester, whither he had gone after missing Keats in Lon-
don—he was evidently not following him to Rome. The next
day they sailed on, but about October 1 Keats and Severn
again went ashore, perhaps at Lulworth Cove in Dorset. At
this time Keats wrote, in his volume of Shakespeare's *Poems,*
the revised version of his sonnet to Fanny Brawne, "Bright
star."

After ten days or more in the Channel the *Maria Crowther*
at last, on or about October 2, reached the open sea, to en-
counter a three-day storm in the Bay of Biscay. It arrived at
Naples on October 21 and was held in quarantine for ten
days, days mostly spent, because of bad weather, in the small

.G

and stifling cabin. During this imprisonment, which was worse than uncomfortable for Keats, he, "in a sort of desperation" (as he said to Brown in his last letter), made more puns than in any year of his life before. On November 7 or 8 he and Severn left Naples in a hired carriage and on the fifteenth they got to Rome. They settled in lodgings in the Piazza di Spagna, in what is now the Keats-Shelley Memorial House. The rooms had been engaged for them by Dr. James Clark, who was to attend Keats, with very kind and zealous care, through the remaining months (he later achieved enough professional distinction to become physician to Queen Victoria and a baronet).

We have no detailed account of the main part of the voyage, but at the beginning and end, at least, Keats managed to display fortitude and even a kind of gaiety. His few letters, however, reveal his hopelessness. On September 30 he wrote to Brown at some length and more openly, in regard to death and Fanny Brawne, than he had ever done before (II, 345–346):

The very thing which I want to live most for will be a great occasion of my death. I cannot help it. Who can help it? Were I in health it would make me ill, and how can I bear it in my state? . . . I wish for death every day and night to deliver me from these pains, and then I wish death away, for death would destroy even those pains which are better than nothing. . . . I think without my mentioning it for my sake you would be a friend to Miss Brawne when I am dead. You think she has many faults—but, for my sake, think she has not one. . . .

While in his present condition he can have no feeling for "woman merely as woman,"

yet the difference of my sensations with respect to Miss Brawne and my Sister is amazing. The one seems to absorb the other to a degree incredible. I seldom think of my Brother and Sister in america. The thought of leaving Miss Brawne is beyond every thing horrible—the sense of darkness coming over me—I eternally see her figure eternally vanishing. Some of the phrases she was in the habit of using during my last nursing at Wentworth place ring in my ears—Is there another Life? Shall I awake and find all this a dream? There must be we cannot be created for this sort of suffering.

Keats was able to write restrainedly to Mrs. Brawne (October 24?), though he put in a postscript, "Good bye Fanny! god bless you." In a letter to Brown on November 1 he broke out again (II, 351–252):

My dear Brown, I should have had her when I was in health, and I should have remained well. I can bear to die—I cannot bear to leave her. Oh, God! God! God! Every thing I have in my trunks that reminds me of her goes through me like a spear. The silk lining she put in my travelling cap scalds my head. My imagination is horribly vivid about her—I see her—I hear her. There is nothing in the world of sufficient interest to divert me from her a moment. This was the case when I was in England; I cannot recollect, without shuddering, the time that I was prisoner at Hunt's, and used to keep my eyes fixed on Hampstead all day. Then there was a good hope of seeing her again—Now!—O that I could be buried near where she lives! I am afraid to write to her—to receive a letter from her—to see her hand writing would break my heart—even to hear of her any how, to see her name written would be more than I can bear. My dear Brown, what am I to do? Where can I look for consolation or ease? If I had any chance of recovery, this passion would kill me. . . .

For a time Keats was able, in good weather, to take walks in the neighborhood of the Piazza or to ride horseback, slowly. He read some Italian and listened to Severn's playing on a rented piano. The poor food sent in from a restaurant became markedly better after Keats, in the porter's presence, emptied each dish out of the window. Rent and other expenses were high and Severn grew desperate for money. When they arrived in Rome the pair had, on their Italian banker's advice, thought to save banking costs by drawing cash for most of Taylor's letter of credit, and Taylor, who had expected no such procedure, stopped payment. The agitated Severn appealed to Dr. Clark, who explained the situation to Taylor; Taylor raised a subscription of £150, but this sum did not become available until after Keats was dead.

On November 30 Keats wrote his last known letter, to

Charles Brown. "I have an habitual feeling of my real life having past, and that I am leading a posthumous existence." Brown's letter had followed him from Naples to Rome, but he is afraid to look over it again: "I am so weak (in mind) that I cannot bear the sight of any hand writing of a friend I love so much as I do you. . . . There is one thought enough to kill me—I have been well, healthy, alert &c, walking with her—and now. . . ." Dr. Clark tells him that "there is very little the matter with my lungs, but my stomach, he says, is very bad." The last words are these:

> Write to George as soon as you receive this, and tell him how I am, as far as you can guess;—and also a note to my sister—who walks about my imagination like a ghost—she is so like Tom. I can scarcely bid you good bye even in a letter. I always made an awkward bow.
>
> God bless you!
> John Keats[3]

The medical opinion Keats quoted—a much mistaken one, of course—had been put somewhat differently in a letter from Dr. Clark to an unidentified person. Clark said that Keats's disease appeared to be seated chiefly in his stomach, though he had suspicions about his heart and perhaps lungs, and that it had been caused by his "mental exertions" and by anxiety over living at others' expense. Clark showed warm human as well as medical concern for his exceptional patient: according to Severn, he once went all over Rome looking for a certain kind of fish, and got it; and Mrs. Clark—later Severn—prepared all the meager food Keats was allowed.

[3] In replying on December 21, Brown began: "And so you still wish me to follow you to Rome? and truly I wish to go,—nothing detains me but prudence. Little could be gained, if any thing, by letting my house at this time of the year, and the consequence would be a heavy additional expence which I cannot possibly afford,—unless it were a matter of necessity, and I see none while you are in such good hands as Severn's. . . ."
As Hyder Rollins noted (II, 364, n. 2), "He afforded it later when such a move was not necessary." Yet Brown was, in his own limited way, a loving friend. In a letter of August 14, 1820, Keats had said: "You must think of my faults as lightly as you can." Brown's later comment was: "Sixteen years have not changed my opinion. I thought then, and I think now, he had no fault. On the faulty side he was scarcely human." (II, 321)

Severn devoted himself wholeheartedly to prolonged and extremely wearing service, day and night, and he would have been more than human if some consciousness of what he was doing had not gone along with his indefatigable care. But his highly emotional letters to his and Keats's friends seem to confirm Clark's doubts of his being the most suitable companion for Keats during this indescribably difficult time.

Keats could no longer write himself and it is Severn's letters that tell us nearly all we know of the last months. Keats "never quite lost the play of his cheerful and elastic mind," Severn said, and he later wondered if such moments of brightness were not a great effort made on his account. On December 10, when Severn thought him almost convalescent, Keats had "a most unlooked for" and severe relapse, which "confined him to his bed—with every chance against him." After the hemorrhage Dr. Clark employed the prescribed bleeding. Keats was "so alarmed and dejected" that Severn removed any possible means of suicide and kept the closest watch on him. Another hemorrhage occurred the next day and was followed by more bleeding. For some days Keats continued to bring up blood in coughing. And he was kept on such a diet that he said he would die of starvation. "Then his mind is worse than all—despair in every shape." Dr. Clark said in a letter of January 3 that Keats was in such a state—stomach, lungs, and mind—that he feared the prospect was hopeless. A few weeks later he told Severn that Keats should never have left England, that his disease had been too far advanced for him to get any benefit from the Italian climate.

Both Severn and Clark wished—from religious principles but still more from human sympathy—that Keats had some religious support against his afflictions of body and mind. "I think," he said to Severn,

a malignant being must have power over us—over whom the Almighty has little or no influence—yet you know Severn I cannot believe in your book—the Bible—but I feel the horrible want of some faith—some hope—something to rest on now—their must be such a book. . . . (K.C., I, 181)

He "set his mind upon" Jeremy Taylor (Benjamin Bailey's old favorite), and Dr. Clark was able to find *Holy Living* and *Holy Dying*, from which Severn read aloud. In his letter to Haslam of January 15, Severn told of Keats's exclaiming:

miserable wretch I am—this last cheap comfort—which every rogue and fool have—is deny'd me in my last moments—why is this—O! I have serv'd every one with my utmost good—yet why is this—I cannot understand this. (II, 368)

Ten days later he wrote to Taylor that Keats's "suffering now is beyond description—and it increases with increasing acuteness of his memory and imagination . . . he cannot bear any books—the fact is he cannot bear any thing." Keats begged for the bottle of laudanum—bought before they had left England—so that he might cut short his misery: but for Severn he would have swallowed it three months earlier, on the ship—"he says 3 wretched months I have kept him alive." Severn dared not trust himself to hold out and gave the bottle to Dr. Clark. "Keats is desiring his death with dreadfull earnestness—the idea of death seems his only comfort—the only prospect of ease—he talks of it with delight—it sooths his present torture."

Keats was increasingly concerned about Severn's exhaustion; he got some relief when an English nurse was hired for two hours every other day. Once Keats felt an urgent desire for books, and Severn got together all they had, but the charm did not last beyond three days. Letters from Fanny Brawne and his sister were put aside unopened, but Keats often held in his hand a carnelian Fanny Brawne had given him. On February 14 Severn could report that "his mind is growing to great quietness and peace," whether, as he thought, from bodily weakness, or perhaps from some kind of final acceptance. That evening he enjoined Severn to see that his gravestone bore the inscription, "Here lies one whose name was writ in water."[4] Severn went, at his request, to see

---

[4] The last phrase occurs in various forms in Elizabethan writers, but Keats was probably recalling *Philaster*, V. iii. 83–84.

the Protestant Cemetery, and Keats was pleased with his account of the grass and flowers, "particularly the innumerable violets."

Death came on February 23. Keats's last hours were described in Severn's letter to Taylor of March 6 (II, 378):

Four days previous to his death—the change in him was so great that I passed each moment in dread—not knowing what the next would have—he was calm and firm at its approaches— to a most astonishing degree—he told [me] not to tremble for he did not think that he should be convulsed—he said—"did you ever see any one die" no—"well then I pity you poor Severn— what trouble and danger you have got into for me—now you must be firm for it will not last long—I shall soon be laid in the quiet grave—thank God for the quiet grave—O! I can feel the cold earth upon me—the daisies growing over me—O for this quiet—it will be my first"—when the morning light came and still found him alive—O how bitterly he grieved—I cannot bear his cries—

Each day he would look up in the doctors face to discover how long he should live—he would say—"how long will this posthumous life of mine last"—that look was more than we could ever bear—the extreme brightness of his eyes—with his poor pallid face—were not earthly—

These four nights I watch him—each night expecting his death—on the fifth day the doctor prepared me for it—23rd at 4 oclock afternoon—The poor fellow bade me lift him up in bed —he breathed with great difficulty—and seemd to lose the power of coughing up the phlegm—an immense sweat came over him so that my breath felt cold to him—"dont breath on me—it comes like Ice"—he clasped my hand very fast as I held him in my arms—the mucus was boiling within him—it gurgled in his throat—this increased—but yet he seem'd without pain— his eyes look'd upon me with extrem[e] sensibility but without pain—at 11 he died in my arms.

Some other details had been given in Severn's letter to Brown of February 27 (*K.C.*, II, 94):

He is gone—he died with the most perfect ease—he seemed to go to sleep. On the 23rd, about 4, the approaches of death came on. "Severn—I—lift me up—I am dying—I shall die easy—don't be frightened—be firm, and thank God it has come!" I lifted him up in my arms. The phlegm seemed boiling in his throat, and

increased until 11, when he gradually sunk into death—so quiet
—that I still thought he slept.

The next day casts were taken from Keats's face, hand, and
foot. An autopsy revealed that his lungs were entirely gone;
it seemed a miracle that he had lived as long as he had. On
February 26 he was buried in the Protestant Cemetery. The
funeral was attended by Severn, Dr. Clark, and several mem-
bers of the English colony in Rome. Since Keats had died of
tuberculosis, the Italian authorities immediately required
the destruction of everything that had been in the rooms, not
only furniture and clothes but "windows, doors, walls, ceil-
ing, floors."

Severn remained in Italy to go on with his painting. In
May, 1823, after consultation with Keats's friends at home,
he had a monument put up in the Cemetery. The design
Severn had first sketched in England, from Keats's idea, in
Brown's copy of *Endymion,* so that it must have been done
before May, 1820, when Keats left Wentworth Place—a fact
that tells us something of his early loss of hope. The design,
with Brown's inscription, Severn thus described (*K.C.,* I, 273;
cf. 242, 252):

Our Keats Tomb is simply this—a Greek Lyre in Basso relievo—
with only half the Strings.—to show his Classical Genius cut off
by death before its maturity.—the Inscription is this "This Grave
contains all that was Mortal of a Young English Poet—who on
his death-bed—in the bitterness of his heart—at the malicious
power of his enemies—desired these words to be engraven on his
Tomb Stone"

"Here lies one whose name was writ in Water."

9

Conclusion

1

A T T H E R I S K of an anticlimactic interlude, the subsequent lives and fortunes of some of the *dramatis personae* may be briefly recorded.

In his *Life, Letters and Literary Remains of John Keats* (1848) Richard Monckton Milnes (later Lord Houghton) did not name Fanny Brawne, since she was still alive; but the prejudice against her held by Keats's friends came out in the Dilke papers (published in 1875) and seemed to be validated by his fevered letters to her (published in 1878 and widely deplored). The righting of injustice was begun by Amy Lowell, who had seen Fanny's letters of 1820–1824 to Fanny Keats, and was completed by the publication of these letters (1937). They revealed a young woman who, whatever the youthful faults Keats saw at first, had become well worthy of our respect. He had asked her to write to his sister and she began the day his ship sailed. Her letters before and after his death are marked by dignified restraint, at first in her hopelessness—"If I am to lose him I lose every thing"—and later in her grief and her devotion to Keats's memory. His sister was the only person with whom she could, up to a point, share her feelings. If Keats had returned from Italy, she said, they were to have married and lived with Mrs. Brawne. Not the least touching thing is the way she echoes his literary opinions as authoritative. Along with her pro-

tracted "widowhood," Fanny had other trials: her brother
died in 1828 at the age of twenty-three, and in 1829 her
mother died after her clothes caught fire from a candle. In
1833 Fanny married a man of Spanish descent, Louis Lindo
(who later changed his name to Lindon); she lived chiefly on
the Continent, had three children, and died in 1865.

Fanny Keats, who lives in our minds as a schoolgirl, came
of age in 1824 and in 1826 married a Spaniard, Valentin
Llanos, who was said to have called on Keats in Rome, and
who now lived in England and had written a couple of nov-
els. Fanny was able to get her share of the Keats inheritance
from Chancery and from Richard Abbey, whose fortunes,
already crippled by reverses in business, could barely meet
this new demand. The Llanoses spent some years on the
Continent and in England (in Brown's half of Wentworth
Place), and then settled in Madrid, where Fanny died in
1889. She had been a good wife, mother, and grandmother;
she had faithfully cherished her brother's memory and kept
the letters she had received from him and from Fanny
Brawne. She never understood or forgave Fanny Brawne's
marriage.

Something was said in the previous chapter about George
Keats's financial arrangements with Abbey in January, 1820.
In reply to charges made by some of Keats's friends, George
affirmed that he had expected—as he had written to John on
June 18, 1820—to help with the cost of the Italian journey
but had found himself too pinched to do so. (In his later days
of prosperity he paid all of Keats's debts.) Brown and others
remained hostile, but Dilke defended George. In Louisville,
George rapidly surmounted his initial misfortunes and be-
came a rich, prominent, and highly esteemed citizen. He and
Georgiana had eight children. He died in 1841, having just
been ruined through backing a note for Audubon's brother-
in-law. In 1843 his widow married John Jeffrey, a Scottish
civil engineer who lived in Lexington, Kentucky; he made
very inaccurate transcripts of fifteen of Keats's letters. Georgi-
ana died in 1879.

Charles Brown—who in 1819–1820 carried on rather shabby relations with his housekeeper, Abigail O'Donaghue ("our irish servant," in Keats's phrase)—in 1822 took his infant son, with a nurse, to Italy. There he became acquainted with Byron, Trelawny, Landor, Monckton Milnes, and other notable figures. In 1835, with his son, he settled in England. He wrote an account of his and Keats's northern tour (printed in Rollins' edition of the *Letters*) and went on with a biography that was to include unpublished poems. Biographies had been planned by John Taylor, Reynolds, and Charles Cowden Clarke, but these were given up for various reasons, and Brown's project was frustrated by quarrels with Taylor, Reynolds, Dilke, and George Keats. However, Brown printed a number of Keats's poems in periodicals and wrote a biographical sketch. In 1841 he turned over the sketch and his important manuscripts to Milnes for him to use, and then emigrated to New Zealand, where he died in 1842. A short, candid, but very fair summary of Brown's virtues and faults was written, in spite of their breach, by Dilke, who called him "the most scrupulously honest man I ever knew" (I, 71). Keats's testimonies of his "love" for Brown have been cited in earlier pages. Brown's drawing of Keats, done in the summer of 1819, is the most authentic likeness we have, and has been often reproduced.

Joseph Severn—who did not suffer from nursing Keats as Keats had suffered from nursing his brother Tom—remained in Italy for twenty years and achieved some success as a painter. He married in 1828 and had six children. He spent twenty years (1841–1860) in England and returned to Rome as British consul (1861–1872); he was until his death in 1879 the respected and popular doyen of the English colony. He was liked partly on his own account, partly because, as his tombstone was to record, he had been the "Devoted friend and death-bed companion of John Keats, whom he lived to see numbered among The Immortal Poets of England. . . ." In 1881 his body was reinterred beside that of Keats.

Apart from Severn's personal care, of all Keats's friends

JOHN KEATS

Richard Woodhouse deserves the most gratitude from posterity. His discerning admiration and faith led him from the start to collect and copy Keats's poems, and his transcripts have been invaluable to modern editors. From him also come our only texts of twenty letters. Woodhouse's selfless literary and personal attachment included a readiness to strain his modest means to give aid—concealed aid—to Keats. After Keats's death Woodhouse continued his literary collecting, in the expectation that either Taylor or Brown would write a biography. He died in 1834, of tuberculosis, after five years of illness.

John Hamilton Reynolds, in 1817 and 1818 an especially congenial companion and correspondent and the recipient of some of Keats's best letters, was much less conspicuous during 1819–1820. He had become immersed in the law and in a prolonged courtship (he was married in 1822), but he had not given up writing and had not lost his admiring affection for Keats, who had gone so far beyond him. We noticed his efforts (July, 1820) to prod Francis Jeffrey into reviewing Keats's poems in the *Edinburgh Review*. In 1818 Reynolds had not been able to furnish the poems that were, with *Isabella* and other pieces Keats was to do, to make a joint volume; and when in 1821 he published two Italian tales in verse (*The Garden of Florence*) he included a heartfelt tribute to Keats's character and genius. His later life did not fulfill his early promise. Not long before his death, in reply to Milnes' request for information, he paid further tributes to Keats—and described himself as "that poor obscure—baffled Thing." He died in 1852; his gravestone carried the phrase "The friend of Keats."

This partial roll call may end with the man who had first given unstinted and important encouragement to Keats, and who, whatever the faults that somewhat alienated his disciple, remained a generous and loyal admirer (though he was wounded by Keats's references to himself when these appeared in Milnes' *Life*). In the distressing summer of 1820 Leigh Hunt and his wife took Keats into their house for seven weeks and ministered to his comfort as well as they could, and he, though much distraught, was grateful. On March 8, 1821, Hunt, thinking that Keats was still alive, wrote to Severn, explaining that he had not written because he had heard of Keats's shrinking from letters and also because he himself had been seriously ill. If, Hunt said to Severn, Keats cannot bear to be told of hopes for his recovery,

tell him—tell that great poet and noble-hearted man, that we shall all bear his memory in the most precious part of our hearts, and that the world shall bow their heads to it as our loves do. . . . Tell him he is only before us on the road, as he was in every thing else: or whether you tell him the latter or no, tell him the former, and add, that we shall never forget he was so, and that we are coming after him.

Such words show Hunt at his best.

2

The story of Keats's rise from the status of a very minor poet, in orthodox circles a despised minor poet, to major rank comprises the evidence of editions, biographical, critical, and scholarly studies, and influence on succeeding poets. There is room here for only the briefest outline, one that must ignore not only a vast amount of material in English but the large fact of Keats's international fame and the always growing body of criticism in Continental Europe and in Asia, notably Japan.

At first it did seem as if Keats's name had been writ in water. For one thing, his best poetry required more sophisticated taste and insight than most early readers possessed. In 1819 the canonical poets whom Byron—himself the Titan of the age—set up against Wordsworth, Coleridge, and Southey were "Scott, Rogers, Campbell, Moore, and Crabbe" (*Don Juan*, i.7), and below these there was a swarm of smaller but more or less popular writers; all alike were transparently simple and clear, as easy to read as a newspaper. Keats himself had begun on that level, but he had not stayed there. Roughly, it may be said that during the first decades after 1821 his general reputation grew very slowly, but did grow, and by the time of the *Life, Letters and Literary Remains* (1848) the climate had changed, Tennyson was established, and Milnes' several kinds of prestige gave his presentation of Keats an auspicious start. In a letter to Bailey of December 18, 1848, Milnes reported that, while the sale of the book had naturally not been large, all the reviews had spoken of Keats with respect and interest; but he agreed with Shelley that Keats "will never be a popular poet," because he can be enjoyed only by the few who possess the poetic faculty.

The most concrete index is the record of editions. Keats's first appearance in an important anthology was in Hazlitt's *Select British Poets* (1824). The first collected edition—*The Poetical Works of Coleridge, Shelley, and Keats*—was published in Paris in 1829; the second (taken from the French one) in Philadelphia in 1831. The first English edition, a paperback given to Keats alone, did not come until 1840. From 1846 onward Edward Moxon published a number of editions; those of 1854 and later years had a memoir by Milnes. (We might remember that the *Fall of Hyperion* was not generally accessible until it was included in the 1867 edition of Milnes' *Life*.) The first full and scholarly edition of the poems and letters was that of H. B. Forman (4 vols., 1883). By 1900 there had been, in England and the United States, over ninety editions of the poetical works. Much the fullest commentary was in the edition of Ernest de Selincourt (1905); this, in its final form (1926), remains the standard annotated edition. The standard textual edition is that of H. W. Garrod (1939; revised, 1958).

To turn to biography, the belief that Keats's illness and death had been largely caused by reviewers' abuse of *Endymion* was strongly held by most of Keats's friends (and Fanny Brawne), as Brown's inscription for the gravestone and his biography partly indicate. Their conviction may have been aggravated by some feeling that they had not done

enough to help Keats through his last year, especially the
Italian ordeal. Byron and Shelley, in Italy, reacted to the idea
in different ways: it evoked two insensitive stanzas from
Byron (one in *Don Juan*, xi.60) and shrill anger from Shelley,
who in *Adonais* (1821) wept not only Keats's fate but his own
sense of persecution. In our time scholarly opinion has taken
the opposite line and made perhaps too little of the effect of
the reviews. It does not need much imagination to put oneself
in Keats's place and, with the aid of his own references, re-
alize the effect of such powerful attacks upon both his out-
ward career and his poetical and personal life.[1]

The first biographical and critical accounts of Keats after
his death were a section in Leigh Hunt's *Lord Byron and
Some of His Contemporaries* (1828) and Hunt's short sketch
of the same year in a work of reference, John Gorton's *Gen-
eral Biographical Dictionary*, which was published by Hunt's
nephew and Charles Cowden Clarke.[2] Hunt's longer account,
while mainly eulogistic, somewhat stressed Keats's ill health
and, in Brown's unfair view, made him "a whining, puling
boy." Hunt recognized the wounds inflicted by the reviews
but denied that they caused Keats's death.

That idea, and also the common image of the sensuous or
sensual weakling, were expressly rejected in Milnes' biog-
raphy, which did much to establish Keats's real character and
literary stature. Along with over sixty hitherto unprinted or

1 For Keats's allusions to the reviews in general and to attacks on himself
and to his low reputation, see *Letters*, I, 173, 180, 374, 393–394, 415; II, 9, 15–
16, 65, 70f., 78, 125, 135, 144, 174, 186, 200, 211, 220; and more indirect allu-
sions might be added. For the feelings of his friends, see Brown's *Life of John
Keats*, ed. D. H. Bodurtha and W. B. Pope (1937), pp. 24f. Richard Wood-
house recorded Keats's saying (obviously after his illness had set in), "If I die
you must ruin Lockhart" (C. L. Finney, *The Evolution of Keats's Poetry*,
1936, II, 746; *K.C.*, I, 232; A. Ward, *John Keats*, 1963, p. 364, n.).

J. R. MacGillivray has pointed out that, while the *Quarterly Review*, after
Croker's article, almost entirely ignored Keats for nearly ten years, and
Blackwood's Edinburgh Magazine continued its sneers from 1818 through
1824, "the *Quarterly* was from the first condemned as the chief or sole villain"
(*Keats: A Bibliography and Reference Guide*, Toronto, 1949, p. xxv). The
Quarterly had of course much wider and stronger authority.

2 This sketch was reprinted, as "the best we have seen," in G. G. Cunning-
ham's *Lives of Eminent and Illustrious Englishmen* (1837), VIII, 252–254;
reissued under a different title in 1853.

208 JOHN KEATS

uncollected poems (and *Otho* and *King Stephen*), Milnes gave
many letters, which fully confirmed George Keats's assertion
that "John was the very soul of courage and manliness, and
as much like the *holy Ghost* as *Johnny Keats*" (*K.C.*, I, 285).
Materials had been contributed by Brown, Reynolds, Severn,
and other friends, and by John Jeffrey, Georgiana Keats's
second husband. Benjamin Bailey, wrongly said in the first
edition to have died soon after Keats, reported himself as
alive and sent in recollections that were used later. In its first
form and in enlarged editions this was for a long time the
standard biography. In 1887 came two small books by W. M.
Rossetti and Sidney (later Sir Sidney) Colvin. There were
critical biographies in German (1897) and French (1910).
The best book of the early twentieth century was Colvin's
large *John Keats* (1917). Amy Lowell's two-volume work of
1925 added much narrative detail but had small critical
value. The standard critical biography is now W. J. Bate's
masterly *John Keats* (1963).

To follow the critical tradition we must again go back to
the beginning. We observed before that, in contrast with the
general neglect of Keats's *Poems* (1817) and with the attacks
on *Endymion* (1818), reviews of the volume of 1820 were
more numerous and displayed a considerable change of tone
—although praise could still include comments on Keats's
language that to us seem obtuse. It has been shown that, among
all contemporary reviews, the friendly or not unfriendly out-
numbered the hostile by seven or eight to one; but such
figures are misleading, since many small voices were drowned
out by the harsh blasts of authority. However, Keats was be-
ing read and admired, and by such diverse people as the
Quaker writers, William and Mary Howitt, and the piratical
Edward Trelawny, whose popular *Adventures of a Younger
Son* (1831) carried many quotations from Keats as well as
from his friends Byron and Shelley. With Milnes' *Life* began
a distinct upward movement which has continued steadily
down to the present time, with some changes in the concep-
tion of both the man and the poetry. The notion of Keats as

a poet of sensuous luxury appeared in the first reviews, whether friendly or hostile. On a higher level it received support from unhappy phrases in *Adonais;* Shelley could not help sentimentalizing his heroes. Although Milnes' book supplied ample evidence for the robust manliness of Keats, the stereotype lived on. The young Matthew Arnold—who called Clough "a brute" for urging him to read the *Life*—was thinking of the poetry on a more critical plane when he linked Keats and Browning as victims of "the world's multitudinousness," although the former had "a very high gift," the latter a "moderate" one; the comparative ranking is significant. In the Preface to his own *Poems* of 1853 the classicist critic took *Isabella* as an example of exquisite verbal richness and invertebrate slightness. The common image of the word-painter and voluptuary of sensation was indirectly reinforced and worsened by the publication of Keats's letters to Fanny Brawne (1878). Even Arnold, in his essay of 1880, recoiled from what appeared to be unrestrained, ill-bred emotionalism. However, Arnold strongly emphasized Keats's strength of character, the flint and iron in him, as well as his Shakespearian gift of "natural magic" and "rounded perfection and felicity of loveliness." Further, although Keats was not ripe for Shakespeare's "faculty of moral interpretation," his passion for beauty was not that of "the sensuous or sentimental poet"; it was "an intellectual and spiritual passion."

In our own century the view of Keats as wholly or mainly a poet of the senses has had few champions; one was H. W. Garrod (*Keats,* 1926; revised, 1939). The modern view of a poet of philosophic reach and depth—a view to which the letters have of course contributed much—was first fully expounded in Clarence D. Thorpe's *The Mind of John Keats* (1926) and, with sometimes erratic but often penetrating insights, in successive writings of John Middleton Murry (1925f.). During the last forty years the scope and seriousness, the dimensions and tensions, of Keats's mind and major poems have been thoroughly appreciated; indeed the modern temptation has been to fuse or confuse the actual with the

potential poet—a quite understandable impulse, although
the actual poet might be thought great enough. The poems
have had their full share of the close analysis that has been
a main method of modern criticism; and, like many other
poets, Keats has at times suffered from off-center or over-
subtle explication.

Victorian critics and poets gave relatively scant attention
to the letters and to the belatedly printed *Fall of Hyperion*,
and it was naturally the sensuous poet whose influence was
most clearly discernible. The first noteworthy imitator was
Thomas Hood (who married Reynolds' sister Jane); disciple-
ship was very obvious in his poems of the 1820's. Tennyson
may have read Keats at Cambridge (1827–1831), when he and
Milnes and Arthur Hallam belonged to the advanced group
of "Apostles." It was, we may assume, through affinity and
the cultural situation rather than influence that, in a number
of his best early poems, Tennyson dealt with the especially
Keatsian problem of aesthetic detachment versus social re-
sponsibility. At any rate the young Tennyson's sensuous
prodigality quickly linked him with Keats. Arthur Hallam, in
reviewing Tennyson's *Poems, Chiefly Lyrical* (1830), was for
the moment an advocate of art for art's sake and insisted on
"the desire of beauty" as the only valid motive for the poet;
hence he placed Tennyson with Shelley and Keats, the "poets
of sensation," as against the Wordsworthian poetry of re-
flection. On the other side, in 1833 a reviewer, probably
Bulwer Lytton, described *The Hesperides* and *Œnone* as "of
the best Cockney classic; and Keatesian [*sic*] to the marrow."
In his *New Timon* (1846) Lytton saw "School-Miss Alfred"
as "Outbabying Wordsworth, and outglittering Keates." But
that was the voice of the dead past. In general, the growth of
Tennyson's fame did much for Keats's also. Tennyson him-
self ranked Keats above all other poets of the century.

The course of Arnold's critical reactions we have noticed.
His poetic response to Keats, to the *Nightingale* and *Autumn*
in particular, is most abundantly clear in the sensuous and
imaginative opulence of *The Scholar-Gipsy*.

In 1872 the *Quarterly Review,* which in 1818 had been
Keats's great enemy, admitted that his writings had "done
more to determine the subsequent course of English poetry
than those of any other poet."[3] The fact had long been plain,
and this remark was made in a review of books by Swinburne,
Morris, and Rossetti. Rossetti and Morris and many lesser
poets represent a distinct phase of Keats's reputation and in-
fluence, in the third quarter of the century and beyond. The
Pre-Raphaelites and aesthetes, up through Oscar Wilde, saw
Keats as the great modern poet and their own forerunner, a
pioneer of art for art's sake, a priest of pure beauty, an ex-
emplar of aesthetic alienation from the bourgeois world. In
keeping with this attenuated and distorted view, the Pre-
Raphaelites—both poets and painters—were especially drawn
to Keats's romantic medievalism and pictorial richness, that
is, to *La Belle Dame sans Merci* and the *Eve of Saint Mark*
and in a lesser degree to the *Eve of St. Agnes* and *Isabella* (if
the taste of Rossetti, the leader of the Keatsian cult, may be
taken as typical). In Morris, if not Rossetti, Keatsian color
was likely to be much diluted with water, in Wilde with
exotic juices. Some bright sharp colors rubbed off on a very
different kind of poet, the young Gerard Manley Hopkins.
To jump over a few decades, it was the Pre-Raphaelite in
Yeats who saw Keats as a schoolboy with his face and nose
pressed to a sweetshop window.

Among later poets perhaps the most remarkable devotee
of Keats was the one who most powerfully felt and rendered
the horror and the pity of the First World War, Wilfred
Owen. In the last fifty years poetic modes have taken various
non-Keatsian directions, and "influence" would be hard to
trace. Yet it is safe to assume that Keats's chief poems and
letters have been assimilated by all serious modern poets; one
eloquent testimony is the final discourse in Archibald Mac-
Leish's *Poetry and Experience* (1961). But by way of conclu-

[3] *Quarterly Review,* 132 (1872), 60; quoted in George H. Ford, *Keats and
the Victorians* (New Haven, Conn.: Yale University Press, 1944), p. 21. These
paragraphs are much indebted to Professor Ford's excellent book.

sion I may perhaps fall back on a paragraph of my own, since it seems to fit this book better than more notable utterances:

For most readers and some critics Keats remains a poet of miraculous sensuous apprehension and magical expression, and in much or most of his poetry his negative capability seems to stop well short of Shakespearian exploration of life and man, to be mainly confined to aesthetic sensation and intuition. But even if we share that conventional estimate, we must say that his poetry is not all of a piece. Keats's Shakespearian or humanitarian ambitions, his critical and self-critical insights, his acute awareness of the conditions enveloping the modern poet, his struggles toward a vision that would comprehend all experience, joy and suffering, the natural and the ideal, the transient and the eternal—all this made him capable of greater poetry than he actually wrote, and makes him, more than his fellow romantics, our contemporary. And if these "ideas" did not get into his poems very often or very far, their overshadowing presence distinguishes his major from his minor achievements. Though his poetry in general was in some measure limited and even weakened by the romantic preoccupation with "beauty," his finest writing is not merely beautiful, because he had seen "the boredom, and the horror" as well as "the glory."[4]

[4] "Keats and His Ideas," *The Major English Romantic Poets*, eds. C. D. Thorpe, Carlos Baker, and Bennett Weaver (Carbondale, Ill.: Southern Illinois University Press, 1957); reprinted in *English Romantic Poets*, ed. M. H. Abrams (London: Oxford University Press, 1960).

Suggestions for Further Reading

S O M E B O O K S O N Keats, cited above in the text or notes, may be located through the index (Beyer, Colvin, N. F. Ford, Gittings, D. Hewlett, A. Lowell, B. Slote, Thorpe, and others), but a few titles are repeated here. The standard textual edition of the poems is by H. W. Garrod (rev., 1958), who also edited the poems without the apparatus (1956). The standard edition with a commentary is that of E. de Selincourt (rev., 1926). There are many small editions of the poems or of selected poems and letters: *e.g.*, those of C. D. Thorpe (1935), H. E. Briggs (1951), R. H. Fogle (1951), J. R. Caldwell (1954), D. Bush (1959), H. Moss (1959), C. Baker (1962). M. B. Forman's editions of the letters have been superseded by that of H. E. Rollins (2 vols., 1958). L. Trilling edited *Selected Letters,* with an essay (1951). The sumptuous Hampstead Edition, eds. H. B. and M. B. Forman (8 vols., 1939), includes, with the poems and letters, Keats's notes on Burton and Milton and other materials. H. E. Rollins edited *The Keats Circle: Letters and Papers 1816–1878* (2 vols., 1948) and the supplementary *More Letters* (1955). F. Edgcumbe edited *Letters of Fanny Brawne to Fanny Keats 1820–1824* (1937).

The latest survey of the romantic age is Ian Jack, *English Literature 1815–1832* (Oxford History of English Literature, X, 1963); this has full general and special bibliographies, including of course one on Keats. Keats is more or less prominent in the many studies of the theory and practice of romantic poetry, such as: M. Sherwood, *Undercurrents of Influence in English Romantic Poetry* (1934); D. Bush, *Mythology and the Romantic Tradition in English Poetry* (1937); D. G. James, *Scepticism and Poetry* (1937) and *The Romantic Comedy* (1948); S. A. Larrabee, *English Bards and Grecian Marbles* (1943); W. J. Bate, *From Classic to Romantic* (1946); Sir Maurice Bowra, *The Romantic Imagination* (1949); H. N. Fairchild, *Religious Trends in English Poetry*, III (1949); M. H. Abrams, *The Mirror and the Lamp* (1953); G. Hough, *The Romantic Poets* (1953); Albert Gérard, *L'Idée Romantique de la Poésie en Angleterre* (1955); D. D. Perkins, *The Quest for Permanence* (1959); M. H. Abrams, ed., *English Romantic Poets* (1960); H. Bloom, *The Visionary Company* (1961); J. Benziger, *Images of Eternity* (1962); E. E. Bostetter, *The Romantic Ventriloquists* (1963); K. Kroeber, *The Artifice of Reality* (1964).

The standard critical biography, a work of rare quality, is W. J. Bate, *John Keats* (1963). Aileen Ward, *John Keats* (1963), uses the poetry, with informed insight, mainly for interpretation of the man and the poet. To these books may be added Joanna Richardson's *Fanny Brawne* (1952).

Some wholly or almost wholly critical books are: M. R. Ridley, *Keats' Craftsmanship* (1933); C. L. Finney, *The Evolution of Keats's Poetry* (2 vols., 1936); W. J. Bate, *The Stylistic Development of Keats* (1945); R. H. Fogle, *The Imagery of Keats and Shelley* (1949); E. R. Wasserman, *The Finer Tone* (1953); J. M. Murry, *Keats* (1955), a final enlargement of an earlier book; E. C. Pettet, *On the Poetry of Keats* (1957); K. Muir, ed., *John Keats: A Reassessment* (1958). W. J. Bate edited *Keats* (1964), a collection of modern critical essays. H. T. Lyon edited *Keats' Well-Read Urn* (1958), an anthology of criticism of one ode. C. D. Thorpe had a critical survey of Keatsian scholarship and criticism in *The English Romantic Poets*, ed. T. M. Raysor (rev., 1956). Some more special books and countless articles and essays are recorded in the larger bibliographies and in the annual bibliographies in the *Keats-Shelley Journal* and *Publications of the Modern Language Association*. The first twelve bibliographies from the former (1950–1962) have been edited by David B. Green and E. G. Wilson as *Keats, Shelley, Byron, Hunt, and Their Circles: A Bibliography* (1964).

On Keats's fame and influence from his day to ours, two books were cited in the Conclusion above, G. H. Ford's *Keats and the Victorians* (1944) and J. R. MacGillivray's *Keats: A Bibliography and Reference Guide with an Essay on Keats' Reputation* (1949). With these goes H. E. Rollins' *Keats's Reputation in America to 1848* (1946).

Index